"A MAGNIFICENT ACHIEVEMENT"

"To have got so far as you did by that long and arduous route and with the slender resources at your disposal was a magnificent achievement."
—Eric Shipton

"You will appreciate the do-it-yourself nature of this ardent adventure in a lonely, frigid, windy corner of the world."
—*New York Times*

"We were at about 22,700 feet. We had no sleeping bags, no stove, and no food. In the early expeditions it was thought that a man would surely die if he were caught out at night away from camp on Everest's North Face. But now the new types of clothing might give a man a chance to survive. At least I hoped so."
—Woodrow W. Sayre

FOUR AGAINST EVEREST

WOODROW WILSON SAYRE

A TOWER BOOK

FOUR AGAINST EVEREST

Tower Publications, Inc.
185 Madison Avenue
New York, New York 10016

Copyright © MCMLXIV by Woodrow Wilson Sayre

Library of Congress Catalog Card Number 64-15208

Printed in U.S.A.

Published by special arrangement with Prentice-Hall, Inc.

To My Wife, Edith

*There is the high heady flight
of the arrow that travels far.
But for this to be, there must
be the bending of the bow by a
hand that stays behind.*

*Friends and family who helped
unstintingly made up this hand,
but more especially my daughters,
Jennifer and Martha, and most
especially my wife, Edith, who
sacrificed for this trip in
more ways than can be said.*

TO THE AUTHOR

ROYAL GEOGRAPHICAL SOCIETY
Kensington Gore
London S. W. 7

12th June 1963

Dear Mr. Sayre,

Having only recently returned from an expedition to Patagonia, I have only just read your account in "Life" of your attempt to climb Everest by way of the North Col. I would like to offer my sincere congratulations on a most courageous and enterprising effort and a really splendid achievement.

I am fairly intimately acquainted with the whole of your route from the Nup La* to the point you reached on Everest, and although I have not myself climbed to the Nup La from the South, Ed Hillary and George Low did so when they were with me in 1952, and I know that they were most impressed with the difficulties. To have got so far as you did by that long and arduous route and with the slender resources at your disposal was a magnificent achievement, and I am truly sorry that the piece of bad luck you had on the North Col robbed you of the success you deserved.

I have always been a keen advocate of light-weight expeditions as the most satisfactory and enjoyable way of approaching the mountains; so it is with particular pleasure that I read the account of your great adventure.

Yours sincerely,

Eric Shipton

* The Nup La is the notch below Gyachung Kang which we used to cross over from Nepal into Tibet at 19,400 feet.   W.W.S.

CONTENTS

Appendices

PREFACE

Mountaineering literature falls short, I think, in two areas. The first of these areas has to do with what I would call the "internals" of mountain climbing. These are the hopes, the fears, the despairs, the gladnesses, the numbnesses, the excitements—all the innermost personal reactions. In all too many books I have found these strangely missing. We are told that the climbers, carrying thirty pounds each, proceeded from *A* to *B* on a given day and that they were almost caught in two avalanches and the wind blew very hard. But these are externals. They make up only part of the story. Indeed, the questions I am most frequently asked in public lectures, as well as in private conversations, concern my inner psychological reactions. How did you *feel?* What did you *think?* The public craves information on this aspect of climbing.

Here, perhaps, the four of us have a special advantage. The fact of our inexperience puts us closer to the public who has never climbed. Their questions and puzzlement are only too recently our questions and puzzlement. If a man has cut thousands of ice steps, it is going to be hard for him to remember his initial reactions and emotions. But if, as was the case with us, we are cutting our very first ice step, the inner feelings and thoughts are going to be very fresh indeed. In addition, therefore, to being an adventure story—which it is—this book will be a story of the inner life of men under stress.

The second gap I find in the literature has to do with completeness. When we were planning our trip, we had to gather our information from dozens of sources. Endless questions concerning equipment and its relative performance at different altitudes and under disparate conditions, innumerable questions of diet, medical care, route, climbing technique, customs, porters, official requirements to be met, and a host of other important items of information: all these had to be researched from an immense collection of books and journals scattered over many countries and many years. We would certainly have appreciated a single source where all this information was collated. And even if we had remained arm-chair strategists, we would have welcomed such a source. There is, therefore, included in this volume an appendix which tries to gather all the essential information a group would need in order to make a major Himalayan climb. The material is organized as far as possible chronologically, with specific details of what must be done at each successive stage. It will be noticed that the requirements are stated for the small expedition only. Naturally we would not be competent to set forth the requirements for the large expedition.

This brings up the last comment I would like to make here. I personally favor the small well-knit expedition that makes no pretense to be anything other than it is, namely, a band of good friends out to see what they can do on a mountain and to enjoy themselves as much as possible in the process. There is a fine tradition of the small expedition advocated by Tilman, Shipton, and others. I would like to see it continue. The pendulum has swung too far in recent years toward the gigantic national-effort-type expedition. The central problems then become problems of finance and logistics rather than problems of climbing. An army must be moved through difficult territory up to the mountain, whereupon there is a full-scale siege and assault. National pride and "success" in the "conquest" of the mountain become the prime considerations. It seems to me that in such expeditions all the overdeveloped competitive and organizational tendencies of modern civilization cannot help but reappear. Yet, one of the joys of climbing is to escape these.

At any rate, I think there is a valid alternative to such grand-scale climbing. It is one of the purposes of this book to support and substantiate this alternative. The book could almost be dedicated to the tradition of the small expedition and the hope that they may continue to attract men who love mountains.

Woodrow Wilson Sayre

I

PROLOGUE

On June 21, 1962, *The New York Times* published the following headline and article, which was repeated in newspapers across the country:

3 AMERICAN CLIMBERS MISSING IN ATTEMPT ON A NEPALESE PEAK

"KATMANDU, Nepal, June 20 (Reuters)—An American mountaineering team was reported today to be lost in bad weather in the Himalaya Mountains in Nepal.

Nepalese officials said the team, led by Prof. Woodrow Wilson Sayre, grandson of President Wilson, had not been heard from since it left a base camp May 3 with rations for only twenty days.

The four-member expedition was feared to have lost its way while trying to conquer the 25,910-foot Gyachung Kang. The peak has never been reached.

Professor Sayre is on the faculty of Tufts University in Medford, Mass. His address was given as Lincoln, Mass.

The other Americans were identified as Roger Alan Hart, a student, and Norman Christian Hansen, a lawyer, both of Boston.

The fourth member of the expedition was identified as HansPeter Duttle, a Swiss citizen.

A Nepalese government outpost at the Sherpa village of Namche Bazar, near Mr. Everest, informed Katmandu that the four climbers had left a Government liaison officer attached to them and their Sherpa guides at the base camp on May 3.

The liaison officer had been instructed to wait at the base camp until June 1.

He stayed until June 9, awaiting the party's return. Then he and the Sherpas returned to Namche Bazar to report that it was missing.

Today's message said that it had been impossible to send out search parties because of bad weather.

Teacher, Student and Lawyer. Three members of the expedition are from the Boston area.

Mr. Sayre, 43 years old, is an Assistant Professor of Philosophy at Tufts University, in Medford, Mass., a suburb of Boston. He has been teaching there since 1957. His home is in Lexington, another suburb.

Roger Alan Hart, 21, was to have been graduated in January, but left on the expedition with only one credit to make up. His geology professor, Robert Nichols, said yesterday that the youth had planned to make up the credit later in the summer and go on to graduate study in geology at Yale.

Norman C. Hansen, 36, is a Boston lawyer. His office phone has been disconnected. He is reported to have climbed Mt. McKinley in 1954 with Mr. Sayre.

A spokesman for Tufts said last night that it was understood that the fourth member of the expedition, HansPeter Duttle, a school teacher with Swiss citizenship, had been recruited for the expedition in Switzerland.

Mr. Sayre is a member of a distinguished family. His father, Francis Bowes Sayre, was Commissioner to the Philippines before World War II. He later was a delegate to the United Nations with the rank of Ambassador.

His mother, Jessie Wilson, was a daughter of President Woodrow Wilson. Mr. Sayre's sister is on the staff of the Fine Arts Museum in Boston, and his brother, Francis Bowes Sayre, Jr., is dean of the Episcopalian National Cathedral in Washington.

Professor Sayre was educated at St. Albans School in Washington and at Williams College in Williamstown, Mass. He was graduated in 1940 and was a member of the Phi Beta Kappa there. In 1942, he received his master's degree from Harvard.

The same year, he married Edith Warren Chase in the First Parish Church of Milton, Mass. Among the two ministers who officiated was the bridegroom's brother.

Mrs. Sayre was graduated from Milton Academy in 1936 and from Smith College, Northampton, Mass., in 1940. She is a member of the Junior League in Boston.

The Sayres have two daughters—Martha, 10 years old, and Jennifer, 11.

From 1942 to 1947 Mr. Sayre was in the United States Air Force. Then for five years thereafter he was an instructor at Pomona College in California. He received his doctorate at Harvard the year he came to Tufts to teach.

Despite his youth, Roger Hart, son of an electronics engineer for the United States Navy, has twice been on exploratory expeditions to Antarctica. He has had a glacier named after him.

With Professor Nichols and others, Mr. Hart went on expeditions there in 1958-59 and 1960-61, sponsored by Tufts and by the National Science Foundation. Mr. Hart was assistant to Professor Nichols, who led both expeditions.

Professor Nichols said yesterday: "Although Roger is young, he is an experienced resourceful expeditioner. He was captain of the cross-country team, and president of the Tufts University Mountain Climbing Club."

Speaking of the expedition in Nepal, Professor Nichols said he was not disheartened at the lack of communication from the team. "These people may be too busy getting themselves back to send out information at this time."

But others were disheartened. It seemed unlikely that an expedition could be unreported in that kind of country for forty-nine days with only twenty-days' food supply and still be alive and well. Bad storms had been reported in the area. The expedition had no oxygen and no Sherpas, and when it was last seen it was pushing up into altitudes of 20,000 feet and over. Whatever was to be done would need to be done fast.

Within twenty-four hours of the report that the expedition was lost, the first steps had been taken to initiate an air search. My family arranged for a search plane to fly out of Kathmandu, the capital of Nepal, which was some 190 miles from our Base Camp. However, they were worried that the plane might search on the wrong mountain. We might not be on Gyachung Kang. Then the search would be a complete waste. Consequently, the State Department was persuaded to send a cable to our embassy in Kathmandu which read roughly as follows:

SUGGEST POSSIBILITY SAYRE PARTY ACTUALLY
ON NORTH FACE MOUNT EVEREST

After due consultation with some available mountaineering experts in Kathmandu, the embassy replied as gently as possible to Washington. (Central offices are so cut off from reality that almost invariably they must be led by the hand gently.) The message said approximately:

CONSIDER IT HIGHLY UNLIKELY SAYRE PARTY ON EVEREST. BASE CAMP ESTABLISHED ON NGO JUMBO GLACIER 25, REPEAT TWENTY-FIVE, AIR-MILES FROM EVEREST. IMPOSSIBLE TO MOUNT ATTACK ON MOUNTAIN FROM THAT DISTANCE.

This book tells the story of the doing of that "impossible."

II

HOW IT BEGAN

It starts with a dream—a dream of walking on the roof of the world, a dream of empty sky and empty rocks and terribly empty air. The sun is cold. The powder snow swirls off the rock slabs into blue-black space. The body is dead, and still there are endless ups to go. And yet that is where I want to be—struggling upwards. The dream fades before I know whether or not I succeed, but I know it will come again to tantalize me. It will come again to goad me into trying what has already been tried unsuccessfully eight times by the best —the great unclimbed North Face of Everest.

That is how it began, with a dream. But if you ask me why this dream and not some other, surely it is somewhat of an accident. What captures a man's imagination depends on time and place, on what books he happens to read, on who his friends are, and much else besides. The man must be just the kind of person to whom the dream can appeal. And the dream must come at just the right time so that he can indeed be attracted to it. After the man and the dream meet, then it is less of an accident. For whether the dream is nourished or not is up to him.

At any rate, as far back as college, climbing on Everest was one of my dreams. And because I let my mind dwell on it, it was nourished, and it grew. I read all about the great British expeditions that first tried the North Face of Mt. Everest. I knew the climbers' names and their exploits, their successes and their failures. I studied their guesses about what ought to be done "next time". I sorrowed over the loss of the great climber, Leigh-Mallory, and speculated with everyone else over what might have become of him and Irvine when they disappeared into the mists on their final try for the top. I admired their whole approach. A few extra sweaters, a muffler or two, knee britches, leggings, and ordinary leather climbing boots, and off they went to have a go at the world's highest mountain. They treated it as casually, it almost seemed, as they would a mere stroll on the Scottish moors. Many of them insisted without too much logic, but with, I think, the right spirit, that the use of oxygen was not "sporting". And they almost made it without it. On two expeditions climbers without oxygen came within 900 feet of the top. And in spite of their inadequate equipment—at least by present standards—no one has done better.*

But part of my dream was to do better. So I studied the literature. I thought I saw where mistakes had been made that could be corrected. I thought I saw new approaches that would make it possible to surmount the obstacles. I made my general plan and was impatient to test it. But I knew it would be a few years yet before I would have the time and the finances to do so. So I sat back and waited.

In Harvard Graduate School I roomed next door to

---

* No one without oxygen, that is. In 1952 the Swiss had oxygen sets which worked only when they were not climbing. Lambert and Tenzing, only half using oxygen, as it were, did reach, in an amazing effort, a point about 90 feet higher.

the Christ Church Parish House. Hearing intriguing noises one evening, I went over to investigate. A gang of boys were engaged in a full-fledged hockey game. For a puck they were using a heavy water tumbler. Every four or five minutes an especially hard shot would shatter the glass so that eventually they ran out of pucks. This all seemed like a fine idea to me. I volunteered to go and get some more glasses from my room. I did and was allowed to join the game. That was how I met Norm Hansen. He and Bob Rose, whom I also met that evening, became my friends. We bowled, we competed in touch football, we went camping together, and we went hunting. Dreams are usually private affairs, but I kept talking about Everest, and eventually Norm Hansen began talking seriously of climbing Everest too.

World War II came and went. Then I read that Tibet had been taken over by the Chinese Communists. This meant that the North Face could no longer be tried by Westerners, since all the approaches to it, as well as the North Face itself, now lay in Communist controlled territory. I was half sorry and half glad: sorry that the great tradition of the British expeditions must now come to an end, that politics should soil mountain climbing, but glad that the North Face would now probably remain untouched until we were ready for it. For I still intended to climb it. I believed I knew how we could get to it in spite of the Communists.

My plan, however, depended on moving considerable distances completely on our own, carrying all the essentials with us for at least a month. This needed checking out. Norm Hansen had already shown a gift for equipment. He enjoyed sifting through the catalogues and then testing and modifying the various individual items. So I was fortunate that he was free to make a test trial with me early in 1950. We climbed Mt. Whitney (14,495 feet) in early June while there was still deep snow and made a 60-mile cross-country circuit. We learned a lot and wrote down all the information we had gained.

Then in 1954 we put ourselves to a more rugged test. We tackled Mt. McKinley in Alaska. Rising 20,320 feet, it is the highest peak in North America. Because it is not far from the Arctic Circle, its weather is, in fact more brutal than the weather on Everest. Forty below is not unusual even in the warmest months, whereas ten below is unusual during the climbing season—April to early June—on Everest. Of course, the altitude is not comparable, but the ice and snow conditions are. It would be a good test.

In view of things to come, certain aspects of the climb are interesting. In the first place there was the question of experience. So far, we had done some rock climbing with the Appalachian Mountain Club and acquired a very fine training in the fundamentals. But apparently it was not considered enough. For when we applied for permission to go on the practice trip to Mt. Washington (6,288 feet), where the basics of the crampon, the ice axe, step cutting, belaying and self-arrest on a snow slope, and other techniques, are taught, we were told that we could not come, since we had not been checked out on the continuous rock-climbing practice trips. So we had to make our try on McKinley—which above 5,000 feet is entirely snow, ice, and glacier—without ever having used an ice axe.

This lack of experience continued to be a problem for the Everest trip. For on McKinley we had not slipped or fallen. We thus had no occasion to learn the rope techniques for getting back out of a crevasse or the techniques for stopping oneself after a slip. Furthermore, there had not even been the need to cut a single ice-step. The consistency of the snow and the route made it unnecessary. Naturally, this inexperience of ours was a worry to us in planning the Everest trip. On the other hand, the fact that we had been so successful on McKinley, even without experience, undoubtedly reinforced my natural skepticism concerning just how important experience really is.

Another attitude which was reinforced was my dislike of busybody rules and regulations, and my inclination to nullify them whenever possible. This arose especially on the question of permission. McKinley is a national park, and national parks "belong to the public." Since the public puts safety as one of its highest values, the park regulations inevitably do also. Thus a climbing party must have at least four members, have adequate experience, have adequate equipment, and have a standby party of at least four people who will go and rescue them if they get into trouble. Well, we had superb equipment, thanks in large part to Norm's excellent research. But in all other respects we were lacking. We joined up, sight unseen, with three University of California at Los Angeles students, and that satisfied the first requirement. Then I made up an impressive list of my European climbing experience, such as the ascent of Austria's highest peak, the Gross Glockner (12,461 feet). Of course, I neglected to mention the fact that there is a very good road to the top, feeling that the park officials would be unlikely to know this. Such turned out to be the case, so the third requirement was satisfied. But how do you drum up a rescue party in a country you have never been in before? I remember in Anchorage, Alaska, going from one bar to another in the wee hours setting up drinks for the barflies, and then extracting their addresses and a promise that they would indeed *love* to come and rescue us if we ever got in any trouble. Later our UCLA friends turned out to have some more genuine candidates for the rescue party. Still, I have always smiled at the thought of the faces of these drinking companions if some weeks later they had suddenly received notification to report to McKinley National Park for rescue operations.

At any event, the man-made obstacles were finally overcome. However, we gained a healthy respect for this kind of difficulty. And just as the lack of experience continued as an added hazard of the Everest trip, so the rules and regulations—man's intransigence to man—continued to be a very real problem also.

On McKinley itself we were pleased to find that several of our theories worked out. First, my reading and study of the mountain paid off. We met no unexpected difficulties, our preparations were sufficient, and I was able to recognize the correct route throughout. So study of a mountain can at least be a partial substitute for experience on it.

Secondly, we found that we could be self-sufficient for at least thirty days. We could carry everything we needed on our backs. This included our cold-weather clothing plus extras; our sleeping bags and air mattresses; our tents; our climbing gear—crampons, pitons, ice axe, and rope; our cooking gear, including thirty days of fuel supply for the stoves; our first-aid kits and repair kits, and lastly (and exasperatingly heavy) our photographic gear, including a movie camera and 1,500 feet of film. Now add a few personal effects, and the food itself, amounting to about 55 pounds, or just under 2 pounds per day per person. We made the trip in twenty-three days, but could have extended it to thirty if necessary. This self-sufficiency for thirty days, now proved under arctic conditions, was the most essential fact. Without it, there could be no trip to Everest's North Face.

Thirdly, we found that our theories of diet were workable. Norm had the idea of a no-nonsense diet consisting essentially of sugar and meat bars. Variety is a psychological luxury, and he argued that, if you only make up your mind to it in advance, you can not only accept it, but enjoy it. After all, people eat the same breakfasts for years. I can't say that I enjoyed it, but I did accept it, and it worked. This also allowed a promising simplification in one aspect of our Everest plans.

Finally, my theory of the movable camp, or what I

call the snail-shell theory of progress, seemed to check out. This is the idea that, with a small party, fixed camps are unnecessary. Like the snail, our total home should be carried with us. Some days, perhaps, we might go only a hundred yards or so, the next, maybe a mile or two. But everything should go with us. On McKinley we had to break everything into two loads, but we kept the relays short so that at the end of the day everything was usually back together again. If the same procedure could be worked on Everest, we felt, a huge simplification would take place. Consider, for example, the immense savings in weight, equipment, and personnel if there was only one camp—the one with us—instead of a string of some seven or eight camps stretched up and down the whole mountain and its approaches. In view of the great distance we were planning to cover from our initial Base Camp, moreover, we would require about fourteen camps. Financially and physically, this would make the trip impossible. So we were indeed relieved to find that the principle of the single movable camp seemed to work. Everest looked more and more possible.

And so the time of beginnings came to an end. Now we were definitely planning to climb Everest. I have not yet answered the more general question of why men climb mountains. A lot of foolishness has been written on that subject, mainly, I think, because the question is misinterpreted as a question about motives instead of a question about values. I deal with the general question in Chapter XV. The above is simply the way it started for me. The time of beginnings changed into the time of plans and preparations when I said one day in the fall of 1961, "You know, Norm, we're getting old. It's this year or never."

Less than four months later we were on our way to Everest.

III

PREPARATIONS

But the four months were, to say the least, hectic. Ordinarily, a major climbing expedition takes a year to prepare. A Himalayan expedition takes two. By trying to condense the preparations into so short a time, we were flying in the face of all previous experience. However, we were counting on our carefully prepared lists of food and equipment which we had worked out as a result of our reading and the experience of our McKinley trip. These, in fact, turned out to be very successful. Unlike what we later found in Europe, practically all items, even for very specialized, high-altitude climbing, are regularly stocked in two or three American stores. Thus, the long job of making and ordering special equipment to specification from dozens of individual companies, and then following through on each one of them, was unnecessary. We simply went down our lists, calculated the type and amounts that would be required, and sent in our orders. For the most part they were filled with little or no delay.

Two other decisions helped us cut down our time of preparation. In spite of the expense, I had decided that we should fly ourselves and our equipment to Kathmandu, the capital of Nepal. Most expeditions take the boat to India, then the trains across India and up into Nepal. But it is a slow process to go halfway around the world by boat and train. Adding the expense of stopovers and other incidentals, I felt it might well be just as cheap to fly. Moreover we both had full-time jobs which we needed to keep until the last possible moment. We simply couldn't afford the time.

Similarly, we couldn't afford the time to send our gear by ship. Most expeditions send all their heavy gear this way. But this requires careful special packaging and even more careful personal surveillance. From the time the gear is debarked in India until it reaches Kathmandu, someone has to watch it at all times to see that it is not misrouted, lost or stolen. Lambert, on the Swiss expedition, tells a harrowing tale of riding herd on their special freight car, which contained all the expedition's equipment, all the way across India. Conscientiously, at each stop they got out, walked back, and checked on the car. Everything was always in order. Finally, on the very last stop before the border, they were in the middle of a card game and decided not to bother checking. After all, why should anything go wrong now, the one time they didn't check? Then later, at the border, they did go back to check. They were horrified to find no freight car at all—thousands of francs worth of irreplaceable equipment all disappeared. It surely meant the end of the expedition. For eight days it was undiscoverable. Then, at last, it was found 1,000 miles away on a siding. It had been detached and rerouted for no known reason. That, plus stories of the disappearance of goods from the docks of Bombay, made me choose air transportation. Certainly neither Norm nor I could afford the time to shepherd our goods across India. It would mean leaving the United States in November, the very time we were actually just beginning our preparations.

Secondly, we saved considerable time by my decision to finance everything ourselves. The search for the "gift" dollar is a very time-consuming process. Moreover, it usually involves doing something for someone on the mountain itself, especially if you are receiving the dollar for some scientific research project. I doubted that we would have any time or energy to spare for such activities on the kind of trip we were planning. I even doubted if there would be very much saving if one calculated in the expenses of using, caring for, and transporting all the special paraphernalia which research projects usually involve. We had no pretensions this way. Our sole aim was to climb and enjoy ourselves without the camouflage of doing something useful or constructive for anyone. The idea, for instance, of pedalling a bicycle wheel 500 turns at various altitudes while breathing through a bag, and while having all one's functions electrically recorded; or again, the idea of having studies in depth made of one "under stress", complete with microphones, tape recorders, walkie-talkies, sociologists, and psychologists, and similar such endeavors—these somehow failed to excite me. No doubt the results of such studies will one day help save the world, but someone else was going to have to save it. So we paid our money, we bought our equipment at the full price, and we kept our independence. And, of course, we saved valuable time by this approach.

The physical preparations themselves are fundamentally a dull business for all but those who are doing the preparing. Therefore a complete list of these is given, but I have relegated it to the appendix. On the other hand, the psychological preparation that inevitably goes on beneath the surface is of greater general interest, so I will say a little of what this was for me.

Most obviously, of course, there was a steadily mounting busyness. There were lists and lists of things

28

to be done: passports, medical supplies, dental tools, shots, visas, international drivers licenses, powers-of-attorney, wills to be made, letters to be written, finances to be arranged, items to be packed and shipped to our first stop in Switzerland, and on and on. Each day more items were added to the list than we were able to cross off. "We'll do that when we get to Switzerland," became almost a refrain. These preparations were, in fact, so harassing that I found that I had no time to reflect—no time to think about the trip, savor it, or get excited about it. I felt a bit cheated.

The fact that there was no time to think added to another feeling that was often with me. This was a sense of unreality. That we were actually going to attempt Everest in a few weeks seemed just too absurd. We had talked about it for so long that I just couldn't get used to the idea that now, at last, I was actually *doing* something about it.

On the other hand, there were times when it seemed very real indeed. I found myself thinking such overdramatic thoughts as: will I ever be doing this again? And immediately I would kick myself for the exaggeration, and yet the feeling would not always go away. I know that my wife felt this too. The ordinary business of living became more precious. Moments were intensified. This is the way that it should be always. I think it is good that all things be at their maximum. But inevitably this goes with that which is not so good—a tendency to hang on to the moment too desperately, a tendency to fear the hurt and dwell on the sadness that it may never be again.

These are the more obvious reactions, but there are also deeper and less obvious ones. Mainly, there is an inner girding for battle that goes on in a man before an event of this kind. My friends and family tell me that I was lost on "cloud nine" for some months before the actual take-off. Concurrent with this inner tightening, and perhaps even a part of its cause, are some fairly basic anxieties.

For instance, every climber who plans to go high can't help worrying a bit about what his performance will be. Will he fall flat on his face, will he be a superman, or somewhere in between? Most especially will he be able to hold up his end? There seem to be no tests yet that will predict endurance and performance, so no one knows for sure. It depends too much on "spirit" and other imponderables. But it would be embarrassing indeed to get halfway around the world at considerable expense and then find that you couldn't stir from your tent.

Again, there is the worry about acclimatization. Acclimatization is the tolerance for unusually high altitude as a result of various physiological changes which take place in the body. For some, these changes occur rapidly. For others, they occur so slowly that the climber is just beginning to feel good and achieve his best form as the expedition starts home. Some never acclimatize. Which would I be? I had had some poor days on McKinley when the altitude bothered me. Looking back, I was convinced that these poor days were due to not eating. Altitude makes a man as dependent on food as a baby. He should eat regularly and often. But there were times when I had had to go an extra long time without food. These were the times, I thought, when I suffered most from the altitude. But I was not sure this was the reason. What was my performance going to be at much greater altitudes? I was now forty-two, eight years older than when I was on McKinley. Maybe I could no longer acclimatize even to the altitudes of McKinley, let alone Everest.

At a still deeper level, I wondered why I had delayed so long in applying to the Nepalese government for permission from them to climb the specific peak that they have chosen. This is mainly because an expedition drains off so much local labor that two expeditions in the same area would mean starvation. There would not be enough labor left to raise the crops, and no amount of money could make the loss good. But if only one expedition at a time can climb a given peak, it can be seen that, just as a matter of prudence, one should make one's application as far in advance as possible. A popular peak may already be reserved several years in advance. But I had not applied until November, a scant three months before I would have to leave. Why? I wondered whether secretly I would be just as glad not to go. I didn't think this was so, but I wondered. I also wondered why I had delayed equally long in applying for my official leave of absence from my teaching duties at Tufts University. Was this also due to secret anxiety?

Incidentally, the late application was the source of some additional worries. Originally, I had planned that I would get the permission well in advance, and with the permission in hand I would have an excellent drawing card for recruiting additional personnel for the trip. Now, however, I didn't receive preliminary permission until January 17, hardly more than a month before we were due to leave. Final permission did not in fact come until three days before we were scheduled to fly to India and after we had already been in Switzerland for some three weeks. This was a bit of unnecessary cliff-hanging. The further direct result was that there was no time to recruit additional personnel, while those whom I might have asked earlier were all occupied at this late date. So we were going to have to go with just the three of us and hope to pick up the fourth man in Switzerland. The three of us were myself, Norm Hansen, and Roger Hart. We were lucky to have Roger. I had first come to know him in the rock-climbing group of the Tufts Mountain Club, of which he was president. He had a long lanky build and an infectious smile. In rock climbing he showed unusual ability and judgment. I found that he had been on a trip to the antarctic already. He seemed just the man to come along to

Everest. It was pure luck that he needed only one credit to graduate, so he could take the spring semester off and make up the credit if necessary later in summer school.

But I worried that Norm did not know Roger; they had not climbed together. I foresaw difficulties in being the middle man. And if we now picked up a fourth man in Switzerland who was unknown to any of us, this would be an added hazard. There is no doubt that a four-man expedition should all have climbed extensively together before, so that there are a minimum of unknown and unexpected reactions to deal with during the actual trip. This was a fault at least partly due to my procrastination in securing the necessary official permission.

One other reaction during this time of preparation should perhaps be mentioned. I had gotten fairly used to the total lack of communication between myself and many people on the subject of mountain climbing. Because climbing in fact involves a reordering of many values—things that many put first are pushed quite far down the list, and vice versa—it is just simply incomprehensible to such people. They may give lip service to the toleration of differing sets of values, but in fact they can't believe that anyone brought up in the same culture as their own can value things differently than they do. I was pretty well used to this. But I was not really prepared for open hostility. In some quarters there was an almost undeclared war against me and the whole project. Sometimes this was rather humorous. I remember, for instance, a woman who was a perfect stranger coming up to me at a cocktail party.

"Are you the man who's going off to climb mountains?" she demanded. And then, without waiting for an answer, she continued, "Well, I think it's absolutely irresponsible. You have no right to leave your wife and children, and go running off on such a harebrained adventure. Why don't men ever grow up?"

She was angry and hostile and very serious, and she

talked for quite a while. When, finally, she saw she was not making much of a dent, she drifted off. A little later I saw her giving what looked like the same speech to my long-suffering wife. I wondered if she had a husband whom she had just barely tamed and for whom I would be a too attractive bad example. On the other hand, I felt she was more honest than many. She spoke out and said what others only thought.

On this score I noticed a difference between the women and the men. Of course it was by no means true of *all* the women or of *all* the men. Still, when I sensed resentment, it was usually on the part of the women. I suppose I was challenging the accepted values of society, especially the values of safety and security. But women are the natural guardians of safety and security. Few people welcome an attack on their basic values. So there were some who would have stopped me if there had been any possible way.

On the other hand, the men were usually intrigued rather than offended. A great many expressed by a quiet word—often shyly, it seemed to me—that they wished like hell that they could be along, that they thought it was wonderful, and, anyway, all the luck in the world. These were warm encouraging words which I greatly appreciated.

I noticed that when society was critical, it simply hardened me in my purpose. Conversely, I noticed that as I gradually convinced my family and friends that our plan was feasible, I found that I really was not so sure myself. As Roger once said, "Having convinced everyone else, now I have to convince myself."

So the preparations included a kind of internal dialogue as part of this inner girding for the action ahead, and also it included a deliberate separation of oneself from the mainstream and flow of society.

IV

PLANS

We made three basic decisions in planning for Everest. We were going without permission, we were going without Sherpas,* and we were going without oxygen. Each of these decisions involved some risk. But in our particular situation there were no alternatives.

Basically, we were going without permission, because we couldn't get it. Mt. Everest is on the border between Nepal and Tibet. Hence, permission to climb it would have to come from one country or the other. But it would be useless, I felt, to ask either for it.

It would be useless to ask Nepal for two reasons. In the first place it would be extremely unlikely that they would grant this valuable permission to such a small, amateur party as ours. With a veritable parade of nations lined up waiting to try the peak, our application

---

* Sherpas are the mountain people living in the valleys around Everest. They were trained as high-altitude porters by the British in their first expeditions. They have been loyal and helpful workers on every Everest expedition since.

would surely be tossed aside quickly. In fact, India already had permission for Everest for 1962, and the next year an army of Americans under Norman Dyhrenfurth was scheduled in. We might well have to wait forever.

In the second place, I didn't want to climb Everest from the Nepalese side anyway. The Nepalese side is the southwest side. It is this side that had already been climbed by the British and the Swiss. I wanted to climb the northeast side. This was the old British route, the route that had first caught my imagination, the route nobody had yet climbed. But this route lay entirely in Tibet. Nepalese permission would be entirely useless for that.

On the other hand, it would almost certainly be useless to ask Tibet for the permission. The legal government of Tibet was now in exile. Permission from them would not be effective. The actual rulers of Tibet were the Chinese Communists. But they were notoriously sensitive about letting any foreigners across their borders. We wouldn't stand a chance, especially in the limited time we had before departure.

So we decided to go without permission. But could this be done? What I needed was a crossing point, not too far from Everest, where we could go from Nepal into Tibet without being observed. This meant that we would have to discover a pass, but a pass that nobody actually used. Also the route from the pass to Everest would have to be a barren, deserted stretch where no living person was likely to be. I searched what crude maps there were until I thought I saw a possibility.

About 15 air miles from Everest, also on the border between Nepal and Tibet, was an unclimbed peak named Gyachung Kang (25,910 feet). High on its south shoulder was a notch at about 19,400 feet. This notch looked as if it could serve as our pass into Tibet. Beyond it, the way would be clear to the North Face of Everest. It would involve some 25 miles of travel over various glaciers. But we would be at altitudes of 18,000 feet and over. There would be very little chance of meeting anyone up that high, unless the Chinese, also, were doing some mountain climbing in the area. We would have to take that chance.

The tougher part was going to be getting to the Nepalese side of the pass. The first stage, from Kathmandu to Namche Bazar—the jump-off point for all the recent Everest expeditions—wouldn't be too bad. We expected to hike the 160-mile trail in sixteen days. The second stage, from Namche Bazar to Base Camp, might be a bit more troublesome. But we hoped to cover the 25 to 30 miles up the Dudh Kosi River and the Ngo Jumbo Glacier to the foot of Gyachung Kang in about five days. It was the third stage that looked questionable. We were going to have to climb some 2,000 feet of ice cliffs between Base Camp and the pass. I was not at all sure that we could do it, especially since we would have to make a route safe enough for men carrying up heavy loads.

I searched the literature to see what I could find out about it. First, I found that the earliest accounts of exploration and reconnaissance mentioned making the trip to our notch on the Tibetan side. They described the route as relatively easy. Secondly, I found a discussion of the Nepalese side of the notch in the 1951 reconnaissance by the British. One party had come over from the Khumbu Glacier and had climbed the first half of the ice cliffs. They described the ice as being of such difficulty that it made the worst glacier climbs in Switzerland look like a Sunday stroll. Nevertheless, they climbed the first half in a single morning and stated that they thought the second half would "go". Lastly, I chanced on a New Zealand journal which described a secret dash by Edmund Hillary, who two years later climbed Everest and became Sir Edmund Hillary. He climbed up to the notch and went on through into Tibet via the West Rongbuk Glacier. So now I knew the route could be done. Only I also knew that Hillary was one of the best ice climbers in the business. Just because he had gotten through was no guarantee that I could.

Still, it was our best chance. We certainly weren't going to get to Everest any other way. We would ask, then, for permission from Nepal to go to Gyachung Kang. If all went well, we would climb up to our notch and go on into Tibet. However, if we found we couldn't make it up the ice cliffs, or if the authorities somehow prevented us from continuing on across the border, then we could still give Gyachung Kang a try. It is the highest, or next to highest unclimbed peak in the world and would be a most worthy opponent. If Gyachung Kang also proved too difficult for us, as, judging by its appearance, it well might be, then we could still enjoy ourselves and have a fine vacation climbing some of the many unclimbed peaks that surround the Base Camp.

We decided to do without Sherpas for an entirely different set of reasons. These varied from the practical to the theoretical.

On the practical side, many Sherpas depend for their living on the various expeditions which keep coming to this area. If we took Sherpas with us into Tibet, mightn't these Sherpas be penalized for coming with us? They might be blackballed from future expeditions, which would be a very serious handicap for them. If there was even a chance of this occurring, it would be unfair to take them.

Also on the practical side, it would be very expensive to take them along. As long as they came only to Base Camp, we could get by without furnishing them a complete set of high-altitude equipment and clothing. But, if they went on beyond, we would have to do this, as well as furnish them with the special food they require, since they do not care for much of our European diet. Frankly, our budget could not stand such an expense.

On the theoretical side, I wondered whether it was either necessary or desirable to take Sherpas. Even if we could afford them, maybe we shouldn't. Granted every

Everest expedition so far had taken them and depended heavily on them, but an unbiased reading of the accounts suggested that they had quite often been a liability rather than an asset. In numerous accounts, for instance, various dangers had arisen: blizzards, avalanches, and other hazards. Quite frequently the climbers had had to abandon all their carefully laid plans and rescue the Sherpas, or escort them up or down the mountain, or what not. It was very commendable that the expedition should feel so responsible for the Sherpas. But the result was not commendable; the expedition never got back on schedule.

The point is that, with only a few exceptions, the Sherpas are not trained mountaineers. It is true that they have lived and walked in the mountains all their lives, but they have not spent years acquiring the very specialized techniques of ice and rock climbing. They can thus become a very serious source of concern and worry for the expedition members, and can indeed disrupt the whole plan of the expedition. We did not want this to happen to us.

Another drawback is plain from the accounts. This concerns a lack of motivation. There are numerous detailed descriptions of the attempt to rouse the Sherpas in the morning so that they could carry supplies on up to the next camp. Considerable time and effort were invariably wasted in this effort—often with no success. Even when successful, the start was often so late that the next camp had to be pitched lower than it should have been. I had the distinct impression that the climbers would have done better if they had just carried up what they required themselves. At these altitudes it is hard enough to get yourself going, without the added burden of inspiring others to get going in a language you don't even understand.

Personally I feel that only those who want to be there should be on a mountain. The climbers have their own motivation, but the Sherpas, with only an occasional exception, such as Tenzing, do not have any direct motivation. They come because they are paid, not for the love of it. But when the going gets really rough, an indirect motivation is not enough. Then the climbers waste their energies trying to generate enough motivation for the Sherpas as well as themselves.

In big expeditions some avoidance of this problem can be gained by establishing a kind of competition among the porters. Only the best are given the "opportunity" of going high. They may even be given status as a full-fledged climber as reward for their prowess in carrying. This is all right in a large expedition. But in a small expedition such as ours there would not be enough to choose from.

The usual reply to these drawbacks is to argue necessity. The Sherpas may lack training and they may lack motivation, but the climbers can not get up without them. The loads are simply too heavy. Here is where the modern lightweight equipment has changed matters. I would guess that a climber fully dressed against the cold today is carrying 15 to 20 pounds less than his counterpart was carrying forty years ago; that is, his lighter boots, his down-filled parka and pants, his aluminum canteen and pack frame, and innumerable other improvements, weigh 15 to 20 pounds less than what a climber used to need in order to stay warm. Mufflers and heavy sweaters snowball the weight very quickly. And incidentally, today's climber is far warmer in spite of the lighter weight. Thus, if he carried a 30- to 35-pound pack, he would not really be carrying more on his person than a climber in the 1920s was carrying when he lifted a 15- to 20-pound pack. This means that today you have, as it were, a built-in Sherpa, since the load Sherpas were expected to carry was precisely 15 to 20 pounds. Furthermore, the rest of your equipment is now so lightweight that 35 pounds is sufficient for your needs at even your highest camp, as long as you are not carrying oxygen.

Thus, I felt that Sherpas were unnecessary. A climber *can* carry what he needs by himself. He can carry 35 pounds as easily as climbers in past years carried their 15 or 20 pounds. And that 35 pounds is enough. Some people mistakenly believe that Sherpas are needed as guides as well as porters. But actually they are used only as porters. Beyond Base Camp it is the climbers who must guide the Sherpas, and not vice versa.

My opinion that Sherpas were not needed beyond Base Camp was re-enforced by the fine performance of the Americans on K2 (Mt. Godwin Austen). They carried everything themselves beyond Base Camp and they stocked their highest camp more amply than any expedition previously had been able to do.

Finally, I will only add that I believe the whole theory of using Sherpas at the altitudes above Base Camp is wrong. I think that almost as a matter of habit, at the time the first expeditions went, it was expected that white men wouldn't carry. The concepts of the personal servant and the proper tasks for a gentleman were taken for granted. Reading between the lines I think the first climbers were a little taken aback by all this service. They were used to carrying their own sacks in Wales and Scotland. Maybe they even felt a little guilty. But it is hard to beat the system. If someone is always there to offer to do things for you, then rather soon you let them do it. A justification of this method was expounded in the form of the "save-the-climbers" theory. The idea was that the climbers would carry the absolute minimum of personal gear. They would move up the mountain from established camp to established camp. Finally, from the last camp they would be called on to give forth with their maximum effort and go on to the top. It was claimed that their best chance of making it was to be as fresh as possible. And this meant to have carried as little as possible at all the lower levels.

All the medical reports, however, refuted this theory. It was found that a man acclimatized more rapidly to high altitudes when he did work than when he just sat around. For instance, if you were suddenly transported to, say 20,000 feet, you would be unconscious in a few minutes and dead in a few more. However, if you were carried up there very slowly over a period of weeks, your body would make a series of amazing adjustments and you would be able to live as we did for a month or more without impossible discomfort. But, if instead of being carried up there, you walked up with a good load, your body would cut down this time of adjustment considerably. I felt this extra speed of acclimatization was likely to be more important than "freshness". Thus, as long as you don't absolutely exhaust yourself, the good hard work of load carrying is beneficial. The idea of "saving" the climbers is a mistake.

For all these reasons I decided that we would do without porters. It would be cheaper, they are not necessary, and their lack of motivation and training could be a handicap. If it is argued that we too lacked training, that is so. But actually, that fact constituted another very good reason why we should not take them. We were going to have enough to worry about with ourselves. We certainly didn't want responsibility for the lives of others who would mistakenly trust and depend on us. If mistakes were to be made, we wanted to make them ourselves and, insofar as was possible, suffer the consequences ourselves.

The reasons for not taking oxygen were logistic, financial, and esthetic. Logistically, how would we ever transport the oxygen? For oxygen to do any good there must be a lot of it; it doesn't do much good unless you use it all day. Some argue you need it all night as well. For instance, the second American Everest expedition (1963) planned for both night and day use. Even at a rather slow rate of flow this requires a lot of oxygen cylinders. But oxygen cylinders are heavy. We couldn't possibly carry the many dozens that we would need. So we would have to take porters after all. Then, all the extra porters would themselves need additional food and equipment, which still other porters would have to carry. Very soon we would be traveling with a small army, and I do not like armies. Also, all the reasons that had made us decide not to bring porters into Tibet were still valid.

These oxygen cylinders are expensive. I calculated that the cost of supplying and transporting all the oxygen we would need would at least quadruple the cost of the expedition. We would be squandering a small fortune. This was, of course, out of the question.

Finally, on the esthetic side, all the business of masks and air hoses and oxygen cylinders and such paraphernalia somehow seem out of place to me on a mountain. I am still attracted, almost as an esthetic principle, if you like, to the concept of "sportingness". I admit that there is no logic to it, but the best things in life are not logical. Logically, one could point out that, if oxygen is objected to on the grounds that it is an artificial aid, then why not object to all the other artificial aids, such as cold-weather clothing, pitons, crampons, and even rope? A man would have to climb with nothing at all. This is all true, but the feeling persists nevertheless: climbing with oxygen is more "unnatural" than climbing with the other aids. It detracts a bit from the purity of the adventure by mechanizing the whole effort; it intervenes in the face-to-face encounter between man and mountain.

But is it possible to climb Everest without oxygen? The answer is an unqualified "yes". Already at least six men had come within 900 feet of the top without oxygen, several of them with old-fashioned, inefficient equipment. There was no reason to believe that, with a little extra luck or stamina someone would not make those last 900 feet. That someone could be one of us.

(Personally, I was disappointed that in the year following our expedition at least one team of the Dyhren-

42

furth expedition* didn't try it without oxygen. I think it will not be too long now before it is made. In spite of its inevitability, when it is made, this will be one of the top climbing achievements of all time.)

So we planned to try without oxygen, Sherpas, or permission. These were our main decisions. There were some minor ones, which somehow all seemed also to involve doing without.

We were planning to do without fixed camps. As borne out by our McKinley experience, we would move our complete camp with us.

We were planning to do without medical help. This was a calculated, or perhaps better an uncalculated risk. It was a source of worry, but I had simply not had the time to sift through the various possibilities, to try to find a climber who would like to come on such a trip and who was also a doctor.

Lastly, we were going to do without any conditioning or acclimatization program. Many interested friends told me indignantly that I couldn't just go off and try to climb Everest without putting in a lot of hard work getting myself in condition. Teaching and lawyering are basically sedentary occupations and not really at all compatible with the extreme physical activity of climbing a Himalayan peak.

But I felt that the rugged 185- to 190-mile walk-in with a pack was going to put us in pretty good condition. Then the up-and-down journey from Base Camp to the North Face should serve as an ideal acclimatization trip. Since all this would take at least a month and a half, it should give us ample time for getting in shape. There was no need to punish ourselves now.

* The second American expedition to Everest, under Norman Dyhrenfurth, was somewhat larger than ours. They employed close to a thousand people, carried some 27 tons of supplies, had a budget of over a third of a million dollars. They had a total of twenty-one climbers. Four climbers repeated the ascent by the southeast ridge, and two more accomplished the fine feat of making it to the top over an entirely new route, the northwest ridge. With all those climbers, however, one wonders whether a mere two could not have been spared for a try without oxygen.

Thus all our decisions were made. We found excellent reasons for doing what we wanted to do anyway, as men always do. Now there was just the increasingly impossible job of physically doing all the tasks that had to be done before departure.

V

DEPARTURES

There came a day in February when the hours and the minutes and the seconds had all run out. It was time to leave for the airport whether ready or not. All the remaining items on our lists would have to be improvised somehow when we reached Europe. How far behind we were comes through as I reread my journal for that day. We did not even have our Indian visas. Roger and I went over to the British consulate where we could get them. My passport had just arrived that morning from Washington, where it had been sent to get the Nepalese visa. When we got to the consulate, I found that Norm had failed to sign his passport photographs. Another trip, another few minutes lost.

A large contingent of family had gathered from around the country to see us off. They were all pressed into desperate last-minute service. Two cartons with all our meat bars in them had to be done up for overseas shipment, carried over to the shipper, and paid for. Someone went out and got hamburgers, for there was no time for lunch. With less than an hour to plane time, Norm had to finish writing a will for a client. Someone said they had seen an advertisement about little portable oxygen bottles for heart patients. Why didn't we take a dozen just in case of emergency? Several agreed it would be a fine idea. My brother went out to a drugstore to see if he could get some. He returned and told us it would cost $180. I was skeptical. We couldn't get them on our weight allowance, I argued. Besides, will they work at high altitudes or in great cold? Call the Swiss consulate and see if they have them in Switzerland; we can get them there. Someone called and the consul assured us that they did have them. (We never found any, and after Switzerland it was too late.)

It was snowing. One car wouldn't start. Norm disappeared. We waited. Finally, the whole disorganized caravan left for the airport. How would we ever carry all this baggage onto the plane? More friends were at the airport. Faces and conversation and hurried good-bys—it seemed as disjointed as a wedding reception. There was simply too much to take in. Somehow we boarded the plane. The door clanged shut.

Then, after all the hurry and confusion, we sat for an hour waiting to see if the fog would lift enough for a take-off. But we didn't mind, for we were still high on the crest of the wave. We were actually on our way at last. The great adventure had begun.

In Geneva, we settled in for a three-week stay. We had several important jobs to do. We had to complete our lists. There were some items that we simply had not had time to get in Boston. But there were others that we had planned to get in Switzerland, either because they were less expensive or because they were heavy and we could save that much on transportation costs by not carting them across the Atlantic.

Also we hoped to get a little practice and training in snow and ice techniques. I had read that the Swiss ran a mountain-climbing school where fundamentals were

46

taught. If there was no school, I hoped to check out with a guide for a few days.

Finally, we had to find our fourth man. All our equipment and all our plans were predicated on the assumption of four men who would travel as teams of two. We had two tents, two stoves, two sets of cooking equipment, two climbing ropes, and so forth. If there were only three of us, then one man would be carrying a double load on many items. I wanted very much to get a European, for I felt that a similarity of backgrounds and beliefs could be very important in such a small group. Even more important, whether in French, English, German, or Spanish, I would at least be able to talk with our fourth man. If we had to fall back on taking a Sherpa, the inability to speak each other's language could be very serious. Especially in an emergency, clear, quick, accurate understanding of instructions or directions could make a life-and-death difference for all concerned.

Our very first day we had great good fortune. We were directed to a sporting equipment store run by Hoffstetter, who had been on the Swiss expedition to Everest in 1952. He in turn introduced us to the great climber, Raymond Lambert, who had been to Everest *twice* in that year. Lambert knew every detail of the walk-in route and the obstacles, both human and physical, that we would be encountering. And his wife had the complete lists of all the equipment his expeditions had used, where it was available, and how well it had worked. No one could have been more generous or helpful. We compared our lists with his and were pleased to find that our equipment was adequate in almost every respect. Still, we found that the stoves we were depending on were only reliable up to about 21,000 feet. We had tried to find out about this before, but until we met Lambert, nobody had been able to give us the facts. So we shifted to a butane stove which he recommended, and it worked beautifully.

Lambert lent us his base tent, a flint-and-steel lighter, and a snow shovel. Madame Lambert shopped for us and gave us all kinds of help with our lists. They answered endless questions. Can you get salt in Kathmandu? (Yes.) Good tea? (No. The best is exported, like Swiss cheese.) Canned butter? (Get it in Bombay or New Delhi.)

Sometimes he asked us questions. "Of course, you have all had your appendices out, haven't you? I had mine taken out," he said, "just three weeks before leaving for India—to be on the safe side." Of course, I hadn't had my appendix out, so his question merely gave me an additional worry. Lambert went over each day's march of the walk-in from Kathmandu to Namche Bazar. He gave us all kinds of practical advice, such as to take extra nylon cord for the porter's loads; to take matches and cigarettes from Kathmandu for the porters as part of their unofficial pay; to take along a cook and a *sirdar* (straw-boss), who would be extremely useful and possibly even indispensable in keeping the porters moving.

The Lamberts also turned over their garage to us for the measuring and packing of supplies. All the food had to be packaged in individual plastic bags containing the exact rations required for each day. Then these individual bags—one bag for each item of food—were collected into larger bags containing enough food for one man for two, four, and ten days. All this was essential because the correct measurement and distribution of food is practically impossible under the conditions of living we would be facing on the trip itself. Also, by this method, we would immediately know exactly where we stood on our food supply, we could pack and repack easily, and we would avoid the overuse or underuse of any particular item.

The Swiss were so kind to us. When we tried to thank them, the Lamberts said simply, "We know the prob-

48

lems." And Hoffstetter added, "We are all bitten by the same virus."

If we were lucky in our equipment, we were less so in our plan to acquire some technical training. I found that the climbing school does not operate in winter. When I asked about guides, I was told that this was the wrong time of year for climbing. There was more money to be made taking people skiing. There were a few guides who stuck to the pure sport of climbing even in winter, but these had been reserved long ago by other parties. Regretfully, we decided to go skiing in Zermatt as the only alternative.

Roger had already gone the week before. During the intensive buying of equipment, I rather think that Norm and I were a bit insufferable. "This is the way we did it on McKinley," was thrown at Roger a little too often. Once Roger wanted to buy a crash helmet for protection from falling debris when we got to the ice cliffs above Base Camp. "Extra weight, can't take it," said Norm rather harshly. Roger argued that he would pay for it himself and carry it himself. But we pointed out that all weight carried was, in principle, community weight. Every ounce was going to be vital on this trip. If a man carried an extra ounce of personal gear, then he would carry an ounce less of community gear. Even if he simply carried it over and above his share of the community gear, still he was tiring himself just that much more. It could affect some other vital job that he was called on to do. Therefore, there could be no separation of personal and expedition gear when calculating the weights which we each should carry. No one could be allowed to overload himself.

I felt that Roger was somewhat restless, so I suggested that he go off to Zermatt early, while Norm and I finished ordering the equipment. Roger did so, and when we finally came down on the weekend he told us that he had a prospect for our fourth man. This was exciting news.

His name was HansPeter Duttle. He was twenty-four years old, and he was a schoolteacher. Roger had happened to talk with him while skiing. Norm and I spoke with him a while and got his address, and said that we might call him. He made a good impression, but Roger said he was a little doubtful about his mountaineering experience. The two of them had walked a bit up toward one of the glaciers. As Rogers told it, HansPeter had fallen into a crevasse that even Roger had seen was there. Still, he was free and he was healthy. Also, he spoke English, as well as French, German, and Spanish.

We all went back to Geneva, and finished our lists and our packing. Finally, two days before we were to leave for India, we had a council of war and decided to invite HansPeter to come along. I felt it would give balance to the party. It would give Roger someone else to talk to besides the "two old men", someone in fact who was close to his own age. Knowing nothing of his character, it was a risky decision, but I felt a necessary one.

HansPeter asked the day to think over our offer. Then in the evening he called back and accepted. We agreed that we must see each other before we left for India. I got on the train for Basel the next morning, and we had lunch and a long talk. We agreed on the philosophy of the trip. We would go as far as we could on the mountain, but we would not adopt the almost suicidal do-or-die attitude of some of the German expeditions. We agreed that frictions were sure to develop, but that they should always be brought out in the open and talked over. That way, nine times out of ten, the steam goes out of the controversy. We also discussed the principle of leadership. I explained that we would usually operate by consensus. HansPeter was a little doubtful. He felt that it was better to have a leader, and that it should be me. However, he was willing to try. If he disagreed with our methods, he said he was quite willing to help the expedition in any way that he could, by carrying, maintaining a camp, or what not.

I found he had quite a library on Everest himself and seemed quite familiar with it. All in all, he made a very good impression. He had a ruddy, open face, frank blue eyes, and a nice smile. I was very happy about our good luck in finding him. As I left, I gave him instructions on where and how to meet, on the last date when we would still be in Kathmandu, on what shots and visas he needed, and a host of other details. He was to bring a bundle of supplementary food with him adding up to some 40 pounds. We waved good-bye. "I'll see you in Kathmandu, next week," I said, and immediately felt a sense of absurdity.

The next day we took off for New Delhi, India. As usual we arrived at the last moment. Madame Lambert was there to see us off, and as soon as she caught sight of us she burst out laughing. We wallowed across the airport like pregnant buffaloes. We were carrying eight ski poles, five ice axes, one Air-India bag with 20 pounds of chocolate bars in it, an Air France handbag whose handles were almost being pulled off, so heavily did it sag with pounds and pounds of iron pitons and carabiners, and a box with all our crampons plus 10 pounds of condensed milk tubes. We were each wearing two light sweaters and a heavy sweater, our down parkas, and our overcoats, whose pockets were also stuffed with more chocolate bars and milk tubes. Around our necks were strung five assorted cameras, as well as our walking boots, and on our feet we wore heavy Korean climbing boots. Madame Lambert knew what was hidden in those innocent little handbags.

"You should have seen Raymond when he left for Peru," she laughed. "What a production."

We calculated that we had over 140 pounds of excess weight as hand baggage. I am sure that Air-India knew that we were well over our combined allowance of 60 kilograms, but they were true gentlemen and let us pass.

And so we took off and flew over the Alps in late afternoon sunlight. Over the Mediterranean the sun turned to scorched copper and reflected off the metallic sea far below. Gradually the sea darkened and night came. The reading lights blinked off one by one, but I was wakeful. I thought of all that had happened to bring us this far, and I thought of all that must still happen. The others slept, and I felt that I alone in the world was awake. As we passed into India there was lightning and great clouds. Then later there was a reddening in the east. Gradually the light spread full-circle around the whole rim of the earth. I was moved by it and wrote in my journal, then sat back and dreamed.

On Jets: High above the earth we flee the downgoing of the sun rush so headlong towards its upcoming that night becomes a thin slice of darkness in a sandwich of day. Into the shadow of the earth, and in a few hours only, out again, the great machine sighs silently onwards. When it turns, its great wing rises slowly like some black monster from the depths, blots out the stars, and cuts the heavens open, and then sinks back down. The stars come back on again—each just where it was. At least *they* stay the same.

Murmur of quiet conversation, clink of glasses, a laugh, footsteps, cigarette smoke—so normal, so unconcerned. Yet we are a bit of the whole continent of civilization whirling isolated, imprisoned, disconnected through the night sky. Strange we should give no thought to this miracle.

And down below in Egypt, then Palestine and all that happened there, now Arabia and soon India. Below are people sleeping, living, struggling, in patterns unchanged for centuries. Do they look up and think of us? Do they know, can they even conceive that we are rushing by at 500 miles an hour, 10 miles above their heads, drinking cocktails and writing postcards?

It is too fast, too disconnected. The savor and slow change of countries and customs and climate and the look and feel of the land are lost. The fertile intermingling of peoples and outlooks has been sterilized by these great onrushing machines.

We flee the downgoing of the sun so fast. We rush to its upcoming. We grasp almost the whole earth in its curving and its turning and its changing and its unchanging. For a moment, perhaps, we fly like a god among gods. But better, I would say, to walk on the earth as a man among men.

And so the dawn came and we were in India. How impossible! The bus took us in to a small hotel. We stared at green fields, unknown trees and birds, colorful saris on the women, donkeys, carts, bicycles, turbans, faces, races, people of all sorts, cows and water buffalo —a great flood of impressions. It was the cool of the morning, but each moment it grew noticeably hotter. On the bus a man got up and introduced himself. He was Alf Gregory who had been on many climbing expeditions, including the British Everest expedition. He was headed for Kathmandu later in the week to stay with Major Wylie, also a British Everest expedition veteran. Wylie lived in Kathmandu, and I recognized him immediately as one of the few men in the whole world who had actually climbed on the icefall we would be climbing above Base Camp. I felt again an almost uncanny sense that good luck was glued to my shoulder. Gregory recommended a smaller, less expensive hotel in Kathmandu, the Snow View. We thanked him and arranged to see him later in Nepal. Then we started preparing for our last departure.

The Indian airline agent who had charge of getting our baggage through India unscathed was a genius. "We'll transfer it to the other airport at 5 A.M.," he said. "Official resistance is especially low at that hour." Norm volunteered to go with him while Roger and I made a final effort to reduce at least our major pieces of baggage below the weight limit. We knew that flying into the mountains in a small plane, the load factor was going to be far more critical. So they were going to be much stricter about extra weight carried as hand baggage.

Everything worked. Our seven canvas marine bags and our three cartons of equipment were safely stowed on the plane under Norm's personal supervision, and a little later we were all aboard in good order. I reflected that we had decisively beaten Lambert's predicted four-day minimum for getting through India. We would see how we did in Nepalese customs.

VI

KATHMANDU

The plane flew toward the mountains, climbing slowly. It was hazy, but we strained ahead to catch our first sight of the "big boys". Quite suddenly we rose above the haze and there they were ahead on our left: Annapurna, Dhaulagiri, Gauri Sankar—magic names for me. It was exciting to see them, but also a bit scary. The whole Himalayan range is like a giant storm wave surging out of the north towards the Indian plains. The wave crests over five miles up in the air. Think of the highest peaks in our Rocky Mountains; they will have a little scattered frosting of ice and snow on their highest crags. Now go a half mile vertically straight up and you will have just gotten to the *lower* part of the snow line on the Himalayas. Then imagine two more vertical miles of ice and snow and glacier stretching on up from this snow line. Now maybe you can imagine a bit the unbelievable Himalayas.

Anyway, I suddenly felt how puny our preparations were. How could we hope to surmount any of these giants? It seemed absurd. But then after a while as I stared at them, the eye accustomed itself to the new dimensions. Imagination, the eternal optimist in all of us, took over. For each peak, I would search out a way— follow up that glacier, detour those cliffs, gain the ridge there, camp here, then, maybe, the top. And so I half convinced myself that our peak, too, could be surmounted, and that the preparations were not so bad after all.

The plane skimmed some encircling hills and flew into the lush green valley at the center of which is the sizable city of Kathmandu. My first impression on stepping out of the plane was how hot it was. The temperature was almost as high as it had been in India and the vegetation was semitropical. I would have thought that the 4,600 feet of altitude and the encircling snow-covered mountains would make the climate much cooler. Later, I was told that it almost never snowed here, which again surprised me.

We were eager to get through customs. Blithely we announced that we would be pleased to have our gear examined this very afternoon or even immediately. The young boy who was the chief customs inspector smiled a faraway, oriental smile and told us that storage charges on impounded baggage began at the end of seven days. We felt the first cold breath of apprehension. In addition he told us that it might be wise to visit the Foreign Ministry and the Director of Customs, and secure certain permissions and forms without which no goods could be released.

"It is possible, however," he added, "that they are away at this time tiger hunting." The cold breath became a full-force wind.

We went to our embassy and were given some more bad news. As of the first of the year there was a new schedule of import taxes on every item of equipment. We were going to be one of the first expeditions to be hit with it. The embassy and various mountain groups were protesting, but there was nothing really that could be done, at least at the moment. These new taxes varied from 10 percent to 90 percent, with the average around 60 percent. There was a crazy-quilt pattern of classification set up, and each classification had its own level of tax. Thus, plastics were taxed at 80 percent, cheese 30 percent, meat 50 percent. Shoes, clothing, ironware, toilet paper, hats—every item had its separate tax. We were not allowed to know the rates in advance, so it became a guessing game. Do you classify a plastic-handled knife as "ironware" or as "plastic"? We guessed "plastic", thinking it would have a lower tax. Wrong. Plastics are taxed at 80 percent, ironware at only 60 percent.

The whole affair reminded me of a Gilbert and Sullivan operetta. There were a bunch of young boys playing at government. (The oldest customs inspector was only 28.) They made up a set of rules at random, then they watched with a certain amount of amusement while everyone struggled to conform to them. Only for us it was very serious. The cost of all supplies for the expedition would now jump by about 50 percent. We had never budgeted for this. One of the worst taxes was the 70 percent tax on film. It was claimed that film was expended when exposed and therefore subject to tax. I remember standing by while one irate tourist tried to recover this tax when he left by claiming that he had not exposed his film.

"Ah, so," said the customs inspector, "in that case you will have to pay an additional tax. There is, of course, an export tax on new or unused photographic film."

We thanked our luck that Lambert had warned us to list the lowest possible purchase prices on our gear. It saved us a lot, but I still had to wire home for money.

The climax of this particular obstacle came after two solid days of meticulous, item-by-item examination of our goods. There was a new rule, previously unknown to us, or indeed to anyone, that all beef products were to be confiscated due to religious scruples. Luckily our meat bars had no large labels saying "Beef" on them. But we could see right in the customs shed the corned beef cans that had been confiscated from the Japanese expedition. There was even a picture of a steer on each can. The loss of these essential provisions just about finished their expedition, and it would certainly finish ours. So Norm and I sat literally with our hearts in our mouths while the inspector picked up one of our meat bars and started reading the fine print where it *did* say "beef product." Over $10,000 rode on which way he set that bar down. Finally he put it back in the box and waved it by as okay. Slowly our hearts came back down our throats. We never did know, incidentally, whether he saw the word or not.

Altogether, it took us four days to get through customs, which we understood at the time was a new record. Some of the youngsters were obviously anti-Western and well-indoctrinated with suspicion and even antagonism toward the "rich Americans". They couldn't believe that we were not sponsored by government or industry or something big. They smiled tolerantly at the pretense when I insisted it was just me and Norm who were paying for the trip. Still they worked hard, and considering what they were paid, even the poorest tourist *is* a rich American. Usually patience and good humor won them over eventually. At several points I told the story of Billy Gruff with good effect. I told them we were just the small goat trying to cross the bridge, so please, Mr. Troll, don't eat us. There is a bigger and fatter goat coming next year with lots and lots of money. Eat him. This story invariably brought a genuine smile.

Three of our sacks had been invaded by rats while impounded in the customs shed. Not too much was destroyed, except for our cheese. We found that rats do prefer cheese. When we finally got the sacks through customs and back to our hotel, we found the rats still attacked them. Two of my most uncomfortable nights were spent sharing my bed with two huge, bulky barracks bags of gear while all the lights blazed, so that our precious food supplies would not be eaten during the night.

Still, it was a happy occasion when all our supplies were at last together again. Norm and I made Roger sweat a bit. For at customs, out of one of the sacks, lo and behold, had appeared the very crash helmet which we had told him he could not buy in Geneva. He had secreted it the whole way. We told Roger that the expedition had been fined 200 rupees for having an unlisted item, and that he would have to pay it. We made much of how he had put the whole expedition in jeopardy with customs by not listing it. Actually the inspector was merely amused.

We rushed around Kathmandu for a week, too busy to sightsee. We first hired the Sherpa, Pemba Nordu. It was a rule of the Himalayan Society that there had to be at least one Sherpa. Then Pemba had a friend, Aila. Pemba would be very lonely and unhappy if we didn't hire him. We stretched, and did. Then it turned out that Sherpas don't carry loads at the low altitudes; only ordinary porters do. Furthermore, they advised us not to either. "Very hot, Sahib," they said. The government assigned us our liaison officer. Each expedition has to have one, and must feed and outfit him and pay him a salary. He doesn't carry loads either. All this kept adding up. Extra porters to carry the loads we weren't going to carry, extra porters to carry the Sherpas' gear and the liaison officer's gear, extra porters to carry the cooking utensils and supplementary food for the Sherpas and liaison officer. And then there was another friend, Putharkey. In the end we had to take twenty-two porters instead of the twelve I had planned on.

We were told that Pemba didn't speak English, but he understood it fairly well. He was very well recommended by many well-known climbers as a responsible Sherpa who was particularly good on small expeditions. Among the recommendations, I noticed, was one from Lambert.

One morning, while I was negotiating at the Himalayan Society, I noticed a wild- piratical-looking man with cape flung rakishly across his shoulders and a proud, intelligent look. Impulsively I said to the interpreter, "I like that man, who is he?" The man turned to the interpreter and asked what I had said. Then they jabbered for a bit, until I in turn asked the interpreter what was being said. The interpreter answered, "His name is Chombi. He likes you, too, and he's going with you!"

Immediately I regretted my impulse. To like a man is one thing, but to engage to travel with him on the trail for two weeks is another. Would he expect to be fed, too? But no. It turned out that Chombi was well-known. We were told how lucky we were to have him along with us. "He is a big man in his village, in the whole area around Namche Bazar, where you are going. With him along you will have no trouble on the trail!" In fact, we found out that it was he who had traveled as guardian of the supposed Yeti scalp which was flown from the Thyangboche monastery to Chicago for analysis. He had met President Eisenhower and been feted both in America and Europe. We were indeed lucky to have him along, and we became good friends even though we spoke no word of each other's language.

Kathmandu is a city of uneven contrasts. It is scarcely a decade since tourists have been allowed to enter the city at all, yet it has electricity, telephones, and running water in the newer office buildings. Elsewhere, one feels that nothing has changed in the last ten centuries. For the Westerner it is filled with unusual sights and sounds:

For instance, we are drawn to our hotel window by a catchy drumbeat, a rhythmic clap of hands, and a cymbal. It comes closer, and we see a band of beggars, jongleurs, like ancient troubadors coming down the street. There is a huge crowd behind them. They seem to be leading a procession. All at once it is clear. About a hundred men on two long ropes are dragging an 80-foot tree trunk. Two axles are used as rollers, and the men dance back and forth trying to keep them straight and replacing the back one at the front. There are many stops. Cars come to a standstill. All wait. Then the axles are straight, the music starts up, all heave in time to it, and the tree shoots ahead another 30 yards before the axle jams.

Again, I watch an old woman with claw-like fingers transferring new cow droppings into a bowl. Is it for food, fuel, or fertilizer? Would an American housewife do this?

Daily we cycle past a fine, forward-looking sign hung on the iron gate of a compound surrounded by a brick wall. The sign reads "Nepalese Bureau of Mines." Immediately I think of industry, science, progress, and such. Only if you look over the wall, you see some two dozen children aged seven to twelve sitting in a circle pounding big rocks into smaller rocks. I wonder if this is not actually for the roads, maybe. However, they generously let them swim in their little pond on Sundays.

Each night there is the dog symphony. Every house has at least one half-jackal, half-dog specimen. They trill, they gargle, they roam up and down in a three-octave scale, they are never silent. The noise rolls in waves back and forth across the city. Invading packs of wild dogs promote the most furious and desperate barking. But even when they are absent there is always at least one prima donna who is trying out his voice and who stubbornly decides that he will too get all the other dogs around him barking. He does. You may count on at least two sleepless nights when you first arrive in Kathmandu.

We set Tuesday, April 3, as the date for the expedition to start its 190-mile walk to Base Camp. I felt very satisfied that this was only two days later than I had planned originally. The delay was partly due to customs and partly due to all we still had to do. For instance, here is a partial list of what we still had to do the day before we were to leave:

Arrange to store suitcase and clothes for the eighty or ninety days we would be gone.

Arrange to have the embassy send out any mail we were able to get back by runner to Kathmandu, and hold all incoming mail.

Meet liaison officer and shop for additional items of his equipment. He must have adequate gear or he can cancel the expedition.

11 A.M. Must be at the airport to meet Hans Peter, I hope. He did not come in Friday as planned, and there is no word from him. I am puzzled. It is not like him not to send some word. Is he stuck in India?

Get mail at embassy and enquire especially whether wire with money is there. Otherwise we can't leave tomorrow.

Pick up photographs and take them to embassy as requested by consular officer Rosner.

Get dysentery and antipar pills at hospital. Also arrange for examination of Roger, who has been very sick with dysentery, or a close facsimile thereof, for last four days. Norm has had a bad cough deep in chest; see if there is a recommended cough syrup. Otherwise buy in the marketplace.

12:30. Lunch with Ambassador Stebbins, who has been very kind to us. Turns out he went to Milton Academy with my wife.

Meet Shah, head of Foreign Office, and pay climbing fee, extend temporary visa, pay two months advance salary for liaison officer, and arrange hurry-up of customs for HansPeter if he comes.

4 P.M. Meet with Sherpas for final instructions and purchase of supplies.

Cut 15 pounds of bacon into thin strips on hotel slicer. Mrs. Mendes, wife of the owner, has been most wonderful to us. We love her hotel. She loaned me her own pocket Bible, since I had none.

5 P.M. Pick up pants and shorts made for us by local tailor for march-in.

Pick up crampon straps made for us.

Mail packages home and last letters to all.

Finish weighing out all our gear (1,200 pounds) into 60-pound loads for the porters to carry tomorrow. Put it in sacks and tie it.

This was a crowded day, but not at all unusual for us. Indeed, we were still too busy to anticipate or enjoy the thought of the mountain. Each day had been so full of what must be done, what must be planned, and what must be arranged that we hardly even had time to remember what mountain it is. Norm made an embarrassing slip when we first came into the airport. He couldn't remember "Gyachung Kang", the name of the mountain we were officially going to climb. I had to prompt him. I wonder what they must have thought? Anyway, this all came up when the assistant manager's wife asked me if I wasn't afraid, contemplating what lay ahead. My answer had to be neither "yes" nor "no", but simply that there was no time either to be afraid or to think enough about it to know whether we were afraid.

The request of Rosner for pictures in case of body

identification—"It really does make things so much easier, you know. Wrong body to wrong family can be terribly embarrassing."—cut through the busyness occasionally. It was definitely there, but I think it was still the underneath girding for trial and danger, rather than fear. Life is good and I certainly didn't want to lose it. On the other hand, I didn't expect to lose it on this trip. Still . . . ? And yet without the "still . . . ?" the trip would not have had the savor it had, nor would it have been the climax it was.

The last Sunday before departure, Norm and I went to the English-speaking community church. Norm had to withdraw because of his continual cough, but I stayed through. It was moving to hear the same prayers and forms so far from home. It would be a long time before we would enter a church again. After the service, coffee was served for all, just as it is in churches all over the world. Only here the ladies on the refreshment committee had to boil their water on a little hand-pumped, two-burner kerosene stove. It took a bit of doing. I said to one of them, "If the ladies in our rectory back home could see you here, maybe they wouldn't complain so much about lesser difficulties."

She beamed at me. She was so pleased to have someone notice and sympathize. "People never know how well off they are," she said.

On Tuesday there was a large crowd to see us off. The liaison officer, whom we called "KC", which were the initials of two of his six names, had his family to see him off. They brought flowered leis for us all. Various news correspondents took pictures, then we were off in a pickup truck. It contained all our 1,200 pounds of gear divided into twenty loads. In addition to the driver, there were Norm, Roger, myself, the two Sherpas—Pemba and Aila—and their helper Putharkey, KC, and two guests. One was the local United Press correspondent and the other was Chombi. The truck was to take us some 12 miles to Banepa where the road ends and the trail begins. There we would meet the twenty-two porters who were to carry for us. I felt I had to ask Chombi to ride with us, rather than walk with the porters, although I was still worried that he was going to expect to live off us for the trip. All such anxieties, however, were removed when he offered to pay for the ride. Of course I refused, but the seal was now placed on our friendship.

On a brilliant, sunny day, the porters each chose their load and started off down the trail. The others followed, and our little caravan was on its way. But I turned back to Kathmandu. I was going to give Hans-Peter one last chance to come in on the Wednesday plane. Neither Friday nor Monday had he arrived, and no message of any kind had come through. I couldn't believe that Wednesday wouldn't bring some news. If he should not arrive, we would go on without him. And later we would take one of the Sherpas into Tibet with us to complete our four-man party. But I certainly didn't want this if I could help it. I took Aila and two porters to carry the food I expected HansPeter to be carrying, and we rode back in the truck to Kathmandu over one of the world's worst roads. Whether he came in tomorrow, or not, I would then have to double march to catch up with the expedition. I felt blisters forming already.

The next day HansPeter *was* on the plane. He had failed to bring the food, but I was too glad to see him to care. He *had* sent a cable, but somehow it got buried in the embassy message center, so that he had received a reply stating that no such group as ours existed. In spite of this negative response he had had enough confidence in me to spend all he had and fly on to Nepal anyway. And I had had enough confidence in him to wait the extra day. It was an auspicious beginning.

I made arrangements to hold his mail at the embassy, then I tried to go to the Foreign Office to get his travel permit. But all the offices were closed for the horse races. So I left a note, and we took off in a jeep for Banepa.

I did not like to leave without official clearance, but the others were now already two-days march ahead. We could not wait a moment longer. Since we had no camping equipment it was urgent that we catch up this same day. At 3:00 P.M. we started the long, double trek after the others. But neither of us minded. We felt as gay as two schoolboys off on a holiday. I felt all the pieces for our trip were now in place.

VII

TO BASE CAMP

The trail starts right off as a long climb out of the valley. It was easy walking, but very hot. These trails are the only means of communication available to the general public. For the rivers are impassable, there are no roads, there is no telephone, and radio telegraph and mail service are for official government use only. Thus there is a continual coming and going of men and animals walking the trails. Over the centuries they have become empirical marvels of efficiency, using every available contour. No step is wasted. If the trail descends as little as 10 feet, there will be a reason for it. Indeed, every possible short cut has already been tried.

Each village is responsible for the paths in its own district. They maintain and improve them. This has meant that, in the course of time, considerable distances of many of the trails have been built up with stonework, from simple steppingstones to endless series of complete stone steps. In other places, however, the way is no more than a goat track.

We started our first long climb on stone stairways. The path led through a fertile countryside terraced everywhere to allow irrigation and to cut down erosion. No patch of ground was left unused. It was usually rice in the low ground, barley and wheat on the rougher, high ground. Cactus and bamboo grew in the rocky sterile spots. The houses looked brown, made of a dried mud brick baked by the sun. Indeed, except for the bright green fields, the whole countryside looked brown, dusty, and dry.

By five o'clock HansPeter and I had used up our only canteens of boiled water, and the thirst began to mount. We had nothing to eat but a little bread and cheese, and that didn't help the thirst. According to my rules we could not drink unboiled water, which meant we would have to last until we reached the others. But how long was that going to be? We couldn't communicate well enough with Aila to find out. Meanwhile, the porters gorged themselves greedily on water at every stop. It was torture.

Then it got dark. A man appeared going our way with a lantern. It was lucky, for we had only one set of batteries for our flashlights. But it was hard to see the path and often we stumbled. I felt very tired. As happens so often, a very hard day comes at the beginning when one is least in condition for it. Then the trail climbed up a ravine in what seemed like mountains with pine forests all around. I could hear a fresh brook rushing over rocks along the trail. The temptation to drink was terrible. HansPeter described in detail how, as an officer in the Swiss army, he had been trained to go all day without water. Also he gave me a lecture on the necessity of the slow, even pace of the Swiss guide. I had heard this lecture before.

In spite of my thirst, I continued to feel happy and excited. I soaked up all the new sights and sounds. When we stopped for a moment's rest, there was the flickering lantern light on friendly oriental faces of all different types, there were the keen stars wonderfully bright, and the smell of the warm pines on the soft night air. We shared our tiredness, and for all the lack of words I felt the kinship of man.

On the trail there were others moving in the night. Often one would hear a sad half-song, half-cry repeated every minute or so. Was it to keep the night demons away? Or was it simply to express in music the long, unending way? Occasionally there was a fire or a light at a distance, and answering cries. The dark mountains rose against the sky, the trail climbed endlessly up and down —sounds of rushing water—the tongue now too thick to swallow. And then suddenly far below we saw their light. In twenty minutes we were down. KC was first to meet me, and I felt the warmth of his greeting. Then the others, the excitement that HansPeter had made it, and the comforts of camp. I drank 3½ quarts of liquid before I was able to eat.

The next morning I was introduced to the rhythm of march for our little caravan. At first light, about 5:15, we were awakened by Putharkey and Aila serving us tea in bed. Then we dressed and packed up our gear while the Sherpas broke camp. By six we were on the trail. Around nine we stopped for breakfast in a shady spot with water. By eleven we were on the march again, arriving at our next campsite between two and three in the afternoon. The middle of the day being so hot, we had consumed our canteens by then, so the first order of business was to boil up a lot of water for tea, bouillon, or lemonade. This done, we read or wrote or loafed until supper at five. Then to bed with the dusk, and asleep by eight. The distance covered for the day was the expected 10 miles.

At the end of my first day with the group we camped at Chyaubus almost exactly 7,000 feet above where we had spent the preceding night. I was excited to recognize the spot as the very same used by the British on their successful Everest expedition of 1953. I recog-

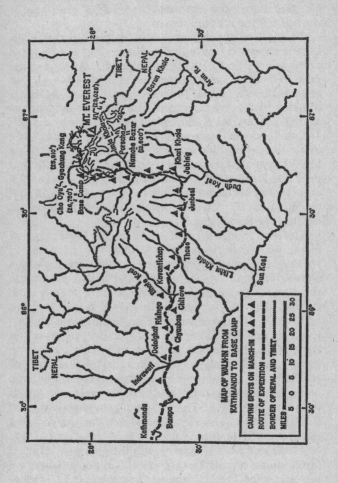

MAP OF WALK-IN FROM
KATHMANDU TO BASE CAMP

CAMPING SPOTS ON MARCH-IN ▲▲▲▲
ROUTE OF EXPEDITION ---------
BORDER OF NEPAL AND TIBET ·········

MILES
5   0   5   10 15 20 25 30

nized the beautiful view as identical with one of the pictures in *Conquest of Everest*. There were even trenches still marked in the ground which they had dug to keep possible water away from the tents.

In camp Norm admitted that the long, hot climb had raised a thirst and he had stopped with Aila for some native beer or *chang*. I was horrified. What had happened to all the strict rules we had set up against eating or drinking any local products? We were out only three days and already we were taking chances that we had agreed not to take. I felt it was irresponsible. Norm said that it was none of my business; he would be the one to suffer if he got sick. I made a speech about the fact that if one flubs, the whole expedition flubs. This was, after all, what we had said to Roger on the issue of carrying extra weight. We cooled down finally. Norm kept on drinking *chang*, and I will say he was the only one that didn't have intestinal troubles, the ubiquitous "turista". Maybe *chang* is an effective preventive. It certainly is tasty.

The next day I took a leaf from one of the earlier climbing parties. I walked the trail in my pajama bottoms. It is the coolest garment that will also keep the sun off. Normally, all the various people and groups you meet on the trail do not greet each other. They pass in silence. Maybe the trails are too steep or there are just too many meetings. I could not help nodding or waving or smiling or saying a greeting in Spanish or what not. Occasionally, they smiled back, but more usually they simply looked startled. But no matter what I did or didn't do, nine out of ten stared in open disbelief at the mere sight of us. Even as we passed within 2 feet of them they would stand stock still watching us. They literally couldn't take their eyes off us. Well, I felt, if I am going to be stared at as an unbelievable freak anyway, I might as well be comfortable about it. Nothing can make them stare any harder. So I wore my pajama bottoms. We were also wearing the tricorn Revolutionary War hats of the Lexington Minutemen. They had been sent us as improbable gifts, but turned out to be one of the most useful items we owned because of the sun and heat. All in all, we would have been stared at even in our own country.

I learned one thing on the trail this day. My regular walking shoes were giving me blisters. They came especially on the toes from the pound, pound, pound of walking downhill. So I had shifted to some light tennis shoes and found an equilibrium with them. But at one point I was sitting on the trail putting on some ointment and Band-Aids. Suddenly a passing group caught sight of me. In no time they surrounded me and were begging me for ointment and Band-Aids too. They needed them for their tough, horny feet about as much as an elephant needs bedroom slippers. But there is prestige in the possession or use of the white man's "medicine". If you allow it, your medicines will be wiped out in a few minutes. So I learned never to apply medicines in public.

Incidentally, I really shocked Pemba and KC by proposing to walk barefoot in order to save my blisters. They were horrified and made up all kinds of dire things that would happen to me if I did. The real reason, I think, is that shoes are a sign of status, just as they were in Abe Lincoln's day. You may carry a pair for days and only wear them when you walk into a village. Even an old pair that is an open latticework and barely hangs to the foot gives importance to the wearer. Putharkey, in spite of the uselessness and the discomfort, insisted on wearing just such a pair. He was a Sherpa. They would lose face if I, as their "Sahib", walked barefoot like a nobody.

That evening we camped in the courtyard of the Risingo monastery for the grand sum of 26 cents. I presented KC with the watch that I had bought for him when I had gone back to wait for HansPeter. He had been complaining loudly about how well all the other liaison officers were equipped.

72

"I poor man," he would say again and again. "Each you have watch. I have none." So now for a while he was happy. But he was always almost pathetically eager to imitate exactly what the "Sahibs" did. He would take salt tablets whenever we did, aspirins if we did—even though he didn't need them—and, most laughably, even sunburn lotion. Since we were low on this item, we had to put our foot down and then he was unhappy again. He appropriated one of the four air mattresses and mattress covers. This evoked quite an argument. I didn't care and slept on the ground. But HansPeter was especially furious. "This is a type. They are poor, and suddenly they have something, and then they want everything. You must stop him now."

But I favored letting it go. Our main job was to keep him reasonably happy until Base Camp. After that it wouldn't matter what he did. But right now he was still writing and sending back reports to Kathmandu by the occasional mail runner that passed by. Norm also felt that I was babying him. I had spent too much on his equipment back to Kathmandu. I argued that we had got off lightly. He could have insisted on absolute equality in everything. We had read of one expedition where the liaison officer was a real problem. He just about cancelled the expedition because he had a V-neck sweater while the "Sahibs" had turtle-necks. Another expedition managed to avoid friction by presenting the liaison officer with an ice axe inscribed in silver with his name, the mountain, and the date. Norm's idea was to take along an old Land camera and give it to the liaison officer to fool with once we reached Base Camp. We did bring along such a camera. The porters were thrilled to see themselves practically instantaneously. On previous expeditions they might have had their picture taken, but they rarely if ever saw it. So they vied for the chance to be taken.

Anyway, KC was stubbornly insistent on doing everything the "Sahibs" did. He would sometimes murmur to me, "I very lucky man. Before very poor. Now you make me rich man. You very kind, very good man." Actually, I rather liked him in spite of the skepticism of the others, and I did my best to defend him. But he made it difficult.

For one thing he insisted on eating our food, even though he obviously didn't like it too well. And he had a tremendous appetite, thereby consuming far more than we could afford or had planned for. Again, he was obnoxiously status conscious. As so often happens, people who are obsequious when looking up, are insufferable when looking down. He aspired to equality with those he considered his superiors, yet he practiced it not at all to those he considered his inferiors. The very first evening it was: Kitchen Boy, bring some more tea; Kitchen Boy, find a spoon; Kitchen Boy this, and Kitchen Boy that. It became a refrain, which we made fun of. But I could feel that Putharkey didn't really like it. And Pemba and Aila were not exactly enthusiastic either over KC's superior ways. It hurt me, and I guess I showed it, because KC noticed that I didn't like this kind of ordering around. He saw it made me sad. But I think he didn't know how else to behave, so he continued.

From the beginning KC had picked me as the boss. He therefore decided that it was me that he was going to walk behind. He was like a leech. He walked just exactly three paces behind me, no more and no less. We were the older men, and he was the oldest. But he was wiry and a great walker. He loved to take the shorter but steeper variations of the trail. So, often, he would arrive at the rejoining of the path before me. But he would never go ahead. He would wait for me to come up and then fall in behind me at the usual three paces. It was highly irritating. I had deliberately to force myself not to walk any faster than I normally would. I definitely didn't want a race. But hundreds of times a day I had to hold myself in. The others asked me how I stood this shadow constantly following my every turn. It was hard, but I just asked myself what difference it really made. Eventually, I became rather used to it. Nevertheless, I was always glad when something detailed him even momentarily and he had to abandon his position as a lamprey securely attached to its host.

I used to kid KC by pointing to every obviously unused fork in the path. I would say with authority, "This way. Yes?" KC would invariably reply, "Oh no, sir, *this* is the way." Eventually he caught on, and rather waited, I think, for another forking where he could say the right way to the "Sahib" who pretended not to know.

Norm just about coughed himself silly that night. He left the tent and had to sit up in order to breathe. I came out and brought over some coverings. I felt sad and tender toward my old friend. He was down and feeling that maybe he should go back. Finally, he made himself comfortable in a sitting position and dozed off. Before I slept I got him to promise to give up, at least for a while, his smoking, especially the Nepalese cigarettes, which are really raw—they would take the epithelial tissue off a dragon.

Just as I was falling off to sleep the big temple gong and other various weird instruments started sounding. It went on for about an hour. We were told that this was roughly our equivalent to evensong. However, there didn't seem to be any congregation—just the priest and a few small boys who manipulated the gongs and drums. It was indeed a unique set of sounds. Roger and HansPeter got up and looked in, but I was sleepy. Finally they quit, and I dropped off.

The next day, at our breakfast stop, Norm performed his first extraction. As usual at every stop a band of villagers surrounded us seeking medical attention. Norm had a fine trailside manner which inspired everyone, except ourselves, with confidence. So he acted as doctor. There might be a horribly burned child, or a man covered with great sores or someone with a mangled hand.

Norm showed great patience with them all. It was an extra effort that he willingly undertook. Once there was a woman with an abscess on her stomach. It was caused, she said, by having cut off a growth a year ago with an old piece of broken bottle. We were horrified. Norm always did what he could, even if it was only to clean and dress the wounds. But of course there were many things he could do nothing about. The sad thing was that with all our abysmal ignorance—the half-remembered bits of medical knowledge that two teachers, a lawyer, and a geology student happened to bring to the surface of their consciousness—we were still paragons of wisdom in a land where the simplest rules of hygiene are unknown. Where are the doctors and dentists for this wonderful, friendly people?

Anyway, this particular day a woman was brought forward with terribly infected gums and at least one tooth that was so abscessed that it seemed about ready to fall out. We argued with Norm that you can't always tell which tooth is the bad one, that he wasn't a dentist, and that there was no local anesthetic. But Norm had a glint in his eye. "I've never done an extraction," he said. "Sort of like to try it." And he did.

At one of the rivers we crossed after a long hot descent we enjoyed a cool swim. Chombi came along and caught sight of us in our shorts. A grin came to his face, and he walked over and quickly reached out with his thumb and forefinger. He squeezed a fold of unnecessary skin that still hung to my middle, then he rolled his eyes up toward the sky. Some of his Tibetan friends who were traveling with him burst out laughing. We didn't need to speak Nepalese to understand that Chombi was asking us how we ever expected to climb the high mountains with all that excess poundage. There was general merriment. I reflected how wonderfully various are the ways in which the human spirit can communicate and how small a part of this total communication is actually dependent on language.

This was demonstrated again that afternoon when we camped on a high plateau. Roger got out some can tops and we initiated the porters in the game of Frisbee. Many of them caught on amazingly fast. They laughed and joked and enjoyed themselves, particularly when the wind would catch the top and curve it. HansPeter told us again that this was an advantage which the Americans enjoyed over the Europeans. "Europeans could not do this," he said. "We are too stiff. We must maintain a distance."

But pantomime, practical jokes, and imitation are international languages, and Norm and I especially enjoyed them. For instance, one of the woman carriers used to sing a sad refrain. I liked it and would repeat it inflection-for-inflection, but in a basso profundo. Immediately the porters would smile and chatter with each other. Again, when the porters stopped for a rest, Norm or I would come up and unload our packs, and groan and make exactly the same gestures and grimaces that they did. This was always good for a laugh. KC told me that the porters were happy with us. He said that when porters smile you will never have any trouble with them. The secret, I believe, is that we genuinely liked and respected these people. And genuine liking transcends the barriers of language and race. I remember that when we finally paid them off in Namche Bazar Norm and I felt sad. It was like breaking up a family. And they showed *their* affection also in the warmth of their handclasps as they said good-by and in the light in their faces. I would have gladly paid them ten times the paltry 75 cents per day which was the going wage, only we just didn't have it.

On the fifth day we camped beneath some huge overspreading trees that reminded me of the great live oaks in the South. A mail runner for the Indian expedition came in. We persuaded him to spend the night so that we would have time to send letters out with him. We thought this might be our last chance, since we could afford no runner of our own. I was feeling poorly from dysentery. Roger, also, was suffering. The flies were terrible, and I noticed them flying directly from fresh droppings to the food we were eating. What's the use? Hygiene is impossible. Only the miraculous power of the body to develop its own defenses can save one. Still I laid down the law to Putharkey. He would boil all our water all right, and wash the cooking utensils in it as we insisted. But then he would rinse them off in a water from the drainage ditch, which had every conceivable filth and disease in it. I stopped him, and also told him that there would be no more "drying" of the eating gear with his old shirttail, which served as handkerchief, covering, and general purpose rag. Still the whole matter is a farce. Cleanliness is impossible, unless you are a millionaire, so you might as well make up your mind to it. Maybe you could get yourself carried in a sterilized nose cone and avoid contamination. But I can't imagine any other way.

In spite of my dysentery I felt high in spirit. I looked up at the great trees above me in the twilight and thought of the loved ones I was writing who were so far away, and felt the mystery and magic of a night in semitropical Nepal. Wasn't it beneath a great tree like this that Buddha received his first great vision?

The days began to melt into one another. After a week what was exciting and new had become routine, and we felt almost as if we had been living this way forever. Only the daily incidents on the trail varied, and, of course, each day's actual trek. The streams that we swam in were colder now as we angled closer to the high mountains north of us. KC, ever imitative, bathed in the streams, too, only he was more modest. I don't think he really enjoyed it, but he had to keep up with the "Sahibs". When he got a bad cough and some dizziness he blamed it on the swimming and urged us to give it up. But we continued swimming, so he had to, too.

One day I hid his watch, which he had left on the

bank. At first he thought it was "teeps", which was how he pronounced "thieves". But then he guessed it was really me. I put on a dowsing act complete with forked stick and special incantations. Sure enough, the stick turned down where the watch was hidden. Some of the porters who were watching were delighted. Long later I could hear them recounting every detail to the others. They brought me forked sticks and wanted me to try it on something of theirs.

One evening I did some coin tricks for the children. A whole group of villagers gathered around. One smart boy saw through every trick and proudly explained them to the crowd. He was right, of course, and knew it. But still everyone wanted me to do the tricks over and over again. In a way they seemed almost more eager to have me do the tricks now that they knew what was taking place than when they had been mystified and puzzled. I wondered why this was so. It is like children begging for their favorite story. Is there a comfort in knowing just how it is going to come out? Or is it simply that all people can feel kinship and equality in their fascination for the world of pretend?

I had brought along a little doll for just such an occasion. It had a beautiful dress and complete set of clothing, including petticoat, nylon slip, panties, and bra. I gave it to the girls to play with and they were fascinated. They dressed her and undressed her endlessly. Inevitably, there was one six-year-old with deep, dark, wonderful eyes that overflowed with her amazement. There was no hope of resistance, so the doll became hers. I reflected that the children of every land in their laughter, their trust, and their natural friendship seem so close to what God intended us to be. But we adults spoil and despoil the world. And gradually, the children, too, are spoiled and despoiled.

I started the walk carrying a mere 20 pounds, intending gradually to work up. Each day I hoped to carry the heavy Bolex movie camera in my load, so that I could take pictures during the day. But I never quite made it. Blisters or dysentery or a pulled muscle allowed me to argue that it would be better to wait until tomorrow. Besides, it was hard to carry when you didn't have to, and were even urged not to by Pemba, Aila, and KC. Anyway, by the end of the march each day I was more than glad to stop, as was everyone. Roger was the tiger. From the beginning he had carried close to 50 pounds in a great pyramid of gear on his back. It was very impressive, even to the porters. He did, suddenly, sometimes tire. But his recuperation rate was very fast. He ran up and down the hills, went exploring for rocks and specimens, stayed behind, then caught up and roared on ahead impatiently. Once he took the wrong turning and walked an extra mile. But that didn't seem to tame him.

Norm went only a little heavier than I. He argued that there would be time enough for the really heavy loads later. HansPeter carried a good-sized load, but less than Roger. KC carried a load almost exactly the same as mine in HansPeter's small rucksack that he had brought from Switzerland. Going up to the higher passes Norm had trouble with his breathing. He lagged behind and wondered aloud if he was going to make it. He had what I considered a crazy theory that one should breathe only through the nose; it keeps the throat from drying out. But with the sniffles one can't possibly get enough air just through the nose. I should think that oxygen would be more important than moisture. Also Norm believed that phlegm must be coughed up at all costs. So he hacked and hacked hopelessly. I told him to forget it and rely on nature. But he said that that was just another Sayre theory.

We reached the village of Those, our halfway point to Namche Bazar. I noticed that the houses were all whitewashed and cleaner looking now. Also the mountains were covered with many varieties of pines. We were definitely getting into higher country.

We crossed a 9,000-foot pass. Coming down the

other side I noticed some large, stratified rock outcroppings to the left of the trail. They seemed familiar. Suddenly I recognized the spot. I had been playing the game of trying to spot each place from which photographs had been taken and published in the various climbing accounts. It had been here that a lovely colored shot had been made of a climber in shorts standing on a rocky trail with what looked in the picture like a tremendous blue drop-off below him. I now saw that the picture was actually taken from one of the lower horizontal strata, so that the drop-off to grass and dirt was actually only a mere 10 feet. Furthermore, the spot was not on the actual trail at all. I was amused; it appears that even the British can exaggerate just a tiny bit.

We spent the night in another monastery yard, and the next day we started climbing our highest pass, roughly 12,000 feet high. Just below the pass, we stopped for the night in still another monastery. In the evening I virtuously slept while the others went "in town" to the nearby village and sampled the local *rakshi,* a homemade brandy, and *chang.* Norm was asked to help a dying woman, but there was no hope. We chided him that he had now lost his first patient. We speculated that maybe we'd better come back by a different route. The extra delay we would charge to him. The others came back from the village after dark, feeling gay. They persuaded me to sample the *rakshi.* I took a little. It was not too bad; it tasted a little like kirsch. However, I was still skeptical of the wisdom of all this. My skepticism got me nowhere.

The next day was the loveliest day of the walk-in. We climbed to the ridge, then walked easily along through beautiful forests of Rhododendrons. In the open spots there were views to the north of several of the famous big peaks. They were in bright sun with not a single cloud hiding them. We stared at them through the binoculars and were awed by the series of impossible precipices that seemed to guard each summit. We felt we were getting close now. Under the thickets of Rhododendron there were old banks of corn snow. It was the first we had touched, so of course we pelted each other, and some of the porters, with snowballs. The air was alive and fresh, and the sun was bright. The blood-red blossoms seemed to float against the blue depths below us and the pale milk-white distances. Then, as we started down, we ran into forests shrouded with Spanish moss. For the first time we noticed a white-blossomed tree, like a tulip or wild magnolia. A pale afternoon sunlight seemed to spotlight each flower.

The first open spot we came to that Pemba and Aila had picked as a campsite was a solid bed of manure. So we ordered them to push on. Finally we camped in the yard of a house. But it was still definitely ripe.

On our thirteenth day out we reached a major landmark, the Dudh Kosi River. It is a tremendous, milky, brawling glacial stream which foams through one rocky gorge after another. We were excited to be here, for it was another dreamt-of name to be seen with our own eyes. The waters of this river flow directly out of the Ngo Jumbo Glacier, which itself starts from the high ice bowl where we were planning to put our Base Camp. But, more especially, a tributary of this river comes from Everest itself. This, in a sense, we were starting the ascent of Everest right now. We were at 5,000 feet, and every step was a step up the great Everest massif. "Only 24,000 more feet to go," we told ourselves. Follow the river until it turns to ice. Follow the ice until it turns to rock. Follow the rock until it turns to sky. Then we will be there.

I had hopes that the generally upward walking now would rest my blisters and give them a chance to heal. It was impossible to descend the steep trails without re-irritating the blisters on my toes. But going up pulls the toes away from the front of the shoe and, so, does not rub them.

We began to notice the Everest weather pattern for

this time of year. It is clear until around ten in the morning. Then there are increasing clouds, with the peaks obscured. By noon it is likely to rain a bit, and one can see that not too far above it is snowing. In the late afternoon it tends to clear again, but not always. We heard that the settled, clear weather seemed to be very late this year. This gave us satisfaction, for our coming to the area later than any of the other expeditions was thereby justified; we couldn't have done anything up high anyway. We also felt a natural, if somewhat guilty, sense of pleasure that no other expedition could have been successful yet. Still, remembering that some years the weather pattern never had become settled, we did hope that this wouldn't go on forever. Also we worried that if there was snow down this low, it would be impossible for the porters to carry in to our Base Camp.

Speaking of worries, Putharkey came forward with a fine set. He warned us that refugee Tibetans and some renegade Sherpas had banded together to hijack expeditions' supplies. Like purse snatchers they would grab and run—knock a man down, and then make off with his load before he could defend himself. Stragglers were especially vulnerable. They also tried bribery. When I thought how little the porters were paid, I felt it must be a real temptation to a porter to sell a few items from his pack. The "Sahibs" would never miss them. But actually we encountered no thievery of any sort.

Even on the march I would have expected to have to institute a complex check-in system at the beginning and end of each march, along with rear and side guards during the march to make sure the porters didn't appropriate equipment from their loads, and then sell it later. However, nothing like this had been necessary, for which we were very grateful. The Nepalese seemed basically trustworthy, as far as I could tell. Once on the trail we met some burly fellows who were pushy and aggressive, and demanded cigarettes. I refused, because of their attitude, pretending I didn't understand them. Later, we were told that they were bandits. But who knows? Also KC often warned about letting gear lie outside the tent at night because of "teeps". Still we never lost anything, and I rather think his fears were the typical fears of the city dweller, where thievery is quite common, imported unnecessarily into the country, where thievery is exceedingly rare.

Indeed, the basic safety of the trail was illustrated on our last day before Namche Bazar. We found ourselves traveling for a time with a band of children. They were up to fourteen years old, of mixed sexes, and simply camping out wherever they were at nightfall. They were out for many days at a time, cutting and selling firewood, and trading various items from village to village. Some of the girls were quite attractive, yet they had no fear of attack or molestation. Such security in these primitive surroundings was really quite impressive to me. I wondered how our suburban parents would react to letting children that age wander around for days with no baby sitters and no supervision in the "wilds" of Nepal.

At Namche Bazar we would be paying off all our porters and would engage a new set of high-altitude porters who would carry us the five days' journey up to Base Camp at 16,500 feet. The porters with us now were not equipped to withstand the cold and the altitude. We felt sad at the prospect of breaking up our happy traveling family. In addition, we disliked the prospect of having to break up the habits and routine which had become so comfortably established during the last sixteen days of travel.

We cheered up quite a bit when we stopped at Pemba's mother-in-law's. She lived in one of the wonderful old timber and stone houses of the region. She served us pitchers of *chang* in the traditional upstairs living room. Pemba, as the favorite son, was plied unremittingly. According to tradition, if you drink even a sip your glass is immediately refilled to the brim. In fact it is made to overflow onto the table or floor. If you don't drink, you are tongue-lashed. Poor Pemba got more and more far gone. Finally, we were off on the march again with Pemba apologizing profusely and repetitively. Next morning he had a king-sized hangover and begged some of the white man's "medicine"—aspirin. Both he and Aila were sick with all kinds of ailments which we *hoped* were just the after effects of the *chang*. So it proved to be. Nevertheless, as far as I myself am concerned, I certainly recommend *chang* as a magnificent way to make the day's hike painless. I can't understand the horror that some of the previous expeditions had for this beverage. I found it delightful. Lambert had said that once we got into Sherpa country, at the higher altitudes, the *chang* would be quite safe. Thus for the first time since I had taken a cup of tea with Chombi out of politeness, and the one taste of *rakshi,* I allowed myself to break the strict rule against partaking of local foods.

And so on our sixteenth day out, after a brutal 2,000-foot climb up out of the Dudhi Kosi gorge we arrived at Namche Bazar in a blinding snowstorm. Pemba took us to a fine cozy inn made of the usual hand-hewn timbers and beautifully fitted stone. You enter through a heavy plank door into absolute blackness which is where the yaks and the chickens and the other animals bed down. You grope your way through the warm barn smells to a steep ladder which you climb, but watch your head. Then you step out into the spacious living room which occupies the whole second floor, except for curtained alcoves at either end for sleeping. A chimneyless central fireplace made of stone serves for cooking and warmth. Some of the smoke escapes through a hole in the roof, but the rest of it you inhale. The windows have no panes and they seem too small when the fire is lit, as you choke on the smoke. But later, when the fire is dead, the cold seeps in and you feel they are too big. Along the whole length of the back wall are a collection of great pots and bowls made of brass and copper. Many are beautifully decorated, and they are kept polished and clean. They represent some of the permanent wealth of the family. A few are at least four feet across. The whole impression is one of cleanliness and comfort.

We stowed all our gear safely in one of the alcoves and then paid off the porters. We treated each to a glass of *chang*. They clasped our hands warmly. I sensed their real regret, but they had to hurry back down the trail to get below the snow before dark. Asman, the youngest porter was really just a boy—about thirteen or fourteen. I gave him a note; I wanted him to look us up when we returned to Kathmandu. I gave him one of my shirts and other things. He was an orphan and had nothing, and was in tatters. Often he had been sick on the trail with no one to take care of him. And yet he always had an infectious grin. I don't see how he did it, but he was always gay. I thought of adopting him, yet I knew that this was probably impossible. Norm was very good to him, too. He kidded him and sort of looked after him. Maybe he reminded Norm of *his* earlier days. Still, it was always a shock to see Asman carrying a full 66-pound load and smoking his regular ration of cigarettes. He was so slight and so young one didn't expect to see him acting like a man.

That night we slept under a roof for the first time in over two weeks. Before sleeping we talked quietly of what had gone before and what was still to come. The safari we had just finished, 160 miles through spring flowers and forests, mountains and terraced fields, reminded me most of what I had read of hunting trips in the West in the late 1800s, or an African expedition before it all became stylized. There was the same sense of being completely on our own. We were a travling community and every obstacle had to be surmounted by our own efforts, for there was no outside help. The unexpected was always around the next corner. It will not be much longer that there will be places left where this kind of trip can be made. I was glad to have seen it and felt it myself. And now, tomorrow, we would leave the last of the man-made obstacles behind. There would be nothing between us and our mountain. "Namche Bazar", a name we had read so often—it made one laugh with disbelief to think that we were actually here.

But the next day we were too busy to leave: extra supplies, cold-weather equipment for KC and the Sherpas, letters to write home, porters to hire, and other endless details. At home, this was Patriot's Day, April 19. Foreign affairs, politics, the "news", local holidays —it all seemed so far away. Yet it was also close. This morning in the early dawn sky I watched a satellite wheel by.

The day was sunny and yesterday's snow melted away. We still worried whether we could get through with the porters to Base Camp, but our spirits rose. A series of government officials called on us. We were told one disturbing story. The year before a Japanese expedition had attempted a peak which, like our Gyachung Kang, is on the border between Tibet and Nepal. Apparently they were on a glacier where the border runs right down the middle. A band of brigands, claiming they were Communist soldiers, captured half the climbing party, ostensibly because they had strayed across the border, and held them for ransom. Eventually they were released, but it finished the expedition. We were told that they returned by way of Gyachung Kang and made a reconnaissance of it for a possible climb the following year.

Then KC told us that the Post Border Control Commander had told him that the Communists *did* have patrols at 19,000 feet. This all made us worry even more about what might happen to us during our extended journey into Tibet. I was counting on not meeting anyone at the altitudes at which we would be traveling. Norm wanted to "shoot it out" if we were caught. Since we had no guns, this struck me as being a little difficult.

Anyway, I couldn't quite believe that they would shoot us outright. In fact, it seemed more reasonable that they would simply imprison us or hold us for ransom. It would not be pleasant, but at least we would be alive. To help us over the first difficult moment, if it should arise, I decided to learn how to say in Chinese, "I am Khrushchev's son." Armies are the same the world over. If I could sow even a little doubt about the correct course of action, the matter would be referred to higher authority. No patrol leader would dare act on his own. So we would be taken back with them, and the time for shooting would be past.

KC met the Indian liaison officer, his counterpart of the Indian expedition to climb Everest by the now traditional south route. The liaison officer for the German-Swiss Pumori expedition was also in town. KC began to make noises about how well-equipped the other liaison officers were. I could feel the beginning of additional campaigns. But finances were low. We were going to have to get KC out of Namche Bazar as fast as possible.

In the afternoon, the long-smouldering feud between KC and the Sherpas broke into the open. They refused to serve him tea, and took away his special cup. The Sherpas looked down on the Nepalese as not being real "mountain men". On the other hand, the Nepalese, who, like KC, had come from the capital into the back country, looked down on the local populace as basically unsophisticated and ignorant yokels. There were heated exchanges. We settled it for the moment by giving up one of our cups to KC. However, from then on the war between the Nepalese and the Sherpas intensified.

One of the yaks became a mother during the day. For some reason it took a special dislike to me. Every time I tried to go from the ladder to the outside door it charged me. Since it was pitch black down there, all I could do was hear it coming and jump with all my might. Everyone got a huge laugh, except me. These animals *scare* me. I suppose it was just that she was a new mother and also that "Sahibs" smell strangely, so that all the animals always eye us suspiciously. Anyway, I made no trips out of the house that night.

What a collection of unlikely carriers greeted us next morning! They were mainly young girls and old men. Pemba told us that the supply was depleted from all the other expeditions in the area. I was discouraged. I couldn't believe we would ever make it with these. We made a late start. An hour out on the trail, Pemba stumbled off it and somersaulted end over end down about 40 feet. Amazingly, he was bloody but unhurt. Poor Pemba. Too many relatives and too many toasts in *rakshi* to success and safe return. Pemba apologized again. A little later Chombi appeared on the trail, having come out of his home village of Khumjung to give us a send-off. He had a pitcher of *chang* for us. We partook and then said good-by. It started raining. About noon we turned off the regular expedition route of the south approach to Everest. We turned north up the Dudh Kosi River again. From now on we would be on ground that was new to me as far as my reading went. Even Pemba didn't know this area. We hoped there was a trail at least part of the way.

The next day we lost the trail. The loads were too heavy for the girls, and we ran into banks of snow on the march. We made wretched progress and camped for the night in some yak herder's stone huts. Immediately it started snowing as if it meant business. There was a rumor that the porters would quit tomorrow if conditions did not get better. Again spirits were low.

Then next day there was brilliant sun. The snow melted. We had a council of war, and it was decided that Aila, Roger, and I would push ahead for two days and see if we could find a good Base Camp spot, as well as mark out the easiest trail ahead. In an hour the three of us took off. The pace was fast. We climbed steadily through rocky meadows and along glacial streams. We followed one of the many dozens of crisscrossing yak trails. At lunch we stopped in the deserted village of Tanna. A little later the snow fields began, but they were hard and flat and good walking.

Almost immediately Roger and I, who were ahead, noticed two sets of tracks going our way. They were as wide as a man's foot but a good deal shorter. A third, much smaller set joined the other two. When Aila caught up, he was very excited and said, "Yeti, Yeti" (the "Abominable Snowman"). We laughed skeptically, but the tracks did seem to have what might be a deeper knuckleprint in the front center and they were pretty large. We followed them for about two miles. Being on reconnaissance, we carried no cameras. But I felt that if there were tracks the very first time we hit snow, there would surely be some all over. They were probably very common. Of course, it actually turned out that we never saw another set of tracks the whole trip. It is something you would almost give your right finger to have pictures of.

Ocassionally I thought I saw rocks piled as a cairn on our path. Had the Japanese left them the year before when they reconnoitered Gyachung Kang? That night we found an old campsite with cans still lying around. From their labels I guessed that we were camping on the same spot the Japanese had camped on.

Today the altitude hit me. On McKinley, too, it had hit me at a fairly low level, and then given me much less trouble later. I think it was due to going so fast and far, with very little to eat. After supper I felt a lot better, although the headache persisted.

In the morning the three of us pushed on several miles along the Ngo Jumbo Glacier. We found fairly easy walking on the lateral moraine which forms a kind of terrace along the right bank of the glacier as you look up it. But finally we had to descend onto the glacier itself. It is a 300-foot drop, and we had a hard time finding a way down which porters with loads were going to be able to handle. After we got down, we walked for a half mile on the glacier over loose rock piles balanced on the ice. The footing was impossible. Finally we were able to climb up to the terrace again, and we continued along it.

Three exciting moments occurred this day. The first was when we were crossing a side valley, which is actually the valley of the Guanara Glacier. We looked up it, and there, in a perfect frame, stood Everest. It looked exactly like the aerial shot taken by the Royal Indian Air Force from the northwest, only, of course, from much lower down. This was my first actual view. In a way it was too classical a pose to seem real. Yet there was a surge of excitement to see it looming so close at the end of the valley. Again I was sorry we had no camera. A few minutes after this first perfect view Everest disappeared behind the clouds.

Meanwhile we kept hoping to catch our first full view of Gyachung Kang. At each corner we felt that now at last we would see the peak we were supposed to be climbing. I had become fond of the peak and tremendously impressed with its reported difficulties. I was eager to see it for myself. Then at last we did round a corner from which we could see, and there it was, tremendously impressive and apparently impregnable. Roger and I looked through the glasses at it for a long time. Maybe it could be reached from the western snow slopes, but they looked dangerously subject to avalanche. Still, if we couldn't make the icefall, or if the liaison officer prevented us somehow from going on into Tibet, it certainly would be exciting to give this peak a try.

Finally, we reached a spot near the end of the moraine where we could see down into the basin where we hoped to put our Base Camp. We had our third moment of excitement when we saw that the way down was clear and that this stage of the expedition could be completed successfully.

Roger and I also looked at the ice cliffs we were

going to have to climb from Base Camp. From this distance they didn't look too bad to us. We spotted what looked like a possible route up the extreme right side, looking up. Unfortunately, a big part of it looked like an avalanche track; it was *too* smooth. This would have to be avoided. Also there was one barrier of huge seracs, or ice towers, that would have to be surmounted. But we both felt optimistic that some way could be found.

And so we returned back on our tracks to the Guanara Glacier and found that the main caravan was already camped there. I was very pleased. Norm had done a magnificent job in getting all the porters up this far in just two days. I didn't see how they had been induced to traverse the nasty section on the Ngo Jumbo Glacier. Norm told me that he had had a bit of a set-to with HansPeter. It appeared that HansPeter had gotten tired of the slow pace of the column of porters and had hiked on ahead after Roger and me. Later he had gotten himself lost, and Norm had had to send one of the Sherpas to find him. Norm had then laid down the law to HansPeter rather roughly. When ordered to stay with the column he would do so, or else. HansPeter came to me and said that if we didn't want him he would leave. I reassured HansPeter that we did want him. Norm, in this case, was right. HansPeter had a job to do with the baggage train that he should not have abandoned. Still, I felt that Norm was more autocratic than he needed to be. I didn't feel that any of us should order the others around. Perhaps the most ominous factor, however, was that HansPeter should have become lost in full sunlight in an open valley. I worried that his "Alpinism" might not be as good as I had hoped.

The next morning was again beautiful. We followed the moraine almost to its end, then dropped down onto the Ngo Jumbo Glacier, where Pemba found a rock pile that was well out of the way of potential avalanches. The porters stacked their loads, were paid, and left quickly. As they disappeared from sight, I remembered feeling lonely. There were just the eight of us and our little pile of equipment in the middle of nowhere. Somehow the pile seemed pitifully small. Then, when I thought of just the four of us carrying all this on our backs for a month, the pile suddenly seemed impossibly big.

The mood of loneliness passed, for there was work to be done. We made rock platforms for the tents. We broke open the high altitude gear and distributed it. We set up the sleeping bags and mattresses in the tents. KC was to sleep in the big Base Camp tent of Lambert's with his three enemies, Pemba, Aila, and Putharkey. Norm and I would sleep in one of the high-altitude tents, Roger and HansPeter in the other. We made a windbreak out of the sack of supplies and covered them with a tarpaulin. Finally we were as comfortable as possible. It was Tuesday, April 24, just three days later than we had planned to be here. Not bad, I felt. At five o'clock it started snowing.

VIII

THE ICEFALL

So far, others had been moving us along. Now we were going to have to move them. On the trail the Sherpas picked the route, selected the camps, and generally made the decisions. Now suddenly it was up to us. It was our turn to perform, but could we? From our camp at 16,500 to the notch on the border of Tibet the glacier rises about 3,000 feet in a distance of 3 miles. There are two nearly vertical rises of about 1,000 feet each in this stretch. These two cliffs were going to be our main obstacle.

I looked out at the wilderness of fallen blocks and ice cliffs all crossed and crisscrossed with a thousand blue gashes, which are the crevasses, and felt that the whole business was a bit ridiculous. Someone should hold up their arm and shout, "Charge!" However there was nothing to do but get on with it.

The sun rose early, and we sorted our ropes and crampons and climbing gear. Everything seemed awkward. There was a smoother-looking trough at the right center of the glacier that looked like a possible line of advance. I asked Pemba where he thought we should try first and was pleased that he independently picked the same spot. So we started out in single file, heading toward the trough. Gradually it got steeper. Courteously, I offered Pemba the chance to lead. It was a compliment that he accepted graciously. Then I watched him like a hawk to see how this business is done. Almost immediately I felt relieved. He stepped just about where I would have stepped, he paused just about where I would have paused, and his wielding of the ice axe, while effective, didn't seem to involve anything too impossible. I felt that my feeling of inferiority was unfounded. Then a little later I was leading, and I noticed that Pemba was cautiously enlarging some of the steps I had used to climb on. I felt better and better. In fact I felt elated. My very first step had held. It was respectably flat, not just a chewed-up indentation. Moreover, Pemba and Aila showed no evidence that we were in anyway acting unusual. My confidence grew. In spite of all their experience on ice and snow, I felt our rock-climbing experience would soon give us a decided advantage in skill over the Sherpas.

After an hour we came to a chasm which obviously would take a half day to cut down into and up again. Even if it could be done, there was another beyond it, and another and another. The smooth trough had run out. We split into two groups and tried several lines. All failed. The pattern of the crevasses tended to push us farther and farther toward the right and the route that Roger and I had originally spotted from the moraine on our first reconnaissance together. Finally we circled over completely to the route we had seen. It took us up about halfway, where we faced the huge avalanche track that we had also noted before. This chute rose about 500 feet vertically above us. It was obviously the pathway for a large proportion of the great ice blocks that kept tumbling down from the heights above. Equally obviously, it was a good place to stay away from. We named it the "Toboggan Slide". We spotted a possible route that circumvented the slide to the left. But by now it was broiling hot in the glacier, our skin was burning up from the sun, and we still had a good long walk back to camp. So we quit for the day.

Well, we had survived our first day. Roger, Norm, and I felt pretty good about it. I had been apprehensive about how we would appear to the Sherpas. But even with all their experience they were at most only equal. So we could lead and direct with good conscience. The icefall was going to be long and difficult, but we didn't think it was going to be impossible. As to its dangers, I felt the crevasses were relatively harmless. Basically, the glacier was bare of snow, so that the crevasses could easily be seen and prepared for. The falling debris was another matter. At all times the glacier was tremendously noisy. Sudden roars, as a section of cliff sheared off and pulverized all below it, creaks, groans, subterranean rumbles, a sudden snap and the tinkle of ice chips falling away as a smaller block collapsed—all these noises warned us that the glacier was in constant movement. A safe passage today might perfectly well be bombed from above tomorrow, or fatally weakened from below. There was not much that could be done about these dangers, except try to avoid the chutes where avalanches had obviously come down regularly. One trouble, however, was that these very chutes were often the only practicable path upwards.

I think the aspect that worried me most about the glacier, however, was its length. Somehow I had imagined that the two cliffs would be short sharp obstacles which, once surmounted, would then be done with. Instead we were going to have to contend with at least two miles of difficult ground. Standing in Base Camp, the whole glacier flowed down upon us like a great Niagara. Imagine this huge flood as water spuming and writhing down two miles of rapids, thundering out and down over cliffs, spouting from ledge to ledge. Now wave a wand and freeze the whole torrent. Only it is not frozen hard enough to stop it absolutely. It still writhes, but piece by piece. It still thunders out and down, but only a bit at a time. This, then, was going to mean a long job of route finding and a still longer job of load carrying, even if the route was found. Because of the carrying, it would not be sufficient just to climb this icefall once. We had to find a route good enough to be traveled by heavily loaded men again and again. I began to think that the ten days I had estimated for surmounting this obstacle was going to be far too short. We had yet to climb the icefall even once.

Next morning we set out directly for the point we had reached the day before at the foot of the Toboggan Slide. I had studied the whole area through the glasses and was sure that I had spotted a route that would go at least as far as the top of the slide. It by-passed the chute on its left, looking up. We appeared with a set of weird face masks. I was the surgeon with gauze taped across my face from the eyes down. Norm sported a large, white nose guard, HansPeter swathed in white was the ghost, and Roger with a red cloth face mask and his crash helmet looked the part of a Martian.

We split up into two parties. Roger, Aila, and I tried the line I had spotted from camp. Pemba, Norm, and HansPeter tried alternative possibilities. My route seemed to work pretty well; we surmounted several steep pitches. Then we came to a bigger wall. I wanted to try one crack, Roger another. Since we were both on an end of the rope, with Aila in the middle, we decided to save time by each doing the preliminary work on our own crack while Aila belayed us from below. I worked up and into an ice tunnel. I called to Roger that my way would go. Roger said he would be over. Then we called down to Aila. Only there wasn't any Aila. Incredibly, Aila had decided that he knew a better way. He had unroped and gone off on his own, and was nowhere to be seen. It was a bit of a shock. Here we were moving precariously up a cliff, each depending on a third man for support—only the third man didn't exist. Without a word, he had simply walked off. We couldn't help laughing, and yet I felt that I should be furious. It would make a fine story for the climbing clubs at home.

Roger and I continued up by ourselves and eventually reached the level of the top of the Toboggan Slide. But now in front of us lay a terribly shattered area with an unbroken line of overhanging ice blocks barring the way on the far side. I saw no way over or through them. As we were standing there Aila appeared. He had gone over to the chute and walked directly up it. We scolded him, but I had the feeling that he didn't understand too much of what we said. So we roped him in the middle again and headed back for camp. We decided to come down the Toboggan Slide to save time. We felt we would be in the line of fire for so short a time that the risk was justified.

That evening I was discouraged. Our highest point was still quite possibly a dead end. The huge barrier of overhanging blocks lay between us and the top of the first icefall, and I saw no promising way through them. Tomorrow we would somehow just have to chop our way over or through. Once we were up, we would have, I felt, fairly easy going along the right bank until we got to the second icefall. But the cliffs on this fall looked even more forbidding than those of the first fall. As insurance we decided that one group should try an entirely new route all the way over on the left bank, looking up, of the glacier. Roger and I would continue from where we left off. We would take Pemba with us and send Aila with the others. Pemba might be more reliable.

In the morning the three of us walked directly to the foot of the Toboggan Slide in a little over an hour. We looked up the slide. Everything was quiet. It lay in blue shadow, frosty and cold. We were tempted to go directly up. It *would* save a lot of time. Besides, it should be at its safest in the early morning before the sun loosened things up. Temptation won. We went up the slide. At every rest we moved to the left, off the slide, and picked out some large ice block that we felt would protect us from anything coming down from above. At the top of the slide was a kind of gateway made by two hotel-sized blocks. If they came down, there would be no hope.

But nothing happened. We arrived safely at the gateway and passed through onto the more level ground beyond. Roger made a fine lead across the fractured area, then we faced the problem of the great overhanging ice blocks. Pemba shook his head at every way we suggested. "Some difficult," he said. "Some difficult." But we realized now that every way was going to be "some difficult" and we just had to make it work. We started on a crack which opened out to a little valley, and our hopes rose. Pemba begged off, so we told him to rest in a flat spot, and Roger and I went on.

All went well until we came to a large pair of intersecting crevasses too deep to climb down into and too wide to jump. There was one way possible. A wedged block of ice led to a thin vertical flake, which in turn led to a spot from which the second crevasse could be jumped. Here was the first lead that actually scared me. There was a blue drop on both sides of the flake so deep that I couldn't even see the bottom, and I wasn't at all sure that the wedged block would stay wedged. I went part way, then quit and came back. Then, because there was no other way, I tried again. It was a little easier the second time. I balanced precariously, and gingerly pushed on. And then suddenly I had made it. I grinned back up at Roger and felt wonderful.

After crossing the crevasse, I went on for a bit alone. I jumped two more crevasses and then came to a bigger one. I was excited to see that if I could cross this and descend a 60-foot cliff, the route would be through to the top of the first icefall. I returned for Roger, as I had to see what the cliff looked like, but I didn't want to jump the last crevasse without a rope. Together we went to the crevasse. Neither of us wanted to jump it, so we dawdled around trying to outwait the other. Finally we tossed for it and I lost. When I finally jumped, I overjumped it by a good 2 feet. I guess my adrenalin was working well. I looked over the edge of the cliff and saw that the route would "go". The first icefall had been climbed.

We made our way back to camp through the usual snowfall. The others were very pleased with our success, since they had gotten nowhere with their route. But when the sun came out again at supper time, I spent a long time with the binoculars trying to search out an easier route. I was still worried that there were too many crevasses to be crossed. We had no extension ladders, logs, and other bridging materials that seem to be necessary equipment on the Everest expeditions nowadays. This meant that every large crevasse was going to cause a long delay, for roping each man and each load across a crevasse separately literally eats up the time. In the long run it would mean days of extra carrying time, unless we could simplify the route. I thought I saw something, but I decided to wait until morning before broaching it to the others.

That night I lay awake for a while in my tent. The warm glow of all we had accomplished today lingered with me. I thought back over the crevasse I had led across, and how wonderful I had felt when I got across it. I wondered to myself why such a thing should make a man feel so good. Certainly it is one of the things that bring men back to climbing again and again. But what causes it? I reflected that one requirement seems to be that you have to have sweated a bit—probably the more the better. And what makes you sweat is primarily physical danger. Of course, there are other dangers—psychological anxieties, threats to the person of all kinds—but only physical danger has the sharp immediacy which can prick the hide or make a quick clutch for the stomach. So these other dangers won't do.

I was sleepy, but I wrote in my diary how ironic it was that if physical danger can make you feel so good, nevertheless there are thousands of people who seem to do nothing else in the world except try to eliminate it. Personally, I think a man needs physical danger. It cleans him and it tests him. If he is protected from it entirely, he loses something important, whether he knows it or not. Instinctively, primitive societies recognize this. They abound with customs and rituals where physical danger provides the keen cutting edge—the knife that tests. Today, as individuals, we still try to satisfy this need. It may be something rather spectacular, such as surfboarding, parachute jumping, car racing, gang wars, or it may be something more ordinary, such as simply taking a ski run faster than you are sure you can do it. But to a greater or lesser degree, all share the same goodness: they can all give us the rather unpleasant tightness of before and the relaxed, proud feeling of after.

But for the feeling to be proud, demands must be made on your nerve and especially your skill. Just danger by itself is not enough. That is why, for instance, I never derived any particular satisfaction from climbing up and down the Toboggan Slide. For it was luck, not skill, that nothing big came down on us. The only pleasure, then, was simply to be rid of it.

The dangers that can arouse the real sense of satisfaction are not to be confused with what simply seem to the public to be dangers. Many things that seem very dangerous to the outsider are actually routine, and this shift to the routine goes on all the time. A man fixing the roof of his house, for instance, will walk the third or fourth time over places he crawled the first time. In fact, a man can get used to just about anything. We fear what we are not used to. Put a mountain climber on a high steel girder and let him try to carry a heavy plank in a stiff breeze, and he is likely to be petrified. But the same would go for the high-steel worker if he were put on a vertical rock face. Generally, if you know what your body can do and what your skill can handle, you will not be afraid of the obstacles within your power, even though to others they may seem terrifying.

That is why the crevasses did not particularly bother me. After a short period of experiment, I found that the climbing problems on ice were not too different from the climbing problems on rock. A few modifications of technique and a lot of practice were all that was required. Since I already had the techniques for rock climbing, the crevasses were in fact routine obstacles.

What was left? The crevasses were routine, the avalanches were out of my control. So what was left that could give me a satisfaction such as I had had today? Well, every climber has his own limits of technique. The satisfaction comes when one walks the feather edge of these limits, when one pushes forward in a spot that one suspects may be too much for one's particular level of skill. And always in the background is the knowledge that there may be a good stiff penalty if, in fact, it *is* too much.

You can't fake this. Some, indeed, postpone and avoid any problem that would really push them to the limits of their skill. But then they don't get the full feeling of satisfaction. Anyway, although both Roger and I did more difficult leads later on, both of us had pushed *our* limits today. Indeed there were several times each of us could turn and grin at the other.

And this brings up one last point. The people with whom you have grinned this way, the people with whom you have shared the tension and later shared the proud afterglow—they make up a very special group. It is as if only they and you are really alive. You walk the heights, while the rest of the world sleeps dully below. True or not, this is the way you *feel*.

Thinking about the rest of the world being asleep

suddenly seemed like a good idea. So I closed my ears to the noises of the glacier and joined them.

Next morning Roger and I went off to work on improving the route to make it safe for the load carriers. The others were to start moving supplies from Base Camp to a cache at the foot of the Toboggan Slide. But Norm decided to stay in camp, and clean and repackage equipment, and HansPeter turned up with a sick stomach. So Roger and I found ourselves climbing the Toboggan Slide alone. It was muggy and the icefall was an incinerator in a brutal sun. Both of us were tired from the day before and neither felt like undertaking the dull routine of improving an old route. Only something new could stir me, so I broached my idea.

From the gateway, I thought we could traverse all the way to the side of the glacier underneath the rampart of overhanging blocks, and turn the rampart at the very juncture between it and the side wall of the glacier. This way I believed there would be no big crevasses to cross. But it was risky. The overhanging blocks were festooned with icicles. Some of these weighed at least 200 pounds, so that, even if the whole block didn't topple over on us, there was imminent danger of being caught by any of these hundreds of icicles.

Roger was not enthusiastic, but it was a way to avoid working on the old route. So we tried it. I must say it was a nasty route. We went from one uncomfortable spot to another, where all we could do was glance anxiously upward and then hurry on. But the route did go, and it did turn out to be free of major crevasses. We reached the top of the icefall, chose a campsite—to be called Camp I—from which to scout the second icefall, and returned the long march to Base Camp. For me it was a tiring eight-hour day of practically continuous climbing. In spite of the long day, Roger volunteered to go back up to the base of the "Toboggan Slide" with Aila and HansPeter in order to get an early start the next day for climbing up and establishing Camp I.

103

Again I was impressed by his tremendous energy. They took off after supper.

Personally, I felt that I had been overdoing and that I need a day of semi-rest. So I would join with the others in donkeying supplies from Base Camp up to our cache at the foot of the Toboggan Slide. In the morning I felt so good that I decided to carry a double load. The Sherpas had claimed that from Base Camp on the normal load should be 25 pounds. So yesterday they and Norm had divided all the supplies into packets of that amount. But I didn't want to have to make the three-hour round trip twice on my "day of rest". So I shouldered the double load and set off. I was pleased to find that the pace was only a little slower than with a single load. Norm followed along with a double load also. But he fell behind and had a terrible time with it. At the cache I waited for a long time, and finally went back and helped him over the last bit. Again I realized that Norm was having the hardest time of the four in acclimatizing. He had headaches, and difficulty in breathing, and tired quickly. I worried that this would make Norm feel guilty and inferior. Actually, no one can predict who will be affected badly by altitude and who will not, so that it is nothing to blame oneself for. But, unavoidably, the psychology of the situation is that you do. At the time I merely felt grateful it was someone else, and not me, who had to struggle so hard. I also felt how dangerous in terms of pride it would be to sympathize or help too much. I gave a silent prayer that the symptoms would go away.

In the afternoon, back at Base Camp, KC talked to me about the possibility of his retiring down the valley to Khumjung during the time we would be climbing high. I had told him that we planned to be gone for around thirty days after we reached the top of the icefall. The Sherpas were to stay at Base Camp in case we needed their help. We would be pushing upward on Gyachung Kang on the back side of a ridge that could not be seen from Base Camp. All along I had been afraid that KC might insist on coming with us at least far enough to discover that there was no route up to Gyachung Kang on the back side of the ridge, and that actually we were going to be making a stab all the way to Everest during those thirty days. I was hoping he would retire down the valley, as everything would be much easier then. But I didn't dare suggest it outright, as he might immediately balk. So I was very happy that at last he had made the suggestion himself. The good life lower down had sung sweetly to him. His official position as liaison officer would make him an important figure. On the other hand, the prospect of spending a whole month alone in Base Camp with his enemies was completely unappealing. So, rather hesitantly, he asked me if it would be all right. I agreed, but without letting my enthusiasm show, and so the matter was settled.

Incidentally, during the whole walk-in we had hidden our one map of the Everest region from KC. Whenever we looked at it, we would do it in secret, when he was not around. For I hoped that KC might not be aware that Gyachung Kang *was* on the border of Tibet. If so, he might not object, even if he did insist on coming beyond Base Camp with us. Maybe we could convince him that Everest was actually Gyachung Kang. However er KC seemed to be pretty smart about these things. The other day, in fact, he asked us why, since we had come this far, we didn't climb Everest. We answered hastily that that was much too hard for us, and anyway we didn't have permission for it. But he also told us again that there were Communist patrols up at the high passes, so the thought kept crossing my mind that maybe he suspected us a bit. I couldn't believe that the idea of our climbing Everest had occurred to him. If anything, it was simply that he guessed we might be crossing the border for at least a little way.

During the next few days we were all busy ferrying loads from the Base Camp to the cache at the foot of the "Toboggan Slide", from the "Toboggan Slide" on up to Camp I, and from Camp I on to a new cache at the foot of the second icefall. Two occurrences stood out particularly. In the first, I had come with the Sherpas to the cache below the "Toboggan Slide". We were resting and loading up for the climb to Camp I. In another fifteen minutes we would be on the slide itself. Suddenly, the whole left side of the chute came down. It was started by a huge block that toppled majestically, then literally pulverized everything below it. Every one of our "safe" resting places was wiped out, including the route that Roger and I had taken on the second day when Aila abandoned us. We stood there awed by the size of the thing. The pure accident that we were not pulverized also affected us all. I took the opportunity of pointing out to Aila that this was one reason we had told him to avoid the slide in the first place. It seemed to have some effect. By mutual consent we decided that the trip up to Camp I was going to have to wait for another day.

Back in camp, I argued that if we made an early enough start in the morning the ice would be harder and we could make it all right. Also I argued that everything that could come down had come down, so the slide should be safer than ever before. No one was very convinced, but next morning we went up it again without incident.

The second occurrence concerned HansPeter. Roger and I were carrying loads up to Camp I. Just before the camp we ran into HansPeter sitting on the side of the trail. It was ten o'clock and he said he had been there since seven. I was amazed. He was supposed to have come down to the cache that morning to pick up a load and join us in ferrying back up to Camp I. I asked him why he had not come down. He motioned to the ice blocks, "The sun hit the top of the seracs," he said. "The route was no longer safe." I was so astonished that I said nothing. Later he told me that our ways of climbing were not his ways, but that he would be glad to do anything for us he considered safe, such as donkeying supplies from Camp I to the foot of the second icefall. Since he had discussed this very possibility with me back in Geneva, he was perfectly correct. He was under no obligation to do anything he considered to be dangerous. Indeed he was very helpful in the succeeding days doing a job that had to be done.

Meanwhile, everything was moved slowly upward. On the eighth day we finally cleaned out Base Camp. Only the permanent tent and the supplies for the Sherpas were left. Putharkey and KC left for the happier hunting grounds down valley. Pemba and Aila joined the four of us at Camp I.

On the ninth day we brought up all that remained of the cache at the foot of the "Toboggan Slide". I was more than glad to see the last of it, but it had one parting scare for us. We were crossing on the long traverse beneath the ice blocks when suddenly the ground rocked and trembled beneath us. There was a huge roar. A great section must have peeled off directly beneath us, but we could see nothing except a slowly rising cloud of ice powder. There was no telling when something else would go, including the ledges we were standing on, or whether the vibrations might not bring all kinds of debris down from above. Never did fully loaded men scamper faster.

This same day, back up at Camp I, Roger and I started off to complete a route up the second icefall. Roger, almost alone, had pioneered brilliantly up the first half, but the last half was being stubborn. Some serious reconnaissance was required. He took me as far as he had gone, then we explored the various possibilities. By late afternoon there was only one we had not explored. But that one lay over a dome of crusted snow. In trying it earlier, I had half fallen through. Then, looking into the hole I had made, I was upset to see that the whole dome was hollow, simply stretching over a great empty chasm. I felt that three climbers on the rope would be a lot safer in this kind of situation, since two can extricate a third from a crevasse, whereas with just one it is sometimes impossible. So we returned to Camp I with mainly negative results. I was frightfully tired, having back-packed and walked since 6 A.M. I had been going steadily at an altitude of over 18,000 feet for twelve hours.

That night I was so tired that I slept badly for the first time. I felt I was suffocating in the blackness of the tent. Having Pemba in the tent also didn't help. The hours dragged endlessly by. Nevertheless, Norm, Roger, and I set off the next morning early for more reconnaissance. We crossed the dome and eliminated some more possibilities. Typical of this period was what I call the useless lead. For instance, there was a 30- or 40-foot cliff ahead of us. If we could get to the top of it, we might have a way ahead. So I started up. I got too high and realized that there was no turning back, for I did not have enough strength left to cut the better steps that would be needed if I was to descend safely. I gasped for breath and cut steps first with one hand then the other. I stepped up on the bare minimum and hung on. Finally I was almost up, but was stuck below the overhang of the crest. Norm passed up a piton, and I reached over and pounded it in. I thanked heaven the ice was firm. I scratched a few semi-steps, grabbed the piton, and hauled myself over the top. As I lay there gasping, I reflected that I was a crazy fool, for the climb couldn't have been any closer to the "just possible", at least as far as my ability was concerned. It was much too close a margin. As the others came up they could follow a trail of blood where my bare hands had clawed into the ice desperately. And then, when we were all up, we found that the top led us nowhere. Furthermore, some 50 feet farther along there was an easy way down that would have been just as easy up. All that work for nothing.

And yet, as before, it was the part of climbing I enjoyed the most.

On the way back, Roger spotted an ice formation that he thought he recognized. If he was right we could branch off our trail and in fact be above all the particular cliffs we had been trying to climb earlier. I was skeptical, but Roger talked us into trying. He was right again. Roger had a great gift for being able to recognize landmarks and natural features from different angles— above, below, from a direction not hitherto seen, and so forth. His natural skill at this was amazing. So now we had a route that took us three-quarters of the way up the second icefall. Tomorrow we hoped to complete it.

Tomorrow, we did complete it. Roger and I alternated leads. The last cliff was a hundred-footer. I did the first half and Roger the second. It was another bloody one for me, but this time far from useless. We were up. And so, on the eleventh day of effort, we finally had a route from the bottom to the top of the icefall.

During the next three days we managed to move everything to the top, where we established Camp II. To raise the equipment up the last vertical cliff, three men hauled from the top while the fourth tied the loads on at the bottom. It was slow, tiring work. But on our fourteenth day in the icefall, the tents themselves were hauled to the top and Camp II was officially established. On hand, were 480 pounds of food and equipment which would last us for a minimum of thirty days. We sent the Sherpas down for the last time with strict instructions to keep the Base Camp manned against our return in about a month—sometime after the first of June. They went off jubilantly, more than happy to get a paid thirty-day vacation. Originally, I had planned to dismiss all porters the moment we got to Base Camp. But gradually, we had succumbed to the easy temptation of keeping at least Pemba, Aila, and Putharkey for cooking and carrying. In fact they had been very helpful. I had planned ten days to get everything up the icefall. It had actually taken us fourteen. Without the Sherpas helping it might have taken eighteen.

We were now a week behind schedule. We had started two days late from Kathmandu, we had rested a day in Namche Bazar, and we had spent four extra days in the icefall. However, I felt this didn't particularly matter. Extra time had been allowed for contingencies anyway. And who was to say just which week of the ones ahead would be the ideal week for climbing Everest? The delay might even turn out to be a good break.

We watched the Sherpas disappear down the glacier below us. Now it was just the four of us. We felt excited. The liaison officer was gone, the Sherpas were gone, nobody could stop us now. We were well supplied, we were healthy, the next thirty days could be IT. Our hopes soared.

IX

INTO TIBET

Camp II was a little over 19,000 feet high, with a stunning view of the Ngo Jumbo Glacier stretching off for miles below us. Seeming very close to us now were the peaks of Gyachung Kang (25,910 feet) and Cho Oyo (26,400 feet). Mt. Everest was still hidden from view. It lay to the east and south of us about 15 air miles away, but about 25 miles by the circuitous glacier route we would actually be traveling. I planned ten days to get to it, eight days to take our one fling at climbing it, and five days to return from it with the light loads we would then be carrying. The round trip journey would thus be exactly twenty-three days. To this I added seven days simply as a cushion for whatever contingencies might arise. There was no telling what might come up to delay us, but there was a good probability that something would.

For these thirty days each man had a total of 120 pounds to carry with him; 60 of these were food. We planned to break the 120 pounds into three loads of 40 pounds each. At each night's stop we would leave a cache of food for the return trip. Since we would be eating up roughly 2 pounds of food per day per person, I felt that we could eventually carry our supplies in two loads instead of three. This, of course, would speed up our movement considerably.

The morning was cold and clear. We made up our packs and set off. First there was a crevassed area, but this quickly ran out and we found ourselves in a great white empty plain of unbroken snow stretching off for miles to the east. It rose gently to an indeterminate high point, then gradually descended. Somewhere at one of the high points, we stepped over into Tibet. I lifted and held an imaginary strand of barbed wire for the others to pass under, then offered to have my baggage inspected, but no one appeared. Indeed, I reflected that to the best of my knowledge only three human beings had ever crossed the boundary at this point in the history of the world.

Ahead of us we began to see the sharp pyramid which I recognized as the North Peak. And then a little later, to its right, quite suddenly the North Face itself appeared. We photographed madly, but very soon the clouds closed in over it. We continued. I picked out a rocky outcropping on the Gyachung side of the glacier and suggested we have lunch when we got to it. We made bets on how long it would take us to get there. I thought less than an hour, but the highest guess was still only two. We walked for another hour and it seemed no closer at all. Again we made bets. Again we walked. Finally we sat down in the snow and had lunch. Actually, so deceptive are the distances, it took us two full days of walking to reach those rocks.

The walking was exceptionally good. Nevertheless, the first man broke through at each step to a depth of about a foot, and this was tiring. We were grateful it was not 2 or 3 feet, which would have made it a terrible struggle. Naturally, the first man was the martyr. This

112

first day Roger and HansPeter were the martyrs. I felt weak and Norm was lagging behind. We walked about 4 miles and deposited our loads on the edge of a side glacier which came in from the north—actually, the far West Rongbuk Glacier. The mid-morning snowstorm started up, only a good bit harder than usual. As we started back, the snow blew full in our faces and the wind was miserably cold. Our earlier trail was quickly obliterated, so that we had to stamp out a new one. If it really closed in I was afraid that we might not find our way back to camp. Here, we were violating a lesson well-learned on McKinley; namely, that one must never move any great distance from camp without marking the trail. A willow wand every hundred feet does very well and we had some along with us for just that purpose. But it was one more burdensome thing to do. So, as we did so often, we had taken the easier way and simply let it go. Generally, one is too tired to do anything that isn't absolutely necessary at the moment. Again, I had to admire the stamina of Roger. He made trail for us all the way back. Behind him, the rest of us followed in single file, crouching low to take advantage of our human windbreak. We walked with heads bent low and eyes fastened on the two plodding feet in front of us. Anytime you looked up, you received a blast of wind-driven snow directly in the eyes.

Fortunately the weather got no worse and we arrived back at the crevassed area without losing our way. I suggested we rope up. It was a happy suggestion for, twenty steps later, HansPeter walked into an open crevasse. With the rope there was no great difficulty getting him out. Without it, he would have had a serious fall. Here, and later on, I was surprised at the mutual magnetism that seemed to exist between the crevasses and HansPeter.

In camp that night I felt discouraged. It seemed to me that we had walked a long day's journey. We were going to have to walk it twice more. And yet where had

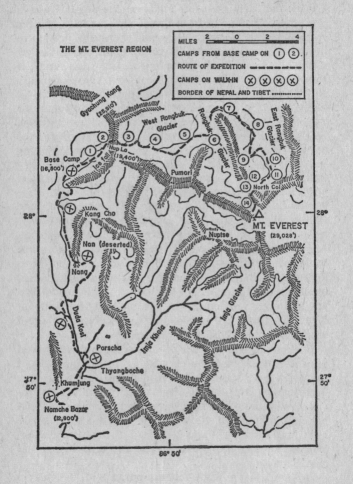

THE MT. EVEREST REGION

MILES 2 0 2 4

CAMPS FROM BASE CAMP ON ① ②
ROUTE OF EXPEDITION ————
CAMPS ON WALK-IN ⓧ ⓧ ⓧ ⓧ
BORDER OF NEPAL AND TIBET ⋯⋯⋯⋯

Gyachung Kang (25,910')
West Rongbuk Glacier
Nup La (19,400')
Ice fall
Base Camp (16,500')
Ronbuk Glacier
East Rongbuk Glacier
Pumori
North Col
Kang Cho
Nan (deserted)
Nang
MT. EVEREST (29,028')
Nuptse
Duda Kosi
Imla Glacier
Imla Khola
Porscha
Thyangboche
Khumjung
Namche Bazar (12,800')

28°
28°
27° 50'
27° 50'
86° 50'

we gotten to? The side glacier looked like a long and fairly tough obstacle to cross. But it wasn't even shown on our rather crude maps. How far was it from there to the Main Rongbuk Glacier? Days maybe. Ten days to the North Col began to look quite inadequate.

I turned to the job of cooking. This was the second night of preparing all our own food. I was glad to be doing it again, as we had on McKinley. There is a routine about the whole business that is really very pleasant. On coming into camp, if it is a new location, Norm and I both worked first to smooth and clear a reasonably flat tent site, either in the snow or on rocks. Then we would pitch the tent together. I would crawl in first and Norm would pass in the packs and other gear. I would pull out the air mattresses and sleeping bags, blow up the former, and arrange the latter on top. Then I would stow all special night articles—flashlight, cough drops, canteens, handkerchief, and so forth—in predesignated, easy-to-reach spots. I would take off boots and outer down clothing, and arrange them as supplements to the mattress and pillow. Finally I would crawl at least halfway into my sleeping bag, put on the dry socks carefully stored there, and then call Norm.

Norm had meanwhile been finishing the tightening and adjusting of the tent, and storing all outside equipment so that it didn't disappear if there should be a major snowfall during the night. He would then crawl in and repeat the contortions I had gone through—undressing, storing equipment in its own individually chosen place, and crawling into his sleeping bag. With all this done, we reached for the cooking pot, filled it with previously collected snow or ice, and started melting it into water on our butane gas burner.

If all went well and no one knocked the pot over, to the furious epithets of the other, we would soon have a quart of hot water which we would make either into tea or hot lemonade (with powder) or bouillon. We would melt down some more snow while we consumed our pint apiece. This was always a nice time. The stove gave out its miniature roar that somehow seemed very comforting. It burned blue and just hot enough to take the chill off the air in the tent. Often the sun would come out and the sky would clear. Norm would write in his diary, or we would talk or even doze a bit. The real evening meal still lay pleasurably ahead. It consisted of three meat bars for the two of us. Each meat bar is a pound of meat, mostly beef, reduced by dehydration to three ounces and vacuum wrapped in aluminum foil. Amazingly, even one of them really makes you feel full and satisfied. Usually we boiled this up into a stew with a little powdered egg and milk, or with hot pepper and chile. Sometimes I was too hungry to wait and just gnawed my bar plain. Supper was brought to a close with a third course which was either a pot of hot cocoa or hot tea.

Since our diet called for twelve ounces of sugar a day, we really poured the sugar into these drinks. Two tablespoonfuls in a cup was not at all unusual. At sea level this would simply the nauseating. But up here, working as hard as we were, the body came to crave calories. Even dry sugar spooned down was not too much.

Basically, a man needs 4,200 calories a day just to keep going. Carrying and climbing at over 18,000 feet is equivalent to the hardest kind of physical labor at sea level. In fact, even the 4,200 calories will not prevent a gradual deterioration. The idea is to deteriorate as slowly as possible. To provide these 4,200 calories we relied mainly on the meat bars and the 12 ounces of sugar. We had some extras for taste, in the form of powders and extracts. But no real cooking is possible. With only one pot and limited fuel, we were confined simply to heating up prepared foods. At lunch time we couldn't even do that. It is too cold and windy to cook in the open and it takes too long to raise a tent. So at lunch we would eat a few squares of semisweet chocolate, a handful of nuts and raisins, maybe a little dry biscuit and jam, and finish off with a lemon drop. We carried a pre-filled canteen for liquid.

Breakfast was tea, hot cereal, powdered eggs, and an occasional slice of bacon for fat. At the higher altitudes we left out the fats because they are too indigestible. We took most of our protein at night, since it takes longer to digest. We took our carbohydrates mainly during the day. I had read that a man can tolerate a thousand extra feet of altitude by forcing the carbohydrates during the daytime.

On the day after our first carry down to the far West Rongbuk a fearful lassitude possessed us all. We sorted our clothing, we repacked supplies, we puttered. Finally by mutual consent, we declared a holiday, our first since Namche Bazar, three weeks earlier. This is another advantage of the small expedition. There is no Olympian plan handed down from on high which must be kept to, no matter what; and there is no inexorable competition with other climbers that makes you struggle to appear strong and fit, even when you are not. All you have to do is persuade *three* others to admit that they are tired, and you have a holiday. So we spent the day merely moving our camp a couple of hundred yards beyond the crevassed area, checking over equipment, and lolling around. We also set up a cache for our return and marked it with corner flags and two intersecting lines of willow wands. I had a hunch it might be very important to be able to find it again.

The third day was almost a repeat of the first, except that I felt better and did my share of leading. We stayed over closer to the left wall. The glacier is so featureless that it is discouraging. Near the wall we could at least watch the rocks go by. We jumped on HansPeter for taking such small steps and for walking zigzag when he was leading. Also he stepped sideways with one foot which was irritating, because you either had to do the same or else go to the effort of making a new step yourself. He accused *us* of zigzagging. I guess we all did a bit.

On the way back the blizzard was, if anything, worse than the first time, and we had still not set out the willow wands. Experience is a fickle teacher. This time HansPeter played the part of King Wenceslaus and we followed in his footsteps gratefully. As on the first day it took us four hours down to the cache and three hours back. Seven hours for 4 miles of advance, an 8-mile round trip—it seemed slow, and yet on the trail we moved along at a very good pace with few stops. We were just going to have to face the fact that portering at these altitudes was a slow business. If we averaged a mile an hour we were doing well.

In the morning I started the water for the tea by 5:30. Then, as usual, I called peremptorily over to Roger and HansPeter in the other tent, telling them what a big day lay ahead and how we needed the early start. We were going to move our whole camp down to Camp III on the Far West Rongbuk Glacier. "All right, everybody up! Get a move on!" I kept at it until I got a feeble reply. This was, I am sure, hardly an endearing procedure, but it is still very necessary. There is an overwhelming psychological advantage to being first up, first to move about, first to be nauseatingly gay and cheerful. Every guide—hunting, packing, canoeing, or whatever—knows this. Those who lie in bed while others are getting breakfast never get over a hidden sense of guilt. Even if the guide does nothing for the rest of the day, he has already gained his master points. And it really doesn't take much energy to do this. Basically Roger, at least, knew we were often no nearer being ready to travel than he. Still we did call out first, we did start cooking first, and always came out of the tent first. When possible, we stood around audibly waiting just before the push-off and audibly griping that they were never ready. Anyway, it is a very necessary technique

118

for the older man. It equalizes inevitably the inner estimate of who is in fact doing their share.

It snowed and fogged badly on the way down to Camp III. We had to resort to "line" walking. The back man lines up the first man with the middle two and then calls "left", "right", or "straight" to him. In this way all four can continue in a straight line. If left to himself, the first man, staring ahead at blank whiteness, will fall off badly to one side or the other. At the end we finally had to fan out in an arc, each barely in sight of the other, in order to find our previous cache of supplies.

Then when camp was set up the sun came out and I was quite disturbed at how clearly our trail down the glacier stood out. A patrol could not fail to see it. The tents were a brilliant orange. I hoped that by being in the rocks of the moraine we would be hidden a bit. We looked over to Pumori, which seemed very close. We wondered whether the Swiss-German expedition, who were attempting it at this time, were in position to see us. If so, they must have been somewhat puzzled. Finally, from this point we had a view right up to the South Col, where the Indian expedition was. There was Lhotse, the Geneva Spur, the Western Cwm—all in classic pose. However it required better binoculars than ours to see any actual camps. We hoped they couldn't see us, either. We didn't want any reports drifting back before us as to where we actually were.

Another plan was frustrated today. It is always good to trade around tent-mates so that there are no cliques. Roger, himself, would have liked to be with me or Norm for a time. But Norm insisted that he was too used to me and that he didn't want to change. It is true that eventually one's every gesture and every motion in making and breaking camp, in cooking, and in getting comfortable for the night, becomes habitual and is anticipated by the other. After a while it becomes a very efficient procedure. Getting used to someone else with different preferences and different ways of doing things would be a disruption and a nuisance. Still, it was something that really had to be done. There is much too much danger of breaking up into two separate expeditions if it is not done. But Norm was adamant, and I felt it would be wiser not to cross him in this matter. So we stayed as we were and risked the consequences.

This was our first Tibetan camp. Except that it was windier than usual during the night, it seemed no different than any other. The staccato flutter and thrum of the tent, with occasional wild whipping contortions, kept me awake for a while. I wondered again why it is that those who snore inevitably fall asleep more quickly than those who don't. Surely there is a Ph.D. thesis here somewhere. The tent held up all right and I dropped off. But I woke frequently. We are in our sleeping bags often for fifteen hours. We may doze off after supper at five o'clock when it is still light. It is no wonder then that by 11 or 12 P.M. we should wake up again. Then the idea of staying another six or seven hours in the dark tent seems intolerable. But after a while I usually relax. I doze off and let the hours drift pleasantly by. Norm claims that I can sleep so well because of a lifetime of experience. But he is a practiced sleeper, too. He can fall asleep anytime and anyplace—even in the middle of a sentence. It is Roger and HansPeter surprisingly who depended on sleeping pills. I never needed one.

Today HansPeter came out with a curious idea. He claimed that he read in a dental journal an unverified theory that altitude clears up tartar. I looked around at the others, and I believed it must be true. It had been a month and a half since we had brushed our teeth. During the walk-in, I remember, Norm had developed some really yellow tusks. My teeth had coated up also. Now I noticed that they were pure white—no tartar at all. I checked mine in our one little compass mirror and saw that they looked cleaner than they ever had even just after cleaning at the dentist. It seemed unbelievable.

Perhaps it was extra ultra-violet or other radiation which comes through more strongly at high altitude. Actually, the effect lasted for about five weeks after I came down off the mountain. I reflected that this was a wonderful way to avoid going to the dentist—just climb Everest.

Speaking of ailments, Norm had a persistent itch. We worried that it might be lice left behind by Pemba when he shared our tent at Camp I, and we had no lice powder. Roger and HansPeter both still had some trouble with diarrhea. And we all had persistent coughs which had been with us, to greater or lesser degree, since Kathmandu. I believe it comes from the dust which is unavoidably inhaled there. The wind swirls it up off the street and you breathe it in and swallow it. When you notice what there is on the street, it is a wonder that you only catch a cough. Breathing in that dust practically amounts to the same thing as getting down on your knees and licking the ground. HansPeter, who was in Kathmandu for the shortest time, had the lightest cough.

But it was very tiring. For some reason it hit worst when he stopped to rest on the march. It took a fruit drop to hold it in check. Then, when we started moving again, it went away. At night I often had some very bad sessions. Norm complained that I woke him up. But he fell asleep again so quickly that I really couldn't spare much sympathy.

On our fifth day into Tibet we faced the problem of crossing the side glacier. We were all puzzled as to what it was and where it came from. From a distance it seemed insignificant, then suddenly we saw that it was at least three-quarters of a mile wide with lines of good-sized seracs guarding both edges. I did not remember any mention of such a glacier. Nevertheless, it was good to be on new ground again, and ground with a little variety. Also it was good to be off on reconnaissance with Roger again. We two set off to find a way across. Again

Roger exhibited his sixth sense in choosing a fine route. We took turns leading, and by the end of the day we had a crossing marked out. The others spent the day relaying supplies along our route.

Now we decided to take our camp as far as possible toward the Main Rongbuk Glacier. So we brought everything in one giant load down to the edge of the side glacier. Here we cached all but two days of food and then pushed on with tents and gear to go as far as we could. We carried about 50 pounds. We crossed the whole Far West Rongbuk successfully by the route that Roger and I had scouted out yesterday, cached some more equipment, and then started down the lateral moraine towards the juncture of the West Rongbuk and the Main Rongbuk. Looking up, I recognized the very rocks we had thought we were going to make by lunch time on our first day. That had been five days ago and a good two-days' journey back. We walked on loose rock and snow patches for quite a while, then, on the edge of another smaller side glacier, I decided that we had better camp (Camp IV). I would rather have gone further, but Norm was nowhere in sight, and I thought we had better not stretch ourselves out too thinly.

We camped and I waited around. Time went by and still no Norm. I got more and more worried. The others claimed they had last seen him on the Far West Rongbuk Glacier as they were crossing. He was following slowly. But that was two hours ago. Traveling alone, I envisioned him in all kinds of trouble. Finally I decided to go back and look for him. After a tough day, to get dressed again, pull on your boots, and start back up the trail, is a little bit of hell. I could certainly have used the rest. Besides, it was all, most likely, completely unnecessary. Still, I felt I must go. I climbed slowly back along the moraine calling and whistling every minute or so. Each of us was carrying a police whistle for emergency use. As I got near the crossover point of the side glacier, I became convinced that Norm really must be in trouble. Only an accident could have delayed him this long. All kinds of thoughts raced through my mind. What were we going to do with an injured man, or worse, this far into Tibet? How badly was he injured? Then, suddenly, only a hundred yards away, I saw him. He seemed to be moving all right and I was tremendously relieved. I went up to him and he said that he was fine—just slow and tired. I was shocked to realize that he had taken four hours to cross the side glacier, which had taken the rest of us only a little over an hour. The altitude seemed to be affecting him more as time went by, rather than less. I took his pack and started down toward camp. Norm said that he had not heard my calls or whistles at all. I was again impressed with how poorly sound carried up here. I suppose if it doesn't travel through a vacuum, it is natural that it should do poorly through a semivacuum, which is what we had here.

In camp that night Norm and I had a big fight. It is notorious that mountain climbers quite often flare up at each other. The close living, the strain everyone is under, even perhaps the altitude—all contribute to this effect. Still, it is a mistake to think that these trips are one long argument. They are not. There are some wonderful times of comradeship, which is one of the rewards. Nevertheless, arguments can be quite hot. Usually these are brief flashes which come and go as quickly as summer lightning and with as little permanent effect. Sometimes, on the other hand, the arguments go deeper and leave a longer mark. Norm felt that he was carrying too much and would be exhausted by the time we got to Everest. He felt that if I kept at my present pace, I would be, too. He proposed that Roger and HansPeter, being younger, should carry the lion's share in a crash program until we got to the mountain. I felt that this was wrong in principle, as well as impractical. We would never get to the mountain that way. I felt that the whole argument arose because Norm was so unhappy with his performance up to now. In all the years I had known him he had never been shirker. In fact, quite the reverse—he always did more than his share. But now he could carry less than we, and even that took maximum effort. This, I think, bothered him terribly. Actually the effects of altitude are not a matter of willpower. He didn't *choose* to be more affected than the rest of us, and he couldn't will himself not to be affected. It is, indeed, more a question of good or bad luck, who is affected and who is not, and therefore not something for which to blame oneself. Yet, inevitably, one does. So he reacted by wanting to do something drastic.

The argument continued off and on for two and a half days. It became involved in all kinds of questions of loyalty and pride—loyalty to old friends, loyalty to new friends, loyalty to principles. Norm felt so deeply about it, he was ready to go back alone. I knew he meant it, but told him I didn't see why it was necessary and that I hoped very much he wouldn't. Finally, we came to the only possible solution of really serious arguments: we agreed to disagree. We accepted the fact that neither was going to convince the other. We agreed to go on, each carrying what he could, and no blame. I was grateful to Norm for continuing. Nevertheless, the situation added one more worry to all the others we were juggling.

From Camp IV Norm made a reconnaissance all the way to the elusive Main Rongbuk while Roger, Hans-Peter, and I relayed supplies from caches dumped here and there as far back as the other side of our mysterious side glacier. Both parties came up with some bad news. Norm said it was still a ten-hour round trip to the intersection of the West Rongbuk with the Main Rongbuk. Roger and HansPeter reported that the cache on the edge of the glacier had been looted by the ravens or crows.

Ever since Camp I several large, black, raven-like birds had followed our progress and scavenged our camps. I have no idea what they eat normally at these altitudes, since we saw nothing else living. But they certainly read the sign "meal ticket" written across our backs. One or two were always in sight. Apparently we had underestimated them badly. They went right through the burlap sacks and the plastic bags in our cache with their beaks. Our food was scattered all over. Their favorite was the meat bars. We could ill afford the loss of these precious supplies, transported with such effort so far. We salvaged what we could and piled rocks on top to frustrate any future efforts. And then I started worrying about our essential cache at Camp II. It was not protected by rocks. The ravens were squatting all around as we left. This could be a disaster. Our only hope was that, luckily, we had stored the food in the canvas marine sacks and so far they had not pecked through these much tougher containers.

On the last leg back to camp this day we had a nasty surprise. We found that the snow patches of fine, firm corn snow, which we had been walking over so easily, had turned to mush. Again and again, we would break through, sometimes all the way up to the hip. Near the rocks it was quite dangerous, because you would drop suddenly as the hollow snow collapsed, and a twisted ankle or even a broken leg was an unpleasant possibility. An easy walk became an exhausting struggle. I had to make another cache to lighten my pack. The three of us straggled into camp late and dead tired.

During the next two days we moved our camp to the edge of the Main Rongbuk, and relayed supplies back and forth to it. HansPeter pulled another sit-down on us. Roger found him dozing ten minutes outside camp when he was supposed to be hiking back to clean out one of the back caches. This eventually disrupted our whole carrying schedule, so that a day or so later Roger and HansPeter were a whole day behind the two of us.

On our tenth day, Norm, Roger, and I set out with light packs to try to find a route across the Main Rongbuk. This was actually the day I had hoped to arrive at the foot of the North face. But by now I was resigned to the idea that our extra week of leeway was going to be used up just getting to the mountain. It couldn't be helped. Secretly I felt that our supplies could be stretched for an extra ten days if we had to, so I was not too worried.

We ran into three new problems trying to get across the Rongbuk. First, climbing down to it, we faced a 600-foot drop of loose rock that was swept by avalanches of bounding rocks every few minutes. We found a way that was fairly stable and that was not swept by rock slides from above. Still, we went one at a time in order not to start a fall that would carry the lower man away. Next, we came to an area of loose rock on top of ice, where the footing was unpleasant but reasonably secure. But by ten in the morning the rocks unfreeze. They slip and turn without any warning and the ice underneath is iron hard. Even a gentle slope becomes a horror. You find yourself flat on your face again and again. Finally we came to the problem of the seracs. These ice towers, carved in fantastic forms, are often 90- to 100-feet high. It does no good to climb them, even if you could, since you would simply have to come down the other side and face another one. Thus, the only way is to thread our way between them. But at this season we found that the areas between them were in fact lakes. Some were frozen hard, some had thick ice only in the center—which did us no good—and some had no firm ice at all. One could follow around the borders of these lakes as long as they were flat, but sooner or later one came to a stretch of vertical wall. This meant a long cutting job, making steps across the face of the cliff. And there was never any certainty that it would not be all for nothing—a hopeless deadend.

I had a great respect for those lakes with their vertical walls. If we fell in unroped, we would be like rats in a drainpipe: we would drown or freeze. So we roped up

126

and belayed very carefully. Even so, I went in twice to the waist, and Roger slipped in once. For there was no time to make perfect steps; we were depending on scratch steps and delicate balance. With the rope, we were pulled out safely. Eventually, after trying a half dozen routes, we found one that went through. We put in some fixed ropes, cached our loads, and returned to Camp V.

The day's work was very satisfying. I felt that Roger and I were now pretty competent ice men. We were handling problems neatly and efficiently that we could never have handled when we first walked to the foot of the icefall twenty-four days ago. Also we now had a route to the east side of the Main Rongbuk. There were no further obstacles between us and the old British route up the East Rongbuk to the North Col. Since I knew this route thoroughly from my reading, I felt that it was now practically a certainty that we really would reach the North Face. Only something terribly unforeseen could stop us. This was particularly exciting to me because I had always felt that if we got to Everest at all, the expedition would be a success. Having gotten there, I wanted very much to climb the North Col. If that too were granted, then every step on above it, on the Northeast Ridge, would be extra icing on the cake. The one thin chance that I might go on all the way to the top was something I scarcely allowed myself to think about. It was too remote a possibility and there were too many immediate problems to face simply to get to the first objective.

On the eleventh day Norm and I moved our half of the camp across the Rongbuk and set up Camp VI. Roger went back as far as Camp IV to pick up various partial loads left by HansPeter the day before. HansPeter declared a holiday and stayed in Camp V.

Then on the twelfth day Norm and I set out for the East Rongbuk Glacier. The view of Everest from our camp was particularly stunning. We were at our lowest point since May 1—under 18,000 feet. Immediately to the south of us the Main Rongbuk Glacier headed into the north wall of Everest, which rose a vertical distance of 2 miles. This is the classic view that so impressed Mallory on his first reconnaissance thirty-one years ago.

But we turned our back on it and walked north, heading toward the junction of the Main Rongbuk with the East Rongbuk. Excitement was high, for we were on historic ground here. Indeed, through the glasses we saw far down the valley, what we thought must be the group of buildings that make up the famous Rongbuk monastery. It was very distant and we were not sure. I worried that they might have more powerful glasses than we, so they might be able to see us. I had been told that the monastery has been converted by the Communists into a border patrol post. I worried about our bright orange windproofs and about appearing on the skyline.

Gradually we climbed as we followed the east bank of the Rongbuk. And then, suddenly, we turned a corner and found ourselves looking up the side valley out of which the East Rongbuk Glacier flows into the Main Rongbuk. The ice melts before it gets to the Main Rongbuk, and its end seemed rather small. But very soon we could see it spreading out more and more, until it is a very impressive glacier. I had not realized it was going to be so big. Now all we had to do was follow this glacier to its head and we would arrive at the North Col, which is the beginning of the North Face route.

We climbed upward for a long time following semi-trails that skirted along the south bank of the glacier. Occasionally there even appeared to be a cairn or marker, made of one rock on another, but it could have been an accident. Norm spotted some rusted cans in the rocks. Some had what looked like .22-caliber bullet holes through them. Again I worried that regular patrols might just possibly be coming through here, although I couldn't imagine for what purpose.

128

I caught sight, across the East Rongbuk and below us, of a series of low stone walls. They had obviously been used as windbreaks for a camp. And so we had discovered either the sight of the Old British Camp I or else a more recent Communist camp. Things last indefinitely in this climate, so it was quite possible that one of the very earliest British camps should still be here. Two days earlier, near our Camp V, Roger and Norm had discovered the site of what was definitely a British camp. Norm had appropriated an old-style wooden tent peg he had discovered. I wondered if it wasn't the camp described in the 1921 reconnaissance of the West Rongbuk and the Lho La.

Anyway, the sight of the camp across the glacier was another landmark for us, so I felt pleased. After a long push, we cached our loads, protecting them as we always did now with rocks. Then we returned to Camp VI at the edge of the Main Rongbuk. There, it was wonderful to see a second orange tent pitched beside ours. Roger and HansPeter had done heroic work. They had brought everything forward to the camp, so we were all together again. Characteristically, Roger had also managed to find a much easier *dry* route through the seracs which might well be a big help on the way back.

In the morning I recalculated our food consumption. We still had nine-days supply of high-altitude rations for the North Col and above. Also we had seven-days supply for our journey to the North Col. I noticed that we hadn't consumed as much sugar as we should have. There was enough left over to cache an extra 5 pounds at Camp VI. In other respects we were running exactly as planned. Of course, there were some items we never had enough of. Roger, especially, was enamored of the luncheon foods. Usually within an hour after breakfast he had also consumed all his lunch. Then he would pull a "Fido" on us, watching us swallow each morsel with soulful eyes. Inevitably he cajoled a dividend.

HansPeter loved the hot cereals. He could not stand the eggs and bacon. I could not stand the brand of hot cereal we got in Switzerland—it nauseated me. Also the prunes were horrible. Even the ravens wouldn't touch them. So we made advantageous trades. All in all, I was pleased that we were coming out so close to schedule on the food. By now we had eaten enough and cached enough against our return so that we were down to two slightly heavy loads instead of three. This was a great help. Twice over a route is much less monotonous than three times.

After making our cache, we all moved the tents up the East Rongbuk, about an hour's walk beyond the cache of yesterday. We were chagrined to find the cache broken into and scattered. Norm feared some type of rodent. We tried to make a rodent-proof sanctuary of fitted rocks. But it was obviously impossible. Then I reflected that there weren't supposed to be any rodents up here anyway. It was probably the ravens again. They were strong and they could knock down the lighter rocks. Their long beaks can poke through the holes. So we used really heavy rocks and we made double walls. It turned out that these in fact were successful. But we had lost some more food.

We camped on a little patch of snow on a talus of loose rock. We were still on the south side of the East Rongbuk. We were scarcely stopped when a mob of huge boulders came down from the ridge above, with a vicious pounding by the big ones, and a whizzing and rattling by the littler ones. We hid behind the biggest rocks we could find. A big one went by right beside me. After it was over, HansPeter said, "Move!" So he and Roger moved down to a little patch of snow further away from the line of fire. Norm and I were not happy, but we were too tired to bother; we would take our chances.

This is characteristic of the way you actually feel. At sea level, well fed and well rested, one can work up quite a sweat over some of the dangers one meets. Both in anticipation and even in retrospect, this is so. But when you are actually there, dead tired and hungry, the dangers barely impress you. It takes energy to be afraid, or indeed to have any emotion, and often there just isn't that much energy around. So a brave man may frequently be merely a tired one.

On the fourteenth day Roger and HansPeter went back to Camp VI to clear out the loads left there. I expected them to detour over to the camp we had seen across the glacier to satisfy their curiosity. Meanwhile Norm and I pushed a load on up the glacier. At our furthest point I saw what I thought was a portion of the North Col with the familiar foreshortened view of the North Face and summit above it. I smiled to see another well-known photograph come alive.

Coming up the glacier today and yesterday we could see a large forking ahead of us. This puzzled me, for I had always assumed that the East Rongbuk was a single straightforward trough. For that reason I had never considered that there could be any problem about the route. All the rather crude maps I had seen showed it just as a single trough. But now we were seeing that it was quite otherwise. Several respectably large side glaciers came in from both sides and, in addition, there were at least two forkings where it was not at all clear which was the main glacier. I had argued with Norm and Roger about the first fork. As usual I backed up my opinion with my book knowledge and was quite condescending about their chances of being right. Then, of course, quite some time before we got to the fork, it became obvious that they were right and I was wrong. Actually, I was relieved to be wrong. For the other fork stretched off into the distance and looked as if it would be at least a week's walk to the first opening which might lead to the bowl of the North Col. If this day's view was, indeed, of the North Col, there should be no more problems of route at any rate.

Back at "stonefall" camp, we re-raised the tent which we had laid flat in order to protect it from any rocks that might fall and punch a hole in it. Roger came in at 6 P.M., but not HansPeter. Roger said that he was behind him packing up from Camp VI. We ate supper, darkness fell, but still no HansPeter. We discussed going back for him. Mainly, we were too tired, but also there was no danger or difficulty on the route. So we figured it was just a question of time before he came in. I had just dropped off to sleep, when I heard a halloo and came awake. It was HansPeter. I hallooed back, got one answer, then nothing. I called to Roger and again got one answer, then silence. Suddenly, I saw a dark figure sneaking along the edge of the rocks, and then another. A light winked on and off quickly, like a signal. The conviction seized me that it was a Communist patrol moving into position around us. The hairs literally rose up on the back of my neck. It was an extraordinary feeling, and not at all pleasant. I shook Norm awake and warned him in a low voice. The thought occurred to me that HansPeter might have been caught by a patrol when he went back down and lagged behind. If the Communists had seen us when we first relayed up from Camp VI, it would take them a day or so to get up to us. The timing was just about right. Then it would be just like them to bring HansPeter along and make him call out to us so that we would give our position away. From their point of view they would not know how many we were, or if we were armed, or what. In the dark rocks it is not too easy to see. But when we answered, then they could surround us and grab us. I wondered to myself if this was it—captured by the Chinese Communists.

Incongruously, I struggled into my down pants. I just didn't like the idea of being overrun without my pants on. I called to Roger to watch himself, that HansPeter might not be alone. Then I too kept quiet. There was no need to give my position away further. Norm was skeptical and began to drift off to sleep. I was wide awake. But time went by and nothing happened. I decided I must have been seeing things, or perhaps the sudden awakening had confused me. I relaxed and finally dropped off to sleep also. But I made a silent prayer that if a patrol was to get us, might they please do so in the daytime. It is just too scary at night, and energies are too low.

Next morning HansPeter was angry that we had not sent someone down to look for him once it got dark. It was no correct "Alpinism". I pointed out that there was no danger and what little there was would simply be compounded by sending others out also. If he hadn't stopped for sight-seeing at the old British or Communist camp, he would have been back in good time. Hans-Peter said it was too much to expect anyone not to look at these historic spots and do nothing but donkey-ing. I said that if you can do both, as Roger did, fine. Otherwise, he should cut it out. Now someone was going to have to go all the way back to the corner of the East Rongbuk and the Main Rongbuk to pick up the load he had left there. This was a repeat of what had occurred on the West Rongbuk. The expedition loses another day.

Now Norm and I moved our camp on up to the entrance of the great amphitheater at the end of which was the North Col. We were exceedingly happy to be rid of our present campsite, Camp VII. The rock slides were so frequent here that there was a grey powder which covered the snow, and our water was filled with grit.

There was a choice of ways on the route. We could stay along the south wall as we had been or we could push out into the glacier to one of several median moraines. These are ridges of rock and silt which have been squeezed up by the ice so that they make a continuous pathway up the glacier. Norm and I decided to go high along the south wall. That night we made our

Camp VIII. We kept expecting to see Roger and Hans-Peter, but they were nowhere in sight.

When we came back the following morning to our lowest cache, we found notes from them. They had taken the central moraine route and recommended it. Further, they said that they had come on Communist or British Camp II and had found some cans of bean sprouts which were, they said, delicious. Finally they warned us that we must go "around" the large rock outcropping to get to the true basin of the North Col.

All this worried me about my route. But our camp was up along it, so it was too late to change. We packed back to Camp VIII. I was pleased to see how well Norm was going now. There seemed to be a steady improvement. He still traveled a little light and took it slower, but he kept at it. He is persistent, and he *makes* it. He seemed to be reaching an equilibrium. This was a great relief to me. Things were looking brighter. But where were Roger and HansPeter?

Now we were on our seventeenth day. We should arrive at the foot of the North Col today. Adding the seven days leeway to the ten days I had originally planned, this should bring us out exactly right. Norm and I put in a tremendous day. We scouted a route up through the heavily crevassed area at the mouth of the bowl. We relayed everything up into the bowl in two loads. And then we pushed up across the bowl to within a few hundred yards of the North Col.

Only was it the North Col? It certainly *looked* like the pictures: the same gentler slopes to the right, the steeper swellings to the left, the approximate height of 1,500 feet. I couldn't imagine that there were two walls of ice that would look so similar. Only I remembered my previous mistake. And why was it that there was a glacier over on our right coming in that didn't belong? And why were there no camps visible, left by the British or the Chinese, over on the right wall? And where were Roger and HansPeter? I became more and more con-

134

vinced that I must be wrong. Unfortunately, the small-scale map that we had, along with a description of the route, was in the possession of Roger and HansPeter.

About an hour before we camped (our Camp IX) we heard Roger yodel. I called back, and we thought that we saw them way down on the glacier we had left. It was hard to understand at such a distance. I understood them to shout that they had a better way. I shouted that we would meet them at the North Col. They went on and so did we. I couldn't understand why they seemed to be heading on past the bowl we were in. I wondered if there was another easier way into it beyond the big outcropping of rock to the south of us. My misgivings mounted. I take an account of the next few hours from my journal:

The sun sinks early in the bowl. The twilight shadow advances across the snow toward us, flows over the tent, and moves rapidly on beyond. Behind it the deep cold settles in. The wind sucks at the tent. Great gusts sweep down from the ridge and across the flats, swirling up twisting columns of snow that buffet it viciously as they pass. We are glad to be snugly wrapped in eider down this night. I reflect that we are sleeping at an altitude higher than I have ever been before—over 21,000 feet. It is higher than the highest mountain in Europe, Africa, or North America. I stood on the top of 20,300-foot McKinley for a brief fifteen minutes. Now I am going to try to live for days at this altitude and above. The testing time is near.

But the worry about the separation of our party and the correct route persists. I decide to find out definitely by walking around the outcropping whether there is any other way into this bowl. If not, then we are in the wrong bowl and this is not the North Col, but simply a part of the North Peak. At 3:30 P.M. I struggle awake, get dressed, and set off into the night. It is not easy.

As I step out of the tent, however, I look up to see

135

a bright moon. The wind has dropped, and a great stillness lies over everything. The rocks are pools of blackness, but the snow shines with soft fluorescence. In a few minutes the tent disappears from sight behind a rise and I walk alone in the keen cold moonlight miles above the earth. I let the beauty flow in on me and wonder why I have never made the effort to come out at night before. Here is one reason why men climb.

I walk for about an hour. Gradually the stars fade and the dawn comes alive in the east. God lifts His hand, and the night is turned to day. I give Him thanks for its goodness.

As I turned the corner of the outcropping I saw, at last, that there was no other way into the bowl, so we were in the wrong place. We were going to have to go back down to the moraine where we had seen Roger and HansPeter the day before and follow after them. I walked back to the tent and told Norm the bad news. He was very generous about my mistake. Without complaint he packed up and we started back down to the East Rongbuk. Norm had carried nobly on the big push yesterday. Today he did even better. I was proud of him. Meanwhile, because, no doubt, I felt guilty, I worked like a demon. I carried my whole share down in one gigantic load, leading a new route that cut directly over to where we had last seen Roger and HansPeter. Then, while Norm went back up to get his second load, I went on ahead up the moraine with half my share all the way to the start of the true North Col bowl. Then I came back down and picked up the rest of my load, and with Norm carrying one of his loads we went on up to the campsite I had picked. All in all I was walking almost steadily for twelve hours with a load of well over 60 pounds for part of the time. I couldn't help but feel that our gradual conditioning during the last two months had been very successful.

It was good to know that night that we were on the

right trail at last and that we would be seeing the others tomorrow. Just beyond our camp (Camp X) we could see that the moraine ended, so we would be walking on ice and snow again. I was very happy about this, for I had been concerned about the effect on our boots of constantly walking on the sharp loose rocks of the moraines. This kind of footing must wear out anything, I felt. What if the outer layer of the boot was pierced? Then the air barrier would be broken, and we would have to retreat or else have frozen feet. We were wearing Korea boots, which depend for their warmth on a double layer of rubber with a sealed space in between. One sharp rock could do it. On the ice, one hard slash from a crampon might do it also. But I still preferred the ice.

In the morning I started off first. I was still anxious to nail down the whereabouts of Roger and HansPeter, who we hadn't seen now for four days. So I left at seven. Norm was to come on later. I climbed for an hour and then suddenly I saw a head appearing and disappearing in the distance.

It was Roger! I thought of hiding and surprising him, but I was too happy to wait. I yodeled and he yodeled, and we rushed to each other with big grins, and pulled a Stanley-Livingstone. We were both overjoyed. We gabbled for many minutes, exchanging news and plans. Roger was on his way down to clean out the caches that they had left, some of which were back halfway between Camp VIII and Camp VII. He told me of finding delicious canned crabmeat, as well as cans of pickles, in the Chinese Communist camp. He said they were in fact camped at what seemed to have been the Communist camp. There was an old British camp a little bit beyond, but they had seen no food there. In addition, he said that he had pioneered a route halfway up the North Col to the lower lip of a tremendous crevasse which cut horizontally across a large portion of the col.

I was proud of him. I told him that I would carry this

load on up to their camp——Camp XI for us—and then would come back down to our cache where we emerged from the false bowl, and help him with anything he was bringing up from below. Then I went on.

When I reached Camp XI, HansPeter was resting. He seemed somewhat surprised to see me after all this time. Then he started in on how I could have missed the way. Very easily, I said. But I saw that he was disturbed. I shrugged and asked what was the harm? So we lost a day; it had happened before. But he said that to lose your way is very significant; it is not "Alpinism". I suddenly had the impression that HansPeter had been looking up to me as infallible. Now that I had made a mistake, I could no longer be that for him. Well, it was no loss to me, but I gathered that it was a rather serious loss to him. Now he had no one he could absolutely depend on. I made light of it and refused to shed big tears. He looked puzzled, but at last seemed to accept it.

Now I went all the way back to Camp X, meeting Norm on the way up with his gear. I continued on down to our moraine cache and joined Roger, who was on his way back up. We divided up our two sets of loads and came laboriously back up to Camp X. There, we tried loading on all the gear that Norm had left for me. But it was too much. So we left one load of food and equipment at the camp. As we continued on up, Roger gradually pulled ahead. I was more tired than I had been at any time so far on the trip. This had been a terrific day of work on top of the preceding series of extra tough days. As I got fairly near Camp XI, I honestly felt that I was not going to make it. Then I saw Norm coming back down to help. Bless him. The sun was almost down and I was crying tired. When he finally came up to me, I actually sobbed. I had tried too much today. Norm took my load and we climbed up to the camp. Thus, finally, on the nineteenth day after we had left Camp III at the top of the icefall, I achieved my first major objective: the traditional camping spot close to the foot of the North Col, and the last camp before actually starting up Everest's North Face.

That night we tried the corned beef of the Chinese. It was much too salty, but still a wonderful change. Also the cans of half-sour pickles were out of this world. They had little peppers and water chestnuts and unknown-to-me legumes floating in the can. We worried that the constant thawing and refreezing might have spoiled the beef. Horrible cases of poisoning were quoted. But I remembered that canned goods from the early British expeditions were eaten as much as a decade later with no ill effects, so I hoped all would be well. Still, there was a metallic taste, and the new food didn't sit too well on our stomachs. However, I felt that this was normal. On any expedition a new food is irresistible. You crave variety and the taste of it makes you ravenous. So you are only too likely to eat too much. And also your system is likely to be upset because it has adjusted itself to what you have been eating.

I heard a lot about the delicious crabmeat, but I never saw any, either then or later. I suspected the others were hoarding it for their own delectation, but I didn't really mind too much. I wondered at the extravagance of an expedition that could carry crabmeat and cans which were 99 per cent water, having practically no nutritive value. Why hadn't the cans burst from freezing? The Communist expedition must have been very large and very well-equipped.

So here we were all together again at the foot of the great North Face of Everest. All our supplies, with the exception of one load, were with us in camp. We had nine days' food supply of our own, which should be enough for our one fling at the mountain. We had food cached all the way back to the top of the icefall, which should be enough for the return trip. And we had the extra food of the Chinese, which we could scavenge if we needed to. We were all healthy and our level of performance was, if anything, better than ever. We were excited and eager as we stared through the binoculars at the North Col and Roger's route and the obstacles which must be surmounted. But most of all, incredibly, we were here. Tomorrow, we would begin the ascent of Everest.

X

NORTH COL

But "tomorrow" turned out to be a sultry humid day with intermittent snow flurries. A great lassitude took possession of all of us, quite similar to our feelings at the top of the icefall twenty days earlier. The result was also the same: we declared a holiday, and slept and puttered all day. Norm repaired equipment—a broken zipper, a pulled rivet on the pack, a broken buckle. He has a gift for this. Many of the straps on the crampons were worn through, and we replaced them with nylon cord, which seemed to work very well. HansPeter went down for the other load; he had had his day off yesterday.

The weather disturbed me. The snowflakes were large and wet, unlike the fine, dry snow we were used to. And the clouds were heavy and brooding, instead of the clear, white clouds of earlier. I had first noticed the change two days ago in the false bowl. Now here it was again. This could well be the beginning of the monsoon. The monsoon is the name for the winds that bring the rainy season to India, but a season of heavy snow up here in the mountains. Once they start, high climbing is out. The daily accumulation of snow makes movement difficult and the avalanches make it dangerous. The monsoons come to the Everest region any time from the middle of May to the middle of June. They are the main reason why the climbing season is so short in this area. One must climb after the winter gales have abated in late March but before the monsoons have hit in full force. It being now May 28, the monsoons should be starting anytime.

I hoped they would hold off at least another week. It was not just that the heavy snow would stop us from making a try on Everest; we also had the problem of the long exit march. Really deep snow might make this march impossible. We might not have the supplies or the strength to get back over the pass into Nepal. Hans-Peter blossomed forth with some panic stories on the subject. One expedition had been hit by the monsoon without warning and engulfed with snow; another party had had to turn back from their objective on the West Rongbuk itself because of monsoon snow. He asked me what steps I had taken to meet these eventualities. Mainly, I could only tell him that I had brought my rabbit's foot along. Also I understood that movement below 20,000 was not supposed to be too difficult even during the monsoon. Still, I didn't really know. I must say, I didn't like the idea of being trapped in Tibet any more than he. I told him it was just one more of the many hundreds of things which could go fatally wrong.

During the day I studied the col in detail through the glasses. I wondered why the big crevasse couldn't be avoided if we made a route further to the right. But you can't prove a route at a distance, and Roger had already carried a half-load to the lower edge of the crevasse, so we decided to stick to his route. Basically, the North Col is a saddle or ridge of ice and snow joining the 24,780 foot North Peak to the main body of Everest. It is, itself, 1,500 feet high, rising from the floor of the

142

East Rongbuk Glacier at about 21,500 feet up to its crest of 23,000. The traditional route up the North Face, which we were attempting, starts with the ascent of this col. From its top, we would be able to walk on to the northeast ridge of Everest. We would follow this upward for some 3,000 feet and then traverse out across the North Face to a large gully, called the Great Couloir. If all went well we would cross this and then try to break through the dark band of steeper rock which protects the upper 900 feet of the peak.

As far as timing, we hoped to climb the col in one day, carrying 20 pounds. We would cache it at the top, then return to our Camp XI. The first good day after that we would start back up in pairs. The first pair would go to the top of the col for the night. Each successive day they would climb another 2,000 feet as long as they could, until they either reached the top or had to turn back. Meanwhile, the second pair would be following one day behind with their tent and supplies. They would serve as support for the first pair until the first pair came back safely. If all was well, they would then have their chance. All this would take a minimum of six days, but, more likely, eight or nine.

On the morning of May 29 the four of us started out for the foot of the North Col. Roger told us it was four hours with packs, but that seemed excessive to me. Actually, we made it in three. At the very foot of the col we came upon an old-style tent half buried in the snow. We wondered to whom it could have belonged. Could it possibly be the tent of Maurice Wilson, the religious fanatic who had tried Everest alone back in 1933 and had died at this spot? Later British expeditions had found his tent poles. We took pictures, then Roger led us up the route he had scouted until we came to the large crevasse that crossed this part of the face about two-fifths of the way up. Mallory, in 1924, spoke of the disagreeable surprise of finding a crescent-shaped crevasse about a quarter of a mile long that blocked the ascent of the col halfway up. In 1933 Smythe encountered the same obstacle. The fact that the upper lip of the crevasse was higher than the lower by some 30 or 40 feet, as well as being an overhang, meant that Smythe, too, had had to perform some impressive gymnastics to get up. From their descriptions I thought this might be the same spot. There could be some basic underlying structure of rock that causes the crevasse to reappear year after year.

Roger had spotted the one possible line of advance. A collapsed block furnished a crossing of the crevasse itself, then a diagonal crack that just might get one past the overhang ran up the far wall. I decided to give it a try. I crossed the crevasse and squirmed up the crack about two-thirds of its height. But the overhang kept pushing me out. The wall was really made of granular snow, so that a piton would not hold; only something that penetrated at least a couple of feet would stay put. Cutting steps, too, was fruitless. They would fall away as you put your weight on them. Furthermore the crack angled up the wall in such a way that I was now above the open crevasse instead of above the block I had crossed on. There was no way to protect myself against a fall, and a fall would drop me down the depth of the crevasse as well as the height of the cliff. I didn't like it. Twice I gave up and came back down. But then I thought of how much time and effort would be needed to detour the crevasse, even if it could be done, so I tried again. Eventually, with another "just possible", I pulled myself over the upper edge and lay gasping for breath. Again I left a trail spotted with blood where my bare hands had scraped for holds on the snow and ice. Later, when Roger came up on the rope, I felt good when he commented, "Sayre, you damn fool, how did you ever get up this thing?"

We hauled Norm's pack up the wall by rope, as well as our own. We cached Norm's pack and he went back down. HansPeter had only gone as far as the base of the col where he cached his load. Roger and I continued on. The snow was very deep and the route very steep. The altitude made it a slow and exhausting business. Walking on level ground is tiring in knee-deep snow, even at sea level. When you try climbing in such snow at the steepest possible angle and at an altitude of over 22,000 feet, every dozen steps is a day's work. Someone once commented that it is like running 100-yard dashes all day with no time outs.

By afternoon Roger and I reached a platform from which we could see clearly to the top. There were only some 300 feet more of vertical height to go, which could be surmounted by a long traverse. It was steeper than we liked, but it would definitely go. And so, tired and happy, we cached our loads and returned back to camp, confident that the col was defeated.

At camp HansPeter congratulated us, but then announced that he was staying there. No North Col for him. I told him that that was all right, but we were going to need both tents, so we would help him make an ice cave in one of the seracs where he could stay. Apparently this didn't appeal very much to him, so he said he would come to the top of the North Col after all, but would not go beyond that. I felt this would be all to the good. I had always believed the North Col should be occupied as long as climbers were above it, so that they would have something to fall back on if things went wrong above. Having HansPeter occupy a camp there, then, would be an asset. The rest of us would go on together using one tent for the three of us. This might be a little crowded, but it had this advantage: if anyone fell sick or in any way could not go on, he could simply take his sleeping bag and drop down to the safety of the North Col camp with HansPeter. The others could then still keep climbing.

In the morning everyone was very slow and lethargic, and I was disgusted. Time was running out, and we couldn't spare ourselves now. I wasted a whole hour hunting for my crampons, which I had cached under a rock on the way back the day before. At last I found them and started off for the base of the col. The others followed slowly. I stamped out the route again up to the big crevasse. But the late start had made us late here. So we decided to camp in the crevasse itself. It was nicely sheltered from the wind.

That evening Norm and I figured out that if we kept moving according to schedule we could arrive on the summit on June 3, the very day that the British first made the top. One day should take us to the top of the col, one day to a 25,000-foot camp, one more day to a 27,000-foot camp, and the next day would be the try for the top. The weather seemed to be good again, and the monsoon no longer seemed to be an immediate danger. We had kept watch on the weather around the summit. Some days Everest had its great plume of snow and ice particles which the jet stream winds blew off it. When this banner was flying, you knew that there were terrible conditions around the summit, and you were glad to be below. Other days the banner was absent and the sun seemed extra warm. I thought that we had had an exceptionally large number of these "summit days". Maybe we had arrived at the mountain at the perfect moment. The thirteen days we had spent beyond our original plan—two in Kathmandu, one in Namche Bazar, four in the icefall, and nine on the approach through Tibet—these lost days might turn out to be a blessing. We were optimistic.

On May 31 we all started again for the top of the col. I used the fixed rope I had left and struggled to the top of the crevasse. We hauled the loads up, and the others came up the rope. Roger and I split the load cached there the day before, so we were now carrying between 45 and 50 pounds. This was twice the normal Sherpa load. We stopped for lunch at our highest point of the day before, and again added to our loads, but two light loads were still left. Then I started out on the long upward traverse to the crest. The snow was firm and, although I had to prepare each step and sink the ice axe into the hilt for support, I moved steadily. HansPeter, following me, wanted to go more slowly. I became so impatient that finally I unroped and continued on alone. I was in the shadow with the sun just ahead. It kept receding ahead of me, no matter how fast I tried to go. But I could see that the top of the ridge was in brilliant sun. It glowed with a golden edge against the blue depth of the sky.

Twenty more steps, ten, now five. Then suddenly I took a step that I had dreamt of taking for twenty years. I stepped out onto the crest of Everest's North Col. The sight was thrilling, and I stared at every detail of the North Face, which now lay immediately before me, beautifully lit in the late afternoon sun's glow. The top seemed so close, the route so easy. But actually the summit was still 6,000 vertical feet above me and a lateral distance of at least 2 miles. Roger joined me on my observation platform, and stared and photographed too. The North Face was nicely swept of snow, as it would have to be if we were to have any chance of climbing it. I could see no problems until we got to the top 900 feet of steeper rock. I grinned over at Roger; I could tell that he was excited, too.

At that moment I felt a glow of satisfaction. Our plans had worked out unbelievably well. We had gotten along without oxygen. We had gotten along without Sherpas. We had gotten along without a string of fixed camps to support us. Moreover, we had negotiated the "impossible" distance from Base Camp to our present perch. In the process we had trained ourselves to handle respectable technical difficulties of many kinds. And we had conditioned ourselves to hard, lean effectiveness. Certainly the loads that Roger and I had just carried up to 23,000 feet without undue fatigue bore witness to this. Most of all, in a few more minutes we would all be here on the col together, safe and sound, healthy, eager, and ready to go on. On hand, we would have five full days of food and fuel for the final push. This was more than I had really dared to expect. But now that it was all accomplished, the miracle of the summit was a genuine possibility.

Then the question of the last loads came up. Roger wanted to go down and bring them back up in an extra trip. Then *everything* would be at the col for an early start in the morning. I felt that it was likely to take us until after dark to finish the carry, and I was against the idea of walking on this kind of terrain without visibility. But Roger pointed out that his tent was down there, too, and did I really want to sleep four in a tent? I gave in, and we started down.

Never had I felt so confident, or so full of energy. I literally bounded down the slope. I could do no wrong. I would jam my ice axe into the snow below me up to its hilt, then, using it as a pivot, I would swing myself completely off the slope in a leaping arc. When I landed I would pull the ice axe out and place it in a new spot below me, then leap again. At that hour of that day the snow happened to be perfect; otherwise, it never would have taken such punishment without avalanching off. I realized that I was experimenting with a new technique for descending mountains that, quite likely, would not pass the test of time, but I felt so wonderful and so energetic that I could not resist it. This euphoria may well have been due to the lack of oxygen at the new altitude we had reached. It is one of the typical symptoms of anoxia. On the other hand, I believe that it is equally possible that the sense of elation came simply from the excitement of having surmounted the North Col in such fine style. Several times already on the trip I had had this same feeling: when we first took off for Europe, when I first saw the Himalayas from the plane, when we got through Nepalese customs at last, when our little column actually started walking out of Kathmandu, when we reached the great Dudh Kosi River, when I saw Everest for the first time, and again when I reached major landmarks on the way to the foot of it. Many of these times my sense of well-being certainly could not be blamed on lack of oxygen. Maybe, this time, it was a combination: the euphoria of reaching a goal, together with the euphoria of too little oxygen.

I made it back to the cache in not much more than twenty minutes. This is especially unusual in view of the hours the same trip took me a few days later. Roger was a little more cautious and skeptical, but he made the descent very quickly, too. It was twilight when we arrived. By the time we were all loaded up and roped, it was completely dark. I was amazed at how quickly the change occurred.

We started back up with our loads. I led, following up the old steps at first. But then, in the dark, I lost them. Normally it would be a huge job to make a new set of steps while climbing with loads. But I still felt so good that I didn't mind the extra effort. We moved slowly, but steadily. After some time I came to the spot where I had left some pitons and carabiners stuck in the snow. I called the good news back down to Roger, and boasted a bit that I was a pretty good nighttime navigator to have found them. I was now only about 50 yards from the crest of the ridge. Norm and HansPeter were camped out of sight just beyond the crest, waiting for us. This was the last steep spot, so that from here on we could relax. I stood and waited for Roger to come up to me.

As he came closer, the slack of the rope hung farther and farther down the slope below us. Carelessly, I gave no particular thought to this. In retrospect, I think this was mainly because I had no real feeling that the rope was necessary. I had made most of the traverse up to the col without a rope that afternoon, and both Roger and I had descended easily without ropes only a little while ago. Indeed, we had both become rather blasé about the necessity of a rope. It seems silly to speak of overconfidence on Everest, but that I think was the case. Everything was working so well, it was only from a sense of duty that we roped up at all. So I didn't notice the increasing slack hanging down between us. Nor would I probably have done anything about it even if I had. I did, however, call back to Roger that it was still pretty steep where he was. But I said it more as a mechanical reaction than as a genuine warning.

Roger was now only a step or two away from me. Even with my back turned, I sensed his nearness. Then things happened very suddenly and very fast. I heard a kind of gurgle and a half-spoken something and immediately I had the flash, "My God, Roger is gone!"

A sudden slip, a body tobogganing down the slope with fearful acceleration—I would be next. I grabbed for my ice axe, which was standing upright in the snow. I tried to sink it in deeply so that it would hold the strain when it came. But right here the snow was thin over hard ice. The axe only penetrated a couple of inches— not nearly enough to hold a man after 100 feet of unchecked fall. For with all that slack between us, Roger had to fall the full length of the rope before I could even begin to stop him. Desperately I tried another spot. No luck. Now there was no more time. I hunched down against the axe to hold against the coming impact as well as I could, but I knew it was hopeless. Then the rope seized me, jerked me over backward, and instantly I, too, was tobogganing down the slope.

I had time to turn over on my back and try to brake with my ice axe. For a second or so I was pleased to feel that we were no longer accelerating; maybe we were even slowing up a bit. Then I felt a sudden surge and pull on the rope and a sickening increase in my speed. I thought, "Oh, Oh, Roger's gone over the brink of something big! No braking can do us any good now!" In the last fraction of a second I wondered if this was really *it* for me. I thought it probably was. What could possibly stop us? Then I, too, was in a free fall

150

with nothing to hold onto, and, as in all falls, things were too confused to remember.

My next impression was: I am stopped, unbelievably stopped. Then came an impression also mixed with surprise: I still exist; I am actually alive. A moment later this was followed by a third impression: I am on my back; what are my feet doing up there in the air?

I sat up. A dark patch against the snow a mere 2 feet away sat up also. It was Roger. We had landed beside each other. "What are you doing here?" he asked. The question seemed strange. The thought crossed my mind that he might be out of his head a bit. I asked him if he was all right. We stretched our arms and legs, and were amazed to find that they all seemed to work. Only my left arm felt sore and sort of bent. If this was all that was wrong, we were very lucky. We had slid 150 feet or more and then dropped straight down some 30 or 40 feet.

We were still possessed by a sense of emergency. Lots of urgent things had to be done quickly. Roger wanted to move. I told myself not to panic. "Take it easy and slow. Talk slowly. Move slowly. Stay calm. We have a fight ahead of us, if we are going to survive this night." I suggested in as normal a voice as I could that we should take an inventory of everything in our packs to see what could help us. I thought that doing something constructive might quiet us down. Meanwhile, I got up and took a step to peer downward. I could see just enough to conclude that it dropped off steeply. Another step and we could tumble down another 1,000 feet. On the other hand to try to climb back up the cliff over which we had fallen in our condition of shock, and in the dark, seemed like madness to me. We must simply last where we were until morning; we must endure. But could we?

We were at about 22,700 feet. We had no sleeping bags, no stove, and no food. In the early expeditions it was thought that a man would surely die if he were caught out at night away from camp on Everest's North Face. With the equipment they then had this might very well have been true. But now the new types of more efficient clothing might give a man a chance to survive. At least I hoped so. I knew the Swiss had stayed very high without sleeping bags, but they had a tent. Two men had slept out with no tent on the slopes of Makalu, but they had air mattresses and sleeping bags. Then Buhl had lasted a night near the top of Nanga Parbat simply standing on a ledge with no bag or tent at all. But the night had been absolutely windless—a rare piece of luck. How cold and how windy does it have to be for a man to freeze to death? I honestly didn't know. I remembered from camping trips what my father once told me: "Wrap everything you have around you, get out of the wind, and stay together. Especially stay together. Two men can last at least a night that way."

Looking through the packs, the only useful item was the tent. Our little ledge was much too small to pitch it, but wrapping it around us should give us some help. First, I had to get Roger's crampons off. I had taken mine off already. If the tent was not to be ripped up by the spikes, he would have to take his off, too. I told him to take them off and he started to do it. Ten minutes later they were still on. I urged him to hurry; it was cold. He seemed to agree. Finally I offered to help. Irritably, he said that he was perfectly capable of taking off his own crampons. Again I waited. Finally, a half hour had gone by and not one strap was undone. It was getting colder and colder. I was more and more worried that the fall had affected him. I feared a bad blow to his head. So I took over. The straps were so frozen with ice that I cut them with my jackknife. Then I wrapped the tent around us as well as I could, but not too successfully, because I couldn't get Roger to stand up. We made do, and I curled myself next to him.

It was now 9 P.M. The first rays of the sun would not hit us for another seven and a half hours, at about 4:30

A.M. Our job was to survive until then. I watched myself anxiously to see whether I would go on getting colder and colder. Every sixty seconds or so a great racking shiver would shake me from head to foot. But I began to feel a sense of equilibrium. I was *not* getting any colder. A little bit of optimism crept in. If it went on this way we were going to make it.

Then the tent heaved, and Roger sat up and started to get to his feet. Where was he going? He gave an explanation that didn't make any sense to me. I argued with him that he should lie down. We were losing valuable warmth. I almost had to pull him back down. For another half hour he lay quietly, then tried to get up again. Once more, I argued him back down. A kind of pattern became established. I could count only on about thirty minutes of quiet before Roger would feel he had to do something. Usually, it was enough to say, "Roger, damn it, I'm freezing; get back down!" But other times he was more adamant. He just *had* to do this or that. One time he tried to go down the mountain. "I have to go get the ping-pong balls," he said. "We need some more ping-pong balls."

Other times he had a legitimate reason. For instance, he rolled away from me to the edge of the tent and raised himself on his elbow. When I objected, he asked me why I was making such a fuss. "I just want to be sick," he said. "Leave me alone." Then he leaned over and was. But, of course, I never knew in advance whether he had a good reason or not. What will cut through to a man's consciousness in a situation like this? I remembered what had worked in a somewhat similar situation with Charles Houston, the leader of the American K2 expedition. Adapting it somewhat, I said to Roger with great emphasis, "Roger, if you ever want to see your family again, *you lie still!*"

And so time passed, minute by minute. Each one was lived through separately. There was no sleep, not even a semi-doze. I shivered too much, and I worried about

153

Roger. He had a bad headache and wanted something for the pain. We had the first-aid kit with us, and Roger knew it. But I wouldn't give him anything. I didn't dare take the chance of upsetting the equilibrium. Many painkillers are depressants and could further increase the bad effects of concussion. Roger was resentful of my refusal.

At last the night began to fade, the horizon lightened, and the dawn rose in the sky. I waited impatiently for the sun itself to appear. I craved the warmth of its direct rays. This was almost the longest wait of all—and the coldest. I swore that I would never let myself be cold again. Then, when the sun did rise above the horizon, it rose at the exact spot where the top pyramid of a peak blocked it. I had to wait a full extra fifteen minutes. I could have cried.

When the sunlight touched me, I gave thanks for the morning. How strongly man's spirit is affected by light! I felt we had been very lucky to get through the night. If there had been a strong wind, among other things, we would not have made it. There had been only an occasional swirling gust to bother us. I found out later from Norm that there had been a vicious wind all that night up where they were. But for the most part it didn't reach us. Not only had we survived a night out on Everest, but also we had done so without a trace of frostbite in either hand or foot. This also seemed very lucky to me. I think our feet stayed warm mainly due to the efficiency of our Korea thermal boots. In fact, I don't even remember feeling that my feet were ever any colder than the rest of me.

Now that the sun had risen I got up and moved stiffly about. Roger seemed quieter now, so I gave him his pills and made him as comfortable as possible, and told him to stay put. I loaded my pack, put on my crampons, and then looked about for an escape route. There were two possibilities. I tried one and it went.

I found that I could only move very slowly. My left

arm had stiffened up, so that I could not put much weight on it and could not use it for cutting steps. This made climbing awkward. After an hour or so, I heard calls from above. It was HansPeter and Norm. I told them to come down, that there had been an accident. In an hour we met. I told them of our fall and our night out. They had assumed that we spent the night back at the cache, although they had still worried. I sent them on down for Roger, while I climbed up to the top of the col.

In camp at last, I was starved. I ate, then slept uneasily. Late in the afternoon the others returned with Roger walking on the rope between them. We had a council of war.

I wanted to go on. So did Roger. Roger said that he didn't think he would be up to traveling tomorrow, but he would be all right at the col with HansPeter. Then if he felt better the next day he would come up and join us. Norm and I feared that Roger might be underestimating the seriousness of his condition. Nevertheless, he had made it back up to the col under his own power, and he seemed to talk perfectly coherently now. So, in spite of our setback, we decided to—continue. I wasn't going to give up on Everest because of one knockdown.

XI

ON UP

But we were quite a different group than we had been a mere thirty-six hours earlier. At one blow our effective strength had been cut in half. Norm set down in his diary that I looked dead: white face, puffed eyes, left arm partially immobilized. I failed to answer questions and seemed to be completely uninterested in what went on around me. He wrote that both Roger and I seemed dazed. He hoped that there were no internal injuries. The go, go, go of two days ago was completely gone.

I didn't realize how great a change had taken place. I was aware of feeling bruised and battered all right. I felt as if I had wandered by mistake into the scrimmage line of a professional football game. But I wasn't aware of how my overall condition had done a hard day's work climbing with double loads and then added an extra carry. I had had the shock of the fall, followed by a sleepless night with neither food nor liquid. In the morning, again without food, I had made the solo climb back up the cliff over which I had fallen and on up to the top of the col. All this would have been exhausting even at sea level. But at high altitudes missing one or two meals, or a night's sleep is much more serious. At sea level a day of rest will bring you back pretty well. But up here, unless you are carrying oxygen, you don't come back. Above 19,000 feet a man deteriorates anyway; his alertness, his strength, his endurance, all gradually leave him. An experience such as we had had hastens this deterioration, jumping it ahead several stages. Only by going down to a much lower altitude for a week or so could we recover. The moral is that, if you insist on sleeping out, you should see that you do it on the way down, not on the way up. On the way up you are likely to have nothing left. I had nothing left, but I didn't really know it.

The tip-off should have been that, even after rising late at seven o'clock, we didn't actually set out until noon. Norm and I, however, both convinced ourselves that it was a temporary effect from the fall. Before leaving I looked in on Roger. He said he had vomited again in the night, and had had pain in the back of his neck and head. He had lost his appetite. Still, he felt better this morning. He wasn't up to traveling today, but still hoped to come on up tomorrow. I hoped Roger was not suffering from another dose of optimism and that he really was as well as he said he was. We said we would see him later and set off.

Because we were now another day behind and were starting so late, HansPeter volunteered to help carry part way up the Northeast Ridge. First we descended a hundred feet or so to the low point of the col, then we began to climb more and more steeply. The footing was excellent and there were no problems except the problem of getting enough energy to keep climbing. The wind, however, was a nuisance. It had been very strong for the last two nights, and now it slapped at us in sharp bursts strong enough to knock us down if we weren't braced.

By 3:30 P.M. we had climbed 500 or 600 feet up the ridge. It was a thrill to realize that we were now far enough above the North Col so that we were unequivocably on Everest itself and not just on one of its approaches. HansPeter deposited his load, wished us good luck, and headed back down to Roger at the North Col. We were left alone on our wind-swept ridge.

We tried, not too successfully, to level the tent by cutting into the snow slope. The wind tore at every object. Raising the tent against it was a struggle. We belayed it to the slope with both ice axes and pitons. I had no desire to be blown down the mountain while we were sleeping.

The swelling in my face had subsided and my left arm was improved. However, I noticed a sharp pain over my heart when I breathed deeply. I suspected a cracked or broken rib from the fall. It bothered me, because up here you have to breathe deeply a lot of the time. Unless you force yourself to overbreathe a bit, you get behind, then you have to gasp to catch up. That was when the rib hurt sharply. However, if it *was* a rib, there was nothing that could be done about it; I would just have to ignore it as much as possible.

We did a miserable 600 feet today when we should have done 2,000. At this rate we would never make it. But we would see if we could do better with an early start tomorrow.

The early start began all right with breakfast at 5:15. The sun hit the tent at six and was comforting. But I just couldn't get enough sleep. I grabbed every spare five minutes and went into a deep drowse. I pleaded with Norm for another twenty minutes, then another. The net result was that we didn't actually start climbing until 11:00 A.M. By 3:45 we decided to camp. Again, we had made only about 600 feet.

We spent a very poor night. The tent was half in the rocks and half on the snow. Norm was lying in a trough and I huddled half-sitting on the up side of the tent. I was clumsy and spilled the precious pot of tea we were heating for the night. The wind flapped the tent unmercifully. Norm and I talked our situation over.

I said that I could see no prospect of making a greater distance tomorrow than we had today or yesterday. At this rate it would take another week to get to the top. Even if we had the strength, we certainly didn't have the food for that long a time. We might as well face it: this was going to be our highest camp. Norm seemed to agree. I suggested that we go up without loads as high as we could, to take pictures. Without a load I thought that I might reach the base of the yellow band of rock which cuts across the whole top of the mountain at about 27,000 feet. I would like to bring a rock back from there.

And so, in a little tent a bit over 24,000 feet high, on a rocky wind-swept ridge, two men talked quietly of the end of a dream. Tomorrow would be the last upward day. For me, at least, contrary to what most might think, there was no regret. It is not merely that up here all things are dulled. This, of course, is true. Emotion takes energy, and there was precious little excess energy around to spare on emotions. So even if I had felt regret, it could have had no sharpness to it. On the contrary, what I really felt was relief—relief that the job was finally over, relief that the long struggle upward was now to end. Many Everesters have spoken of the actual relief they felt when they turned back at last. I think one would feel regret only if he felt that there was something more he could have done, or if he felt that he had made a too obviously wrong decision. But in every situation and decision so far I had simply done the best that I knew at the time—and the others had, too. So where was the basis for regret? In these affairs, a man struggles and works toward his goal. Then there comes a time when he knows in his heart that the last ounce of effort has been given, that there is nothing more to give. As long as he does know this in his heart, then he will

159

not regret; he will, in fact, feel happy with the pride of a job well done.

The butane stove burned blue. Our nightcap of tea steamed up around our heads, and we looked like hairy trolls tending a witch's caldron. We drank our tea. The stove was extinguished. The dark wind flowed from off the heights and swirled in black eddies around the tent. We slept fitfully. My rib hurt.

Next morning I set out by myself at ten o'clock. Norm said he wanted to fix the tent so that it would be more comfortable. He would follow along when he could. As I started out, I noticed that the wind had dropped completely. I had my single twinge of regret that if we were now at 27,000 feet, as we might well have been, we would have an ideal day for the summit. Indeed, the weather had been sunny now for five days, but this was the first windless one.

I set out with only a canteen, a little chocolate, and my Bolex 16-millimeter movie camera. It seemed brutally heavy. But no Westerners had ever taken colored movies on the North Face of Everest before. It was an opportunity that must not be missed. I walked up slowly, following the rocks at the edge of the hard snow which forms the crest of the Northeast Ridge up its first half. I did not hurry, but I kept at it. Every twenty or thirty steps I would stand for a bit to rest. I didn't notice any particular trouble in breathing, but within me I felt a deep bone tiredness. It was as if I were half asleep. Disconnected impressions flitted through my mind almost at random, as they do just before you are about to doze off. And they had the same extra vividness that makes you almost think they are real. I talked to myself, I laughed, I spoke in various accents and made up things for the rocks to say back. Fragments of conversations drifted through my consciousness, snatches of music, remembered scenes and voices. I said to myself; "Sayre, it's lucky there's nobody around to hear you; you're out of your head."

160

I left the snow behind and cut over a bit to my right. Time went by and finally it was the middle of the afternoon. I came to an outcropping of rock with a rather comfortable seat on it. I rested there longer than usual. It came to me that I wasn't going to make the yellow band. In fact I wasn't going to make any more upward distance at all. This time there not only was no regret, there wasn't even relief. It was just a fact, accepted almost mechanically, with no emotion at all. The band was still too far away, I was too tired, and it was getting late. So I sat in the warm sun and looked around me. The day was still perfect.

Then, as I looked off to my right, it seemed to me that the whole face was different. From the yellow band up it was the same as I remembered it from photographs; but the lower part looked entirely unfamiliar. Wasn't there supposed to be a steep drop-off? I couldn't see any. Instead I saw a series of descending terraces that seemed to be separated each from the other by man-made stone walls. It looked like a vineyard or even a city. In my heart I was sure that these walls must just be a natural geological formation. Some harder strata of rock were cutting across softer material. I had not seen before, maybe, because pictures had not been taken from just this angle. Or, possibly, a giant landslide had somehow laid them bare. Still I stared at them in disbelief. They looked so regular, so square. They even appeared to have occasional windows or doorways cut through them. The fantastic thought occurred to me that the Communists had been up here doing this. As propaganda for Asia and Africa they were going to make even the most waste places fruitful. How better could they try to show the superiority of Communism than by offering produce grown on the very heights of Everest?

I felt I was surely seeing things. So I got up and walked down toward them. They still looked the same. I aimed my camera and photographed them. At least when I got back home I would know how crazy I had been. I took a last look at the summit. It seemed very close. I looked out at the view. I could see Gyachung Kang, the mountain where we were supposed to be. The top of it still seemed higher than me, but not terribly much. I judged I was about level with the snow fields of its upper plateau. This would put me at somewhere between 25,000 and 25,500 feet. It was not very accurate, but it was the best I could do. I was definitely above the North Peak (24,780) and I was at least a thousand feet below the yellow band (27,000), so I must have been at 25,000-something. My best guess would be 25,400.

Now the sun was getting low and it was time to start down. I found that I was very tired, and walking down over the rocks was slow and fatiguing. So when I got down to the top of the snow crest on the Northeast ridge I was tempted to try a glissade. Others had been similarly tempted in the past, with varying results. I really felt I was too weak to try it. On the other hand it would save a lot of slow laborious descending. Finally I yielded. But I would experiment a little first. I would try sliding down over a little patch of snow some 20 or 30 feet wide. If I could control the slide well enough, I would try the big, open slope. If I lost control on the little patch, I felt that I would safely stop in the rocks at its lower edge. So I sat down as on a toboggan, pressed the point of my axe into the snow as a brake, and pushed off. Immediately, I knew I had made a bad mistake. I accelerated viciously. So much so that the rocks didn't stop me at all. They just bruised and scraped me and tore the ice axe out of my hand. I bounced and tumbled over them and out onto the uninterrupted snow slope beyond. Now there was nothing to stop me except the col itself, if I happened to hit it. Otherwise I could slide off on one side all the way down to the main Rongbuk or, on the other, down to the East Rongbuk.

I yelled for help to Norm down below, but of course he could not hear me that far away. I spun and twisted.

Occasional rocks cut painfully, as did also the rough, granular snow. I managed to roll over on my left elbow and, using it as a kind of brake, I stopped my spin and held myself in one position. I caught sight of the small orange tent below me. It was coming up fast, looming larger and larger. Amazingly, it looked as if I were going to pass right next to it. I yelled even harder for Norm. I thought he might be able to catch me as I went by. Then the tent was upon me. I made a desperate lunge and succeeded in grabbing one corner. It tore out of my hand, but it slowed me slightly. Now the snow was a little flatter, and 30 feet beyond the tent I ran into the rocks. The combination brought me to a jarring stop, but it was a stop. Norm emerged from his tent like a trap-door spider and came down to me.

I was bloody and bruised. My whole left arm was completely skinned in one great friction burn, yet the down jacket was not even torn, impossible as this seems. Otherwise there were no broken bones or sprains. I was again amazed at my luck. I had slid at least 600 feet along the surface of the snow, dropping a vertical distance of more than 300 feet. Yet the total damage was a cut on the head; a bloody left arm; and the shock of the fall. Norm helped me back up to the tent and I crawled into my sleeping bag. We cooked supper and he dressed my arm.

I had arrived at the tent about 4 P.M. Around 5 P.M. there was a shout and I was astonished to hear footsteps right outside the tent. A moment later a grizzled, black-bearded head appeared in the doorway and there was Roger. I was overwhelmed to see him up here.

But he had said he was coming up, if he could, from the col. Now he had done just that. In view of the condition he was in when we left him, I didn't see how he made it up. He had brought along food and now offered to do whatever was most helpful: help the two of us to go on up, go on up with us himself, or help us get back down. I felt this was truly a noble effort, as well as a noble offer. We talked it over in the tent. I said that for me it wasn't even a decision. Even without the fall that afternoon I had been walking exclusively on willpower now for some time. There was no use kidding myself that I could go up anymore. I said that if Norm wanted to try it with Roger, that was fine with me; I could get down. But Norm wasn't too sure how well off Roger really was. It appeared that he too had a sharp rib pain when he breathed deeply. This couldn't help but hurt his performance badly. Also what prospect was there for improving on the 600 feet-per-day upward rate which had been our maximum so far? If it were not improved on, there was no use going on. But this would be Norm's fifth night without oxygen at 23,000 feet or above. If anything, it was likely that he would be making less than 600 feet upward.

So the decision stood. Today would remain our highest clutch upward. Now our eyes were only fixed downward. Even if Roger had come up the day before, I don't think it would have made much difference. At most we might have put one more camp up another thousand feet and someone might have gotten as far as the yellow band. But in our collective condition I don't think we could have done anything more. Without the first fall it would, admittedly, have been different. I feel sure we would have gotten at least to the Great Couloir, given the good weather we had. Beyond that, without oxygen, on a difficult, as-yet-unclimbed route, the chances were probably over 100 to 1 against success.

Now both Norman and I thought only of how relatively uncomfortable it would be in the tent if Roger stayed for the night. How he would disrupt our routine! So we urged him to go back down to the col. This was a scurvy way to treat his great push. Also it was very shortsighted. We did not realize how badly we were going to need help the next day. The comfort of the moment prevailed, and we sent Roger down. We settled in for our second night at over 24,000 feet.

164

The next morning I had deteriorated badly. I had no strength, I was weak, I was dead on my feet. I literally fell asleep every minute that something was not going on. Norm had to bark at me to keep me conscious. He wrote that I was very slow in understanding and very slow in executing what I did understand. It was obvious that I could not carry a pack and Norm could not carry both. So he tied the two packs together on a light line and let them down the slope. They stuck again and again. Each time they did, it was my job to go down the rope and push them on down the slope. Of course, now when we wanted things to slide down, they never would. All this was very slow and tedious. I didn't notice it so much, because at every stop for a new belay I dropped off to sleep. But it was a big strain on Norm. He was getting groggy, too.

Suddenly he slipped and tobogganed down 25 feet, ending up in the rocks. He broke his watch. At that moment I suddenly felt that things were falling apart. We were falling all over the mountain. We were accident prone. We were too close to the edge. "Wake up!" I said to myself. "This is going to be the fight of your life just to get off the mountain. This is for keeps!"

We called down the mountain to the others for help. We could certainly use Roger now. But they were too far away. So we continued our slow struggle downward. By twilight we made it at last to the low point of the col. HansPeter came down and took my pack for the short climb up to camp. It was good to be all four together again. Roger and HansPeter were having their troubles, too. Roger complained of the pain in his chest and HansPeter had an aching tooth. We all looked exhausted.

Tonight was our last night up here. Tomorrow the retreat would begin. But would I have the strength for it? Would any of us have the strength for it? For myself, I knew that I had pushed too far. Instead of going down after the first fall and night out, I had piled on myself five strenuous days of struggling upward. My strength was gone. I could just barely walk. After today's performance I felt pessimistic. It was not just the mild verbal form—of *saying* that, indeed, one or more of us might not get out of this. It was rather the sharp, unpleasant form—the inner tightening that came with *knowing* that disaster was now a very real possibility. The increasing number of falls was one sign. The growing list of our disabilities was another. What had once seemed a very reasonable trip was rapidly becoming a nightmare. The carefree romance was gone. *We must get down!*

XII

RETREAT

Next morning we started the retreat. I think we all knew how serious and difficult it was going to be. We didn't just have to get down the North Col and then relax into the waiting arms of Sherpas and Base Camp personnel, who would take care of us from then on. We had ahead of us the whole long trek all the way back to Nepal, with all the various obstacles that lay between here and there. Until we got back to Nepal we could expect no help of any kind. Yet, looking at the four of us, I was most reminded of a group of sick and wounded war veterans. An observer would have been surprised if we could climb a sand dune at sea level.

And this very morning the monsoon-type clouds seemed to be closing in again. Since it was now June 6, we were lucky it had held off this long. But heavy snow could be a heartbreaking setback. Our caches were a day's journey apart over dry terrain. With heavy snow we might only make a fraction of the necessary distance, and so we would run out of food. We might lose the trail or fail to find the caches or tire ourselves too much trying to struggle through it. Could we get through in heavy snow at all? The caches had food for only five days. What if it took fifteen?

But all these were future worries. Our immediate worry was to get down the col. I was the weakest, so it was decided to send me first. Generally speaking, the first man on a rope going down has the most protected position. Going up, it is the last man. We felt it would take us too long to belay over short distances. So I was to go out a full 200 feet on an extra long rope before I took a stance and brought the next man along. During the next hour or so we gave an excellent exhibition of how not to do things. In fact, so many mistakes were made that perhaps the whole affair is best set down as a tragicomedy on the subject of anti-belaying.

"Belaying" is defined in the mountaineering lexicon as the art of securing one's fellow against the possibility of a fall by means of a rope running from one climber to the other. The art of *insuring* a fall of one's fellow by means of a rope running from one climber to the other has, as far as I know, no name. I can think of some apt ones, but perhaps the most neutral is "anti-belaying". A fair example of the art of anti-belaying comes rather vividly to mind.

Our hero starts on a long traverse over a steep slope of insecure snow on top of ice. His hope is to get some 500 feet of distance across this dangerous section. He starts out. The anti-belayors and he have previously agreed on a set of indispensable signals, since he will be out of sight around the swell of the slope almost as soon as he starts out. One jerk on the rope means keep tension on the rope by hauling in on it; two jerks, give some slack; three jerks, hold fast; four jerks, all okay, proceed. The anti-belayor now firmly sets his ice axe in the snow. Then, as the belayee starts off, the belayor passes the rope between himself and the belayee *around*

168

the ice axe, thereby effectively preventing the sensing of any signals which the desperate belayee may later send.

(Rule: In belaying, the rope should run directly from the belayee to the belayor. The belayor may *independently* secure himself by ice axe, rock, or piton, but this should not be with the rope connecting the two. If it is, not only will the belayor be less sensitive to any signals from the belayee, but also he may make the effects of a fall more serious. The falling man will be jerked to a stop suddenly instead of having the extra spring furnished by the interposition of the belayor's soft, yielding body.)

So our hero proceeds, following old steps which slant down across the slope. One, two, three—everything is going fine. Then the steps turn downward a bit more and stretch a little farther apart. He takes a few quick big steps in succession. The belayor says to himself: "This rope is running out terribly quickly. I wonder if our man is falling. Better give a good tug on the rope and see."

He does so. Result: the belayee is lifted neatly out of the steps he has been following by the rearward pull of the rope, and starts slithering down the mountain.

Belayor: "Guess everything is okay. Give him slack." Having literally been pulled off his feet; the belayee is now glissading with abandon towards a vertical drop-off below. But the backwards slant of his fall gives no sense of strain on the belayor. He smiles happily.

Suddenly, the strain comes, and the belayor becomes aware. "Ah, there is a fall." He heaves in. Squish. The belayee is brought to an absolute halt and is just about cut in two. But he is safe; he falleth not. However, he is being suffocated by the pull of the heavy pack in one direction and the pull of the rope in the other. Helplessly he hangs against the slope, unable to gain his footing. With a desperate effort he tries to attach the pack by one of its straps directly to the rope above, so that the strain will be eased from him. But he hasn't the strength. He calls for help. He jerks urgently on the rope for slack. No response. He is pressed so badly that his wastes are actually squeezed out of him. Finally, he eases the strain in the only way possible. He jettisons the pack and sadly watches it bounce down the slope and disappear over the brink of the cliff below, carrying with it, among other things, a $1,000 movie camera.

The anti-belayor above, feeling a little easing of the strain, nods with satisfaction. "Things must be better," he says to himself. Generously he gives out a little slack. The belayee finds a little purchase for his feet and can breathe again, which, after all, is worth the small price of a $1,000 camera.

The anti-belayor now turns his job over to an accomplice and descends the slope to assess the damage. He peers over the steep drop-off at the belayee and asks what he can do. The belayee has some ideas; but out loud, he merely pleads for some 40 feet of slack to reach a ledge beneath. The belayor disappears and relays the message to the new belayor. Thirty-five feet are given, then the big freeze. Nothing happens. Two jerks, three jerks, four jerks, twenty jerks—all are unanswered and unheeded. Standing on a steep 70-degree slope, his legs tire. When is something going to happen? Another twenty minutes go by. Apparently never.

Craft must be employed. Carefully, he climbs 3 feet upward. Complete slack puzzles the brain trust upstairs. Maybe the belayee doesn't need a belay any more. Maybe the danger is over. Tentatively, a little slack is given. The belayee gathers it in, but ever so gently. A little more, then still a little more. Maybe now he has the 5 extra feet he needs. He starts moving.

But he is exhausted. Who knows what slips first? A little slip increases. He starts careening downwards. Now he hopes the belayor is alert after all. But the belayor has decided that this is the time to neaten and coil the excess rope. He is holding it loosely in one hand. The rope burns out of his hands, whips around and off the ice axe, and falls down the cliff. The belayee drops unchecked, catapults over the brink, falls 40 feet, hits the roof of a crevasse, and falls on through. He finds himself lying on his back with his feet in the air. He stares up at the small sky light he has made 30 feet above his head. He proceeds to curse all belayors thoroughly and carefully, in order to leave nothing out.

He gets up and waits for some kind of action from above. Nothing happens. He decides no one is really interested in him anyway, so he looks around for ways to climb out of the crevasse. He tries two and fails. Then, after what can only be described as one of his most brilliant leads, he makes it out. With surprise he observes that he is only a few feet from the spot where he landed in his first fall almost a week earlier. He starts climbing up the cliff by the same route he had used before. About forty-five minutes go by, and then he hears a cheery call above him: "Hey, are you okay down there?" The answer is mercifully swallowed in the great silent snow slopes of Mt. Everest—playground of the antibelayors.

HansPeter moved grimly toward our original objective, which was the very spot to which Roger and I had returned for the extra load on the night we fell. I followed along as best I could. I had my pack back, as I had found it at the bottom of the crevasse resting beside me. But I had no rope. It was hopelessly snarled in the crevasse, so I had left it there.

If I was exhausted before, the fall had added the finishing touches. I had to rest at each step. Hours went by trying to cover those last few hundred feet. Finally, I was not more than twenty paces from the flatter spot we were heading for. After that, the descent would be fairly easy. But right here was the steepest part of all, and the ice was hard under very thin snow. I just did not have the strength to move carefully enough. Suddenly, I slipped a bit. My reflexes were too slow to recover. The next instant I found myself sliding downwards again. It was getting monotonous. Almost mechanically, I turned over into a sitting position and went into the routine of trying to brake with my ice axe. I passed only a few feet from HansPeter. I can still remember the horrified look on his face—pinched nose, grey face, staring eyes. But by now I was practically blasé about the whole thing and I was just too tired to care. I nodded my head to him as I went by. "Here we go again," I said. "Be seein' you." And down I went. All at once I was over the edge of a big drop tumbling head over heels. I curled myself into as much of a ball as I could and clasped my hands behind my neck to save my head. There was a long fall, followed by a buffeting slide, followed by another free fall, and then a slide that finally came to a stop in deep snow.

This time, I was completely dazed by the fall. I looked up and all around, and felt I should know where I was, but I didn't. Was this McKinley? No, I knew that was wrong. But where was it? I squinted. I furrowed my brow. Somehow it seemed important. I tried to name the ridges and the peaks.

I must have sat in the snow quite a while, because suddenly I heard HansPeter behind me asking if I was all right. At that very instant everything came back to me, and I knew that this was Everest and I had just descended a third of the col in record time. I had fallen about 400 vertical feet. We were just above the big crevasse where we had spent the night on the way up.

My knee was twisted, but I could still walk on it. Otherwise, I was again unharmed. I reflected that in my four falls I had descended over 1,000 vertical feet across the face of Everest, yet I was still able to move around under my own power. This is no doubt a record of some kind, but scarcely an enviable one. Still, I was getting down the mountain. HansPeter told me that on this last fall I had skittered and bounced, and incredibly missed a whole series of huge crevasses.

About this time we heard shouts from above. Norm and Roger wanted us to come up and help them. They were entirely unaware of this last fall of mine and could not understand why HansPeter and I had not waited for them. Norm wanted HansPeter especially to come back and carry the pack he had left there. They could not carry three. I felt that we should go up. If they were in trouble, we must help. Only I knew that I couldn't move upward. Even without my twisted knee I had long ago passed the various degrees of exhaustion; I was at dead bottom. HansPeter urged that we get down. He was undoubtedly right, but I felt guilty to leave. I shouted that my leg was bad. In my own mind I didn't really see how I could help anybody. If I did get back up, they would have to help me. Nevertheless, I felt like a traitor as I called that we couldn't come up; we were going down.

Now it was twilight. We secured some rope that we had cached above the crevasse and roped up together. I belayed HansPeter down the wall of the crevasse and came down on the fixed rope myself. Then we continued on down, HansPeter first, me second. He fell into a crevasse, but I held him and he was able to climb back out. About 200 feet from the bottom of the col it became completely dark. Since we were not sure of the way we decided to stop for the night on a small snow ledge. There was a sleeping bag and a stove in my pack, but no food or tent. We stuffed our feet into the single bag, lit the stove, and huddled ourselves around it as closely as we could.

Time went by slowly. This night in the open, however, was much less cold than the first one had been. The stove made the big difference. For I could turn my hands slowly over the flame and breathe in the hot air above it. But we were sitting on snow and the cold seeped in uncomfortably. Also, the loss of sleep meant a bad blow to my chances of getting out. I dozed off once, and the sleeve of my jacket caught fire, I managed to beat it out. I realized I couldn't afford to sleep. I reflected that I was making unpleasant new records all the time now. No one before on Everest had spent even one night in the open, let alone two.

The sun came up and began to warm us. I blew the stove out and dozed for a while in the snow. But I was still very worried about the others above. Since the calls last night we had heard nothing from them. Now I called several times again without a response. Hans-Peter and I descended the last 200 feet to the snow flats at the foot of the col. Again I called. HansPeter said he would go out onto the flats. Maybe he could spot them better from out there. I sat only half awake in the sun leaning against my pack.

Then HansPeter called to me that he could see them. A great relief flooded through me; I had really begun to fear the worst. I called to them and still had enough emotion to be joyful when they answered. They said they were exhausted and could hardly move. I urged them to at least get down here off the col. They said they would try. I leaned back and dozed again.

It wasn't until four in the afternoon that they made it down. They had also had quite a time. Norm had had to use our aluminum snow shovel instead of an ice axe. He had given me his to replace the one I had lost during my fall on the Northeast Ridge. Twice on the traverse he had slipped, and Roger had slipped once, but in each case they had managed to hold each other. Then they had spent a foodless and waterless night at the cache platform which I had just failed to reach before my last fall.

Roger and Norm pitched the tents, and I crawled in. It was good to get out of the sun, which had been roasting me all day. They asked me where HansPeter was. I didn't know, but guessed he had just gone on to the Communist camp, our Camp XI. I noticed for the first time a disagreeable, rotted smell from the discharge and pus on my scraped left arm. Norm cleaned and dressed it for me. Then we had another meatless supper.

The next morning we all looked sick—Roger with his

chest, Norm with the fatigue of altitude, and I with a twisted knee and a dull lack of comprehension of what was said to me. My knee had stiffened up during the night, so that I was not sure it would hold my weight. Then, when I tried out a few steps, I felt that I could get by on it, but my sense of balance was gone. I wove and staggered like a drunk. I sent the others on towards Camp XI. I knew the trip ahead was going to be a slow, brutal business for me, and I wanted to face it alone. After the others had left, I sat for quite a while in the sun at the foot of the great ice cliff I had come so far to see. I felt relief that it had let us go at last— just barely, it had let us go. At the moment it seemed like the biggest obstacle, for from now on, we would be at lower altitudes. But immediate obstacles always seem like the biggest. I struggled to my feet and started the slow journey to the Communist camp.

At first the footing was good. But then I got into a devilish section. The glacier had melted and softened on its surface since we had last been here nine days ago. There were rivulets and water holes and sudden hollow spots. I would break through to my knee or even go in up to my hip, so that I would have to take my pack off to pull myself out. Since I had no balance anyway, I would slip and stumble and lurch, and every few steps come crashing down. The weight of the pack smashed down on me at each fall. At this rate I knew I could not last very long. Even if I didn't twist or break something, it was too exhausting. I took off my pack and dragged it foot by foot behind me down toward smoother ice. When I sat to rest, there was a hard battle not to stay there indefinitely.

The trip went on for several hours with some terrible stumbles and falls. But finally, I was nearing camp when HansPeter came to meet me and took my pack in for me. Somewhat later I got in, and one more section of the retreat was accomplished. I think the will to exist is more fantastically stubborn than anyone can imagine.

That night we ate full rations for the first time since our highest camp, Camp XIV, four nights ago. Again, the others told me how wonderful the crabmeat was, that elusive crab which I never saw. We gorged ourselves on the too salty beef and the delicious half-sour pickles. I found that HansPeter was sleeping in one of the two emergency survival suits which we had brought with us. Originally, I had thought that these suits might be just the thing for the summit party in case they became benighted. They are extremely light down suits which convert into a sleeping bag and are vacuum packed into a 5-pound package about the size of a soccer ball. But at the last moment we had decided to leave them at the foot of the col; the extra 5 pounds was more than anyone wanted to carry. Actual necessities, and not hypothetical necessities, are the only stimulants which can persuade men to pack loads around this countryside. Since HansPeter now had no sleeping bag or mattress, these having been left in his pack on the col, it was fortunate we had these extras along.

Next morning everyone except me felt much better. Roger bounced back so much that he embarked on the preparation of a sign. In due course it was set up and braced. It said: "THE FIRST AMERICAN EXPEDITION TO MT. EVEREST WELCOMES YOU TO THE NORTH COL." Then, having done our little bit for international understanding, we proceeded to pack up. We jettisoned everything we would not absolutely require. Saddest for me, was to throw out ten reels of perfectly good 16-millimeter movie film, which had cost $10 a roll. But the movie camera was now useless, and it is better to throw away things than not get out at all.

Roger and HansPeter took off first. We agreed to meet at the intersection of the East and Main Rongbuk Glaciers. Norm shepherded me as we started off more slowly. Eventually he went on ahead, and I was left alone with the rock and the sun and the ice. I walked slowly, almost in a dream. After some time, I reached the end of the lateral moraine which made a pathway of loose rocks that can be followed most of the way from there on down. It was another landmark for me. It marked the end of the high ice and snow. There would be some more on the West Rongbuk Glacier, but that would be below 20,000 feet.

Now the moraine became my new obstacle, an unrelenting enemy. It was composed of piles of loose rocks that slid and turned under me as I walked. I had lost my glasses on the col, so I could not see the footing clearly. With my dark glasses on I could not see the footing at all. But when I tried to go without them the glare inflamed my eyes, they watered, and again I could see nothing. So in either case I stumbled and fell continually.

I feared the possibility of snow blindness, which can hit at these altitudes even when you are not on snow. Then I would not be able to see at all. I noticed sometimes as I stared ahead that a kind of spider-shaped crossing of black filaments would appear to one side or the other. It would float slowly upwards across the eyeball and then disappear, only to be followed by another. If I looked directly at them they disappeared. I wondered to myself of what these were the symptom.

When I fell, I tried to relax instantly and catch myself on my hands and arms. I couldn't afford a twisted ankle up here. Certainly the others could never have carried me out. I suppose one person could have gone down and knocked on the monastery door, while the other two went on back to Base Camp. But this would have been a pretty sad ending, not really to be considered.

During the falls I had had no time to think. But here there was too much time. Realistically, I felt that the chances were against getting out. I still had no sense of balance, so that I literally had to learn to walk again. Put one foot forward, transfer the weight, bring the other foot forward—careful, don't catch it on the other. Now repeat. It was a curious feeling to have to will each separate movement of the body. I said, "Move foot." Then there seemed to be a bit of a time lag before the foot eventually moved more or less the way I told it to. I wondered if the foot was really mine. And the lack of coordination increased this feeling. Instinctively, I did the only thing that would help. I completely narrowed my horizon to just the next step. If I allowed myself to think of the thousands of steps still to go, I was through. Just the next step—a new act of concentration, a new act of will. I played the game of naming the steps. One step for each friend or acquaintance I could think of. Then, when I could think of no more, start over.

Toward the middle of the afternoon I had only reached a point opposite our old false col. It was at most only half the distance to where we all had agreed to meet. But I was about ready to quit for the night when ahead, I saw Norm waiting for me. It gave me a lift to see my old friend sitting there. He was tired, too, and we agreed to camp. HansPeter had my pack and my sleeping bag, but I was carrying the tent in an ungainly horseshoe pack around my neck. So we pitched it, and settled in. Norm gave me his sleeping bag and used only the padded mattress cover. It was snowing again quite heavily this afternoon. There was no doubt that the monsoon had started. But it seemed to take several days to build up its full force.

I woke up in the morning feeling better. I still felt as if I were underwater; things and events had a kind of fuzziness to them. But today the feeling was less marked. At one time it was so bad that I had worried that I might have become a "vegetable". Then this morning I had made a pun. It was a very poor pun, but it was a sign that I had just that little bit of surplus energy which would let me search out a double, instead of a single, meaning. It was a small thing and yet it gave me a big lift. Vegetables don't make puns.

I started off first, as I was slower. I was determined to reach the Main Rongbuk today. I would just keep going slowly but steadily until, like the tortoise, I got there. Today was the 10th of June. Since we had left the Sherpas on the 8th of May, we were now two days overdue. I wondered if they would still be in Base Camp when we got there. I didn't see why they wouldn't. For one thing, they could only collect their pay from us. Still, they couldn't stay there forever. How long would they wait?

Very soon after I started the weather began to cloud up. In about an hour it got very dark and stayed that way. Off to my left, I heard a call. It was Roger and HansPeter still in their camp. I went over, and they asked if I had any food. I shared what I had, and we brewed up some tea. It appeared that they had not made much more distance than we had. Because they had not even made our old Camp VII, where there was a small cache of food, they had had a hungry night. Norm and I had carried enough extras from the Communist camp, so that we had dined reasonably well. This was a lesson well learned on McKinley. Never assume you are going to get to where you expect in the time you expect. So always carry extra emergency rations.

Norm and I pushed on together. I was going very well today. About 1 P.M. snow squalls started that became heavy and annoying. At Camp VII rock slides had swept most of the area. We didn't know where Roger and HansPeter had cached the food, but we anxiously hoped that they would find it. The area was so changed I doubted if they could. A little later we came to the site of the cache which the ravens had robbed. I was so hungry that I hunted around in the rocks for raisins and nuts that they might have missed. I actually collected half a dozen. I reflected on the cycles of life. They eat our scraps and we eat theirs. We went on.

Near the intersection of the East and Main Rongbuk Norm and I huddled under a rock to get out of the snow and wait for the others. When they came up, I immediately asked Roger if he had found the cache at Camp

VII. He said he had. I was again impressed with his un-canny sense of location. It was only a cache of leftovers, but it meant that we at least had something to eat that night. I was grateful. I think we were all becoming in-creasingly preoccupied with food now. I calculated that since our highest camp above the North Col, Camp XIV, we had been on short rations, or even no rations at all, for five of the six nights. Camp XI had been the one place we ate really well.

Thus it was a highlight the next day when we found the 5-pound sack of sugar which I had left under a rock at the crossover point of the Main Rongbuk Glacier. This time Norm was the genius who found it. We spooned a good part of it down just as it was. Another growing favorite was invented by Roger. Put a large chunk of canned butter into a plastic bag, then pour in sugar. Now seal the bag and knead it. This can be done as one walks along. The result is a kind of cake mix that is nirvana itself. It gives an almost immediate pickup to a tired body.

I was concerned about the problem of crossing the Main Rongbuk. The lakes had been bad before; what would they be now? We had a really good cache on the other side at our old Camp V. We needed to get there tonight, or else face another foodless bivouac. Roger led us to the good route he had discovered on his last trip across. Anxiously we waited while he reconnoitered to see if it was still passable. When he came back and said it was, we all cheered. Like Moses, he led us across dry-shod.

A little later we had another piece of good luck. There was a large stream with a vertical wall of ice on its far side. We were amazed to find our fixed rope still in place and still usable. After that we climbed the 600 feet up to Camp V, camped, and made merry with our feast of full rations.

Yesterday it had snowed from 1 P.M. to 5 P.M. Today it snowed from 1 P.M. to 7 P.M. Each morning was still cold and fair, but for shorter and shorter periods. We felt very fortunate that the snow as yet did not seem to be accumulating in any depth. Each day I was feeling better and also more optimistic about making it out. But I worried about some of the obstacles ahead. Would our route across the Far West Rongbuk Glacier still be usable? Would the footing on the snow of the West Rongbuk be reasonable, or would it have become like the East Rongbuk had been for me below the North Col? What about our route down the icefalls? And would there be anybody or anything at Base Camp? Most of all, would we continue to find our caches, as we had so far?

In the morning the weather stayed fine for a change. We followed our old route along the rocky bank of the West Rongbuk. Everything went well until we came to the small side glacier on the other side of which was our old Camp IV. The whole landscape had changed. More especially, a large frozen lake that we had walked easily across before was now unfrozen. The weather turned nasty—wind and blowing snow. It was a bleak spot. I scouted two possible routes that would avoid the lake, but neither looked easy. The snow over rock and ice made the footing very tricky. Finally, I decided our best hope was to cross one arm of the lake on some floating ice that was still left. We spent a good deal of time throwing boulders at it to test it. Finally, we gave it a try. It held. We crossed and, after some steep and unpleasant going over slag heaps of moraine rocks, we arrived at the site of our old Camp IV. Again, there was evidence of rock slides and other changes. HansPeter, Norm, and I hunted with increasing feverishness for the cache. Nothing was visible. Then Roger came up. "What are you looking for?" he asked. "If you're looking for the cache, it's over here, under this rock." It was. If I had been a Frenchman, I would have kissed him on both cheeks.

We ate well that night. Norm and I talked until late

on the heady subject of all we would do when we got back to civilization. It continued to snow heavily. But we were snug.

By 6 A.M. the sun hit the tent. Everything was wet from the soggy snow. So we spread and dried equipment. For the last three days HansPeter had been the good Samaritan by carrying my gear and our tent, along with what he had left of his own equipment. Now I felt well enough to start doing some of my share again. We made up the nylon cord into a kind of harness and made a load for me of the two tents. It was awkward and after awhile the cords cut into me uncomfortably, but it worked.

I started on ahead of the others to see if I could find a way across the Far West Rongbuk. I followed along the glacier for an hour or so. There was a line of great ice towers along its edge. I was going to have to find an opening between these towers. I looked at several, but each had an impassable lake behind it. The others joined me and we talked the problem over. It looked as if we were going to have at least a long delay, involving route finding and detours. Immediately I became very pessimistic again. We were never going to get across. But we hadn't yet tried the opening that we had used on the way in. By now I was almost superstitious about sticking to our old route. Every time we tried to vary it we got into trouble. Every time we followed it things went perfectly. The only trouble here was that we were going to have to cut steps around a small lake just to get to a spot where we could see if the route was still passable beyond.

Roger started cutting the steps. Then I said I wanted to give it a try. They all looked at me. I could feel them thinking, "Is he really well enough to do this?" There was also a practical consideration. We were now down to only one ice axe. I had lost one in the fall on the ridge above the col. Another was lost in the last long fall down the col. A third had to be left as an anchor for the fixed rope at the top of the great crevasse on the col. Nothing shorter than an axe had held. So now we were walking with one ice axe, one ski pole, a bamboo pole, and a pointed walking stick from the Communist camp. If I should lose this last axe, we would be in a bad fix. For some obstacles there just is no substitute for an ice axe. Nevertheless, they nodded for me to go ahead.

It felt good to be chopping away again. Route-finder Roger. Step-cutter Sayre. I pushed along the cliff in good style. When I had made it beyond the lake, I climbed up the wall on the far side, almost afraid to look. If there was water, two hours of chopping would go to waste. More important, we would lose at least another day, which we could not afford. Finally I was at the top. I looked and could not believe our luck. There was a clear way ahead. No water at all. And I saw no other way that would have taken us through.

It took another hour to get ourselves and all the loads across this nasty spot. Roger came over last and then found that his rope was jammed back at the starting point. There was no way of pulling the rope through to us without returning to the starting point and untangling it. But it was late and no one felt like crossing this unpleasant cliff twice more. So we rationalized. We had another rope cached at the top of the icefall. We should be able to get to it with luck by tomorrow. Except for crossing the rest of this glacier, the route was fairly free of crevasses, so we should be able to get along without it. Finally, if it turned out that we needed a rope in order to complete the crossing, then we would just have to come back and get it. We all knew that no one was ever going to come back and get this rope, but it sounded rational.

So we continued on across the glacier carrying our bamboo pole, our walking stick, our ski pole, our one ice axe, *and no rope*. Now we couldn't even extract a man from a medium-sized crevasse if he fell in. However, I was glad of one thing. There wasn't any rope left to tie the tents to my back. So I would be traveling without a pack again.

It was almost twilight when we came to the middle trough of the glacier, which made a good flat camping place out of the wind. I was still feeling strong, so I volunteered to scout ahead with Roger to make sure the way ahead was passable. I tried one way and Roger tried another. I found a route all right, but, typically, Roger found a much better one. Both of us reached positions from which we could see that the way on across would be easy. We returned with the good news.

That night my optimism soared. We needed only to find the surface of the West Rongbuk walkable and find our cache at the top of the icefall. My strength was returning. We were definitely going to make it now. The thought crossed my mind that this was our last night in Tibet. We had slept a total of thirty-three nights in this country. One more day and we would be legal again. I wouldn't be sorry.

In the morning we were packed and off by 8:30 A.M. We wanted to start as early as possible to take advantage of the harder snow and the better weather which occurs in the early morning. We crossed the glacier and came to the edge of the West Rongbuk. Anxiously, I climbed up the 20-foot cliff at its edge, then stepped out onto its surface. It held. I took a dozen steps, and it still held; I didn't even sink in. We all let out a whoop of joy. Then I waited while the others scrambled up beside me. We started walking.

On my twentieth step, I broke through to my knee. Another twenty, and another breakthrough. This was going to be hard on the others after all, for they were carrying packs. At least I could feel out the soft spots for them, so I continued leading. I came to a softer area and broke through every ten steps, then every six, then several in a row. I started worrying again. This could be too tiring and slow.

But the going improved. All day it varied, but never deteriorated completely. The weather was less obliging. By ten it was snowing and windy. Visibility dropped to almost nothing at times. Norm moved up and took the lead for a long stretch. He must have become acclimatized at last, or else he simply felt the nearness of our goal, because he disappeared into the distance and no one could keep up with him. We began to notice unpleasant little crevasses appearing occasionally underneath the snow. Norm called back that they seemed to come about every thirty-two steps. Since we had no rope, the leader had to probe ahead at each step. When he found, or half fell into, a crevasse he would slash a cross in the snow with ice axe to mark its location. Then the others coming behind could step warily.

Suddenly I felt the route beginning to drop downhill. I called to the others that we had just crossed the border again. We were back in Nepal. There would be no more worries about Chinese patrols.

After another mile or so visibility ended completely. The crevasses seemed to be getting worse. We thought we should be getting near the cache, but there was no hope of finding it in this weather. So there was nothing to do but camp. A half hour after we were camped it cleared a bit, and there ahead was a black dot. Norm looked through the binoculars and declared it definitely was our cache. Again, there was rejoicing.

I decided to make a try for it. We needed meat and we also craved the comfort of a rope. Roger and I set off. But after a hundred yards or so the weather closed in again. We waited, but it was hopeless. The hidden crevasses were numerous here and the snow was extremely soft. It began to rain. So we returned empty-handed. No real supper tonight. Still, the cache was very close now. To all intents and purposes we had made it back to the top of the icefall. Tomorrow we might even make it to Base Camp. What a fine thought to fill my head as I fell off to sleep.

We were up by 5 A.M. I wanted to use every bit of morning daylight that I could, for only in the early morning was the snow at all frozen. I had found out yesterday that we were in a very bad soft section with many hidden crevasses. HansPeter and I went down to the cache first. I was surprised to find that every one of our flags and all our marker wands were gone. The snow had built up to the very top of the cache. Only the topmost marine sack stuck out above the surface. But for it we might never have found the cache. This, I think, would have finished us. For I doubt very much if we could have gotten down the icefall without a rope. And without the food we would have starved even if we had.

We went back up to the others. Then, roped, we all came down to the cache. These 300 yards were the worst of the whole West Rongbuk. Every third step the crust gave way and we went in up to our knees or even our hips. It was about like trying to walk across a room balancing on a series of high bar stools. Now add a good-sized load on your back and a creature below who, without warning, can pull any given bar stool out from under your foot. I again reflected what might have happened if the whole West Rongbuk had had this kind of footing.

We reached the cache and gorged ourselves. Then we loaded up with another day's supplies. The rest of the food was to be left. Only I was a skeptic. I wasn't at all sure we could make it down in a single day. Also, I still had a premonition about Base Camp. It was now June 15. A month from May 8, when the Sherpas had left us, would mean that we were now a week overdue. But from the June 1 date, when we had told KC to be back, we were two weeks overdue. I felt that they might well have left. Also I felt that it was completely rational that they would have left supplies for us in case we returned, but somehow I had no real confidence that the rational was going to actually happen. So I secreted extra bacon and sugar and butter in my parka. There were no extra meat bars.

Between the cache and the edge of the icefall the crevasses were much worse. Two required a running broad jump for the first man to get across. Then there was the long slow process of passing the packs over one by one, and then bringing each person over one by one. But at the very edge of the fall, we had the luck to spot our old marker flag and there below it was the very piton we had used to come up the last 100-foot cliff.

Now we started a series of rappels down the cliffs. But each was time consuming. In places we had to hunt for a new route. The wind and snow were with us again, as usual. By quitting time we were only halfway down the upper icefall, still a long way from Camp I. Immediately in front of the tent was a long vertical drop that we were going to rappel down first thing in the morning. I said to Roger that I wasn't sure there was any way off the block we would land on after the rappel. I wasn't sure the route would go. Roger replied simply, "It has to."

Next morning it did, but a giant icicle fell on me as I was rappeling down and cut my scalp open. At least it didn't knock me off the rope. We descended a whole series of walls and in between times scouted to make sure our route wasn't going to trap us in a pit with no exit, or a cliff that was too long for our rope. By late afternoon we had just reached our old Camp I, so we camped and decided to try the lower icefall as early as possible in the morning. It was a hungry camp. We had had no meat bars the night before, and the food I had secreted didn't go very far when stretched among four people. The night before Norm had asked whether I didn't think we would get down today. I had been pessimistic. Now he asked again, didn't I feel that we would surely get to Base Camp tomorrow? I still wouldn't admit that it was at all certain.

Our food situation was getting pretty serious. We had been on short rations for nine of the last thirteen days. This meant that, in effect, we were gradually starving. We were using up more energy than we were taking in. And we had no fat or other reserves left to draw upon. Inevitably, this cut into our strength and endurance. So now I was not at all sure that we were going to get all the way to Base Camp in one day. But I felt that we had better; and also, we had better find food there. Food was becoming an obsession with me. It was hard to think of anything else. I felt this was a dangerous sign.

What were the chances that we would find food at Base Camp? I was pessimistic. When we had first reached the top of the icefall we had tried calling down one at a time, then all together. "Pemmm—bah! Pemmm—bah!" we shouted in unison. But only the echoes answered. Several times since we had tried it, also with no response. I was sure they were gone. The cry was loud enough to be heard, and we could have heard the answer. And I just had the hunch that if they were gone, the food would be gone too. If it was, we were going to be in a very tough spot. We would have at least two days with no food at all. Added to our present starvation, what would be the effect? At these altitudes could we keep going at all? I didn't know.

In the morning we started off pretty grimly. Hot water for breakfast didn't fill the stomach very well. After descending for a bit, we moved out onto the rock cliff which forms the side wall of the glacier. The plan was to move out far enough on one of the ledges so that we could rappel directly down the full remaining distance of the icefall. I felt that this plan would allow us to by-pass all the difficult ice surrounding the Toboggan Slide. The ice was sure to have changed. It would involve considerable lost time in route finding. Also, in the

188

soggy weather we were having it was sure to be soft and unstable. I wanted no part of it. At least the rock cliffs would stay put.

The drawback, of course, was that this whole cliff was continually bombarded from above by boulders and rocks of all sizes. They whizzed and spun down with a very nasty snarling noise, for they fell from ledges a thousand or more feet up, and so they swished by at tremendous speeds. We hoped to climb down early enough so that the bombardment would be at a minimum.

Out on the ledge I found a good belay spot protected from above by an overhang. I rigged up a fixed rope so that Norm and HansPeter could come along the ledge using the rope as a kind of handrail. As I came back to them I gave an extra tap to the near piton just to hear it ring and make sure it was well set in the rock. The result was really laughable, but not to Norm and Hans-Peter. The tap of the hammer jarred a small piece of the rock away, then another fell away, and then another. Norm and HansPeter watched horrified. Bit by bit the whole rock fell apart and there on the ledge lay the piton without a stitch of rock around it, completely useless. I could see them thinking: "In fifteen more seconds we were going to be trusting our life to this?" White-faced, HansPeter suggested that maybe we better go down the icefall after all. Norm called Roger and made frantic gestures over my head, suggesting that Roger had better come and pound the piton in. But Roger merely said, "Hell, I don't know any more about hammering pitons than Woody does." He also added that it was the rocks or nothing. So I fixed two pitons at the jump-off spot to satisfy the nervous, and started down the first rappel.

Getting all the way down with the packs and transferring from one rope to another took us several hours. The intensity of the bombardment kept increasing. But there was nothing that we could do about it. We just had to stand and take it. Finally we were down to the ice and moved hastily out away from the cliff. Hans-Peter was the last to make the dash and had the closest call. A rock the size of his head missed his ear by less than an inch.

Hungry or not, I got a real lift from being down. The North Col had let us slip from its grasp, the great glaciers had let us pass unharmed, and now even the icefall had let us go. The objective dangers were over. Now it was just a matter of endurance. When I thought of how I had felt at the foot of the North Col, it seemed impossible that I was actually here. There, I had sat for fifteen minutes in order to get up enough energy to tie my shoelaces. Putting on sunburn lotion was a series of separate acts each taking a half dozen minutes of concentrated effort. Get the lotion out of the pack, sit and rest; unscrew the top, sit and rest; apply the lotion, sit and rest. Everything was in slow motion. There, I had been dazed from the falls. But now here I was, half-starved, but better off each day than the last. I gave thanks to God for being down.

Slowly we walked the mile to our Base Camp. Roger and Norm went on ahead. I was not surprised when they returned with the news that there was absolutely nothing there. No people, no equipment, no food—absolutely nothing. KC had left a note on a stick. It was dated June 9, 1962, and read:

Sir:
With due respect. We beg to state this bascamp because here very bat wither. And we have finished footings [he means "food"] all. And we stoping at bascamp 40 days. Your's order at the mountain 30 days be we stoping after 10 days but win 10 days we went surch to your's party at the sidel but we could not up the mountain because we have now [no] articles clamping up the mountain. Therefore all ice broken and falling then very difficult. We not now your's company cation. [He means

190

that he has received no communication.] Then we back to return at the Khumjung, because we have not footing any things.

your's sincerer

K. C. liaison officer

Well, that was that. The unbelievable had happened. You don't just abandon four people at such altitudes, but they had. I wasn't even particularly angry. Anger might come later. But right now, things were too serious to be angry. We held a council of war. On the way in it had taken the loaded porters three days to march to Base Camp from the last inhabited village. Without loads and going downhill we could hope to do a lot better than that. On the other hand, we were going to be slowed down by our lack of food. Tomorrow, would be our third day with no food at all. And this would be coming on top of two weeks of inadequate rations. At this altitude the human body needs food regularly, just like a baby. And just as a furnace goes out quickly without fuel, so a man must eat or else run out of energy in even a few hours. At sea level one can go many days without eating, as long as there is water. Up here, exercising heavily, it cannot be done. Or, at least, we didn't know how long it could be done. I would have preferred that someone else make the test.

We decided that the next day we would all climb to the top of the side moraine, which was our pathway down the glacier. There we would cache everything except our sleeping bags. Norm and Roger were the strongest, so they would push ahead until they got to the first inhabited village. HansPeter and I would follow along as best we could. We would try to get at least to the deserted village of Tanna. The others were to keep going, no matter how long, until they found help, and then send back for us there.

So we made a very miserable camp in the rain on

dirty ice and loose rock. We boiled and drank our hot water. I noticed that I was beginning to feel the fuzzy, underwater sensation that I had had after my fall on the North Col. I realized the lack of food was exhausting me all over again. I dozed off fitfully. Tomorrow, I knew was going to be the fight of my life.

At first light we get up. It doesn't take long to make breakfast today. We break camp, then start climbing the 300 or 400 feet up to the top of the moraine. It is a sign of our condition that it takes until 9 A.M. to make it. Norm and Roger take off. We wish them luck. "Keep going," I say, "and send food back to us. Don't stop. Just keep going."

Soon they are out of sight, and HansPeter and I make up the cache. Then we leave, too. Mercifully, it is a lovely, sunny day and shows every indication of staying that way. At least the footing will be good. I move very slowly, but with a grim steadiness. I have resolved that I will keep going forever if I have to, but I will get there. I want to go at a pace so slow and steady that I will never have to rest, for I sense that a start-stop, start-stop advance will finish me. Inside I now have a deep weariness that makes everything seem unreal. The foodless days have done their work. I notice that the little spider shapes that floated across my eyes are back again. Only now they look like ants. The thought flits through my mind that this is only right, for I am lower down now and ants can't live as high as spiders. The thought seems perfectly relevant.

HansPeter is ahead, but he stops and rests. Also, he is carrying the pack. So eventually, I catch up and pass him. Then gradually he falls behind and I walk alone down the moraine in the sun. I talk to myself, I upbraid myself for my self-pity. "You could be a lot worse off," I tell myself. Time goes by. I keep going.

I remember a short story I once read back in elementary school. A man failed to run hard enough and died.

He didn't realize that his life was at stake or that he was so close to escape. At the time we were indignant. "Why didn't the man know?" we asked. "It was unfair." I reflect that I am lucky. I do know. And it is not unfair. I keep going.

I play the game again of naming the steps. Anything to keep my mind off how exhausted I feel and how much I would like to stop and rest. Then I come to the Guanara side glacier. This is where I have to go down onto the Ngo Jumbo Glacier itself and negotiate the horrible footing of that section. I find myself falling quite often now. My reflexes are slow. I wish my legs obeyed me better. I keep going.

When I finally reach the spot at which the route climbs back onto the moraine I have a great struggle to get up. It is a high cliff of loose mud and rock. Every step slips back. Once up I decided I better wait for HansPeter. I have about 50 feet of light cord. He may need it up this last pitch, since he has the load. HansPeter appears and I help him up. Now it is straight walking for a few more miles to Tanna. Again I push on ahead. They are very long miles.

The sun begins to set. Since Base Camp, I have been walking for ten hours. I ask myself what I can still notice, what affects me? The emotions are dead, the intellect is feeble. I haven't even felt hunger for some time now, just weakness. But, surprisingly, the sense of beauty is still sharp. The little Alpine flowers are so beautiful they almost make me cry. Purples and blues and buttercup yellows. So bright and graceful, what are their names? They are everywhere so that I can't help stepping on them. I don't like to. I notice the smell and the feel of the turf underfoot. How wonderful to smell earth again! A light evening mist rises from the low spots and softens every outline. I hear some low, throaty birdcalls in the wet twilight that remind me of Martha's Vineyard, or even Killarney in Ireland. How deep the sense of beauty must be within us. Even a man waiting to die will notice the loveliness of trees and sunlight around him.

I feel that I am getting close to Tanna. It will not be long now before the journey is over and I can stop walking. I have the sense that I am floating along in some feverish dream and that I could go on this way forever. I almost have a feeling of contentment. In a little while now the job I set myself this morning will be done—well done.

Then I come into a small glade and see some dark rocks ahead. As I look, one of the rocks seems to move. "Yak," I think. "A herd of yaks." Then I think of mother yaks defending their young against strange creatures that sneak up on them in the evening half-light. Also, I remember how upset they are by the scent of Westerners. If they charge, I could not run two steps. I squint anxiously at them, but my vision is still very poor. Nevertheless, they definitely must be yaks. My sense of contentment disappears. I force myself to make a long climbing detour. The yaks do not charge. I leave them alone and they leave me alone. Gratefully I continue on.

Now, rather suddenly, I see the stone walls and the few deserted huts of Tanna. I walk to the largest and sit down comfortably on the doorstep. HansPeter arrives, then goes off to get water from the stream. It is now seven o'clock, so I have walked a total of twelve hours. I wonder if Norm and Roger will send back food tonight. I know I will get out now, but it would be nice if they sent it back tonight. I think about them sending it back tonight, and I doze.

All at once, I hear shouts. It is incredible. These are the voices of strangers. I haven't heard a strange voice for a month and a half. I answer, I call HansPeter, and I wait impatiently. Two young boys appear. They are wonderfully solicitous and they *do* have food. Quite suddenly I feel ravenous. They have young new potatoes, still warm. They have rice. And they have a kind of wooden gourd filled with a milk-like liquid made from ground barley. HansPeter and I devour everything while the boys stare at us in astonishment. It is absolutely delicious.

It is now very late and completely dark. But I want to get down the valley to Norm and Roger if we can. The boys are willing and they lead the way. They have cat's eyes. We follow closely, but the footing is still very difficult for me and I cannot always keep up. Nevertheless, I feel very gay and foolish. I reflect that a man can always go a few more miles when things are either very bad or very good.

We come to the village where Norm and Roger are; we come to the stone hut itself. I can hear their voices. I call out to them to get the lead out of their tails and mobilize the welcoming committee. I hear Roger say, "Hey, it's them! They're here!" And then a moment later we are in the warm firelit interior of the hut. We all smile at each other. It has been a long time since we smiled.

XIII

RETURN

What luxury it was to sleep on the floor of a house again. Luxury is a relative matter, but just the business of not having to pitch a tent, because there was already a roof over one's head, seemed like a noteworthy comfort to me. And then in the morning, someone else got up and made the fire, and served us tea and *chapatis,* rather like Mexican tortillas. That was luxury, too.

These wonderful Sherpa people could teach most of us lessons in hospitality. I wondered how many American families would take in four strangers in a two-room dwelling, feed their gigantic appetites, send their young children up the mountain in the darkness with food to find two of them, and generally share everything they had with them. It was very moving to me. We found we were in the house of Tensing.* Norm and Roger had been looking for a Sonna Tensing. But he actually lived down the valley at a considerable distance in the village

* Only a very distant relation of Tenzing.

of Porche. We had used Sonna Tensing as a porter on the way to Base Camp, and Norm had mistakenly thought he lived in this village. It turned out Sonna Tensing was a cousin, and so it was agreed that our host would go down and get this cousin the next morning to help porter for us. We wanted to reach Khunjung, the small village adjacent to Namche Bazar. For we understood that all our gear was there, along with KC, Aila, and Pemba. In fact our host had helped carry it there a few weeks earlier. We needed this gear, especially since it included all our low-altitude clothing. Our high-altitude clothing, which we had with us, was now too hot. Also it included our money, film, papers, and other essentials.

Because Sonna Tensing would not be available for a day, and because we were all tired, it was not too hard to declare a holiday. We would just loll around, mend gear, and recuperate. It had been almost a month since our last holiday at the foot of the North Col. The morning was sunny. Idly, I watched a band of sheep being herded down the path. An idea seized me. We needed meat. I *wanted* meat. Why could we not have a sheep? We would buy one. It turned out that the village was a good example of uncontrolled capitalism. One man owned all the sheep. He was called, and we dickered. The price was set at 40 rupees in Nepalese currency ($5.20). This seemed very reasonable to me, although later we were told that we had been had.

Now, it appeared that, because of their religion, the Sherpas do not kill animals. We would have to kill the sheep. This was a blow, since they had never taught any of us in college how to kill sheep. They presented us with a somewhat ancient ewe, rather than the young lamb I tried to promote. I hogtied it in the best Wild West tradition. HansPeter retired to the hut. And there were the three of us standing around—three grown men surrounding one poor sheep—and wondering what to do next. There was considerable hot debate, which they *do* teach you in college, but little action. In the end Norm seized the initiative, or rather the knife, and stabbed the poor creature to death. Then we bled it and started skinning it, whereupon the Sherpas all came out and took over the job very efficiently. The body was quartered and hung in the hut. I put the heart and liver in a bowl of water to keep the flies away, then we sat around and waited.

Tensing had gone off to get some rice, *chang,* and *rakshi.* We didn't realize how far he had to go and so expected him back by lunch. Actually, it was almost dark before he returned. Meanwhile I dozed, and wrote in my journal, and got hungrier and hungrier. At last my appetite got the better of me. I went over to the bowl, took out the heart, cut a thin slice off it, salted it, and ate it. It was delicious. I could feel the nourishment doing me all kinds of good. A few moments later I thought: "I ought to have some more good done to me. I have a duty to try another slice." I did. Soon, it was all gone. It was a lovely large heart. Roger came and saw the trend. Pretty soon we were both cutting off strips of meat from the haunch, salting them, and devouring them. The others came in and haughtily predicted all kinds of dire results if we kept on with this gorging. We agreed wholeheartedly and kept at it. Then, as it was getting dark, we tried to start a fire. All they have up here is a low, damp bush resembling gorse. How they make it burn I will never know. However, some of the small children watching our every move came over and got it burning for us. Then Roger and I put chunks of meat on the steel pick of our one ice axe and burned them a minute or so in the fire. HansPeter decided to try one. I gave him an almost raw piece and, sure enough, he decided he didn't care for any more. Norm was above it all. That left the field to Roger and me. We gluttonized. Never have I tasted anything so juicy, tender, and delicious. A magnificent shish kebab —shish kebab à la ice axe!

What I had written in the journal that day was my immediate reaction to being down safely, as well as my reactions to this last part of the trip. In one sense, it is the most authentic report possible, since it was written at the moment itself. It is not necessarily the way I feel now, but it was the way I felt then. And so I shall quote passages from it as it was written, changing it only enough to make it coherent.

June 19, 1962. At last we are down! ! ! What blessed relief. The mountain has let us go and we have finally made it. Literally to know that you will live and see your loved ones again.

Here we are in a cozy timber and stone house. The four of us doze the day through. We have slaughtered and skinned a sheep. Natives won't kill because of religion. Owner is off to buy chang and rice. There will be a great feast tonight, we hope.

How I hate mountains and glaciers and moraines and walking on rocks and not being able to get out. Today is probably the best ever. For this is the day it is over, OVER! Unbelievable. And we don't have to walk, or push on, or hope desperately to get somewhere where we aren't. The hope of more progress, and the despair of not enough. The snow and the rain and the afternoon storms and the starvation are all over. I munch my potato. I revel in doing nothing.

Outside, it is spring! A warm wind blows like a March sirocco. Everything is green and flowering. Life stirs; how wonderful, how perfect.

How gently the trip turned from a fairly reasonable venture to a real hell. Like the slow movement of water towards a dam and then the sudden sucking acceleration that is almost too strong to fight. The shock of one fall and then with increasing frequency three more. Norm was good to me. Arranged to have my pack carried and prevented me from trying to carry again too soon, while I learned to walk again.

How lucky we were. The snow wasn't deeper, we found our route, no essential equipment broke, and we recovered all our caches. All except the last. We *counted* on food at Base Camp. Why should that damn KC have left us to die? Yesterday I was oh so tired. Meat gone for five days, sugar for three. It is amazing what a man can stand.

I hate crampons and ice axes and glaciers and rock. But it will not stay this way. Already, in even a few hours, a little veneer of nostalgia and subjective manipulation starts painting over some pretty awful things. I will love mountains again. But I will not come back here. Never!

I have learned a few things. A trip like this is too big and too long to keep up a pose or an attitude. Whatever romantic view I held about it, the realities of the people and the events cut through. The carefree and the unplanned approach don't really fit very well. The fear of death and the knowledge of it came sneaking in so gradually. It was a slow throttling that turned the trip into something very unromantic.

The truth is that death is not gay. It creeps up, and suddenly it is very grim and very terrifying and very wasteful seeming—and even disgusting. The romantic and adventurous is all very well, but it doesn't stand up against suffering and death. We can pretend and hope, but something more is needed. Well, why not say it, only God, Himself, can give us the strength to withstand such things.

After the feast that night, we slept late the next morning. Sonna Tensing arrived from Porche, and we gratefully turned over our loads to him and our host, who had agreed to accompany us. The walk down the valley was easy, but the reaction had set in for me, and I was terribly weak. HansPeter vomited on the trail, but Roger and I were pleased that our feasting had none of its predicted aftereffects.

We decided to stay for the night in Porche and walk to Khumjung the next day. All at once we heard calls outside the house, and there were Pemba and KC, who had walked over to meet us. They came upstairs into the big general living room. Then there was a performance. Pemba was contrite and dejected. "Sahib, I wrong, I no good," he said over and over again. But we refused to blame him. It was KC who had the authority. It was KC who had made the decision to leave. I felt the Sherpas might have stayed on their own, but it was probably too much to expect them to resist official authority. However, KC did not want to be blamed. He claimed that we had ordered him to leave in a month. Then he claimed that the Sherpas had ordered the departure. KC and I stood face to face, waving our hands at each other. A large crowd of villagers sat along the walls, gravely turning their heads toward each speaker in turn, like an audience at a ping-pong match. This was a great show and they obviously enjoyed every moment of it. The climax came. "I was your friend," I said. "I take this fur hat which I gave you as symbol of authority, I throw it on the ground, and I step on it." A sigh of expectancy went through the crowd. KC rushed for me; I rushed for him. We were immediately restrained, as expected. KC left, alone and indignant, to make the march back to Khumjung. The show was over.

I was really angry. The emotions were very close to the surface these days. But, curiously, throughout the whole affair there was another part of me that stood off from it all, almost as an observer. To this other part it all seemed a preposterous farce, even while it was happening. But the confrontation had to take place. Each part had to be played. I had the feeling of an inexorable necessity. Tomorrow, or at most the next day, we would play the reconciliation scene.

In the morning we climbed the steep trail toward Khumjung. An hour away Chombi appeared with a big grin, bearing hot tea and *chang*. I felt very moved to see him, and I knew that he felt the same way. He hugged me so hard that my rib hurt again. Then he embraced me on both cheeks. For a while we sat and talked with the help of those who could speak a few words in both languages. He told me one intriguing story. It appeared that he had been very worried over our long absence. A few days ago a holy man had come through the village. This man had a great reputation for reading tea leaves. One paid him a fee and asked him a question, then he would find the answer in the leaves. Chombi had gone to him and asked him whether we were still alive. The holy man had drunk his cup of tea, then stared at the leaves in the bottom for a long time. Then he had thrown them out and drunk a second cup. Again he looked for a long time, and again he threw the leaves out. Finally on the third try, he had looked up at Chombi and said; "I do not see how it is possible, but they are all still alive."

We stayed at Chombi's house and he treated us to a fine supper. It had meat in it, which I gather only occurs on very special occasions. The main diet at this season seems to be potatoes for breakfast, lunch, and supper, washed down with hot buttered tea. We found that KC was staying at Chombi's also, but he wouldn't come out of his room. Then we were presented with the gear that we had left at Base Camp, all carefully kept for us. We felt a twinge when we saw included in the pile some 30 or 40 pounds of food. What a difference just a little of that would have made!

We heard that KC had sent out word over the military wireless the day before that our expedition was overdue by twenty-two days. He reported that we had left Base Camp with only twenty-days' food supply some forty-two days earlier. He requested instructions and of course was ordered to abandon Base Camp, which he had already done. I was puzzled why he should have said we only had twenty-days' food when he knew that we had at least thirty. I noticed also that he had in fact removed the Base Camp only thirty-one days after we left the Sherpas on May 8. If we had been as little as two days late; we would not have found a Base Camp. I still do not know why he did this. Certainly, he wasn't deliberately trying to harm us. Nor was

202

he trying to make off with our supplies. I sup
weather was bad, it was an unpleasant spot,
didn't think very clearly what the consequences of his
decision might be. Actually, he had been in Khumjung
during May, so that he did not even have the long wait
at Base Camp that the Sherpas had had. Again, I could
understand a man deciding he had had enough and
going back down. But why should he take all our supplies with him? Why should he then carefully keep all
these supplies for our return journey to Kathmandu,
having made it just about impossible for there to be any
return journey to Kathmandu? The whole affair must
remain a mystery. My best guess is that he thought the
June 1 date that I had asked *him* to be back at Base
Camp, was the date *we* were going to be back at Base
Camp. He didn't grasp that we would be back in about
a month, which would have meant that we wouldn't return until around June 8. As to why he took the supplies, perhaps it was just his sense of neatness. One
doesn't leave valuable goods scattered unattended over
the countryside. But that is just a guess.

So we had a message sent that the expedition was
safely in Khumjung. We requested helicopter transportation to Kathmandu. This would be expensive, but we
had talked it over. No one relished walking all the way
back to Kathmandu. One hundred sixty miles of mud
and leeches and monsoon rains would be a terrible anti-
climax. And I, at least, was exhausted enough to feel
that it might take me a dismally long time to make it. I
was more tired than I knew.

We all worried what the effect of KC's previous message might be. We hoped it had not been picked up by
the news services. I thought it unlikely. Little did I
know.

The next morning KC and I made peace. There were
no ill feelings. He had meant no harm. All was forgiven.
I was glad to be friends again. Aila came in looking
very sick. There was a German research team in the vil-

lage with a doctor. We took him down and he was diagnosed as having cavernous tuberculosis. Shots were prescribed. HansPeter said he had talked with the German team, and would like to stay with them and come out with them when they returned to Kathmandu a little later. He asked that we not talk about our actually being on Everest until he got back out of Nepal. Then he confessed that he himself had already spilled the story to one of the Germans. I was angry, for I had not yet decided how the illegal aspect of our trip should be handled. I didn't want it to just leak out. The consequences had to be estimated carefully.

On Saturday, June 23, we heard a report that a broadcast out of India had announced that our expedition was found and that helicopters were being sent for us. This meant that the earlier message concerning our disappearance must also have been circulated. There went one hope for anonymity. But we were excited that transportation was being sent. Now that it was a possibility I wanted it desperately. Only now they told us that the monsoon made flying very uncertain. They might not come at all. It might be a week. We debated whether to start walking. We decided to give them a day or so.

I set off on a trip across the ridge to Namche Bazar. I wanted to arrange to pay our debts here if the helicopter should come. Since I had only a little cash, I was going to need a loan until I got to Kathmandu. At Namche Bazar the Post Control Officer met me and invited me to lunch. The food was delicious. All at once we heard the sound of a 'copter. I was tremendously excited. I sent a note off to Norm that I might be flying out very soon. I told him to bring my camera and a few essentials for me when he flew out, too.

A little later the helicopter landed. Aboard was Norman Dyhrenfurth. He had been in Kathmandu making advance preparations for next year's American expedition, which was also going to try Everest. Although very busy, he had kindly offered his services to help direct the pilot to Namche Bazar, since the pilot was unacquainted with the route. A crowd of villagers gathered to watch the great "praying mantis" take off. This was my first ride in such a contraption. I waved good-by to Sonna Tensing and KC, and we lifted off. It was a thrill to see all the country we had walked over so laboriously on the way in from this new angle. The great gorge of the Dudh Kosi was especially impressive. It was also unbelievable to think that we were going to do in an hour and a half what had taken us sixteen days.

Mr. Dyhrenfurth told me that I must have a lot of friends, judging by the fuss that the notice of our being lost had caused. I didn't really grasp what he meant, for I had no inkling of what was in store for us. I suppose I naïvely had thought that we could make a quiet little trip and have our fun. But the notice of our possible death had really let the cat out of the bag. Now there was going to be a spotlight on us. However, I still didn't realize how strong that spotlight was. During the trip I told briefly what had actually happened to us. I felt that as leader of the forthcoming expedition, Dyhrenfurth should know the truth. He was immediately concerned as to how our try for Everest might affect his. I agreed not to say anything publicly until I had discussed the question with the State Department. And so it was left at that.

When we came in over Kathmandu, we flew directly to the hospital grounds. I was amazed to see a large crowd of people waiting for us below. We landed, and correspondents and doctors and representatives from the embassy swarmed around me. A stretcher was brought, which I refused. Although I was slow, I could walk perfectly well. My emotions were very close to the surface, and frankly I was overwhelmed by all the kindness and consideration that were shown. The hospital was so sunny and clean, and the bed was so nice and

205

neat. I reflected that it had been eighty-one days since I last lay in one.

Baskets of mail were brought in: cables and telegrams from friends all over America, and even one or two foreign countries. I began to grasp how extensive the publicity must have been on all this. It amazed me, because I had almost forgotten that there was such a thing as a radio or a newspaper.

The next afternoon Roger and Norm arrived for observation also. It was found that I had contracted amoebic dysentery, I did have a cracked rib, my left arm was still stiff, and I had lost thirty pounds. Otherwise, I was in excellent shape, just a bit run down. Norm and Roger received a clean bill of health also. When we last saw HansPeter he seemed perfectly well. I allowed myself the satisfying thought that our little expedition had come through without permanent damage of any sort. We had advanced, and when the time came we had retreated, and we were all still sound in mind and body. Even though luck is obviously a large factor in such a result, nevertheless every expedition which achieves it takes pride in it. I was no exception.

On the mountain one never sees one's own body. I was really shocked to see the gaunt, bony specimen that was me. Every vein on my legs stood out vividly. The ribs and the hip bones had no padding at all. With my orange beard and hollow cheeks I could easily pass for a hermit or prophet who had lived for forty days and forty nights on locusts and honey in the desert.

My happiest memory was eating my fourth supper of the delicious food they served at the hospital. But the embassy was eager to get us out of Nepal, so we had to cut short our pleasant recuperation.

On June 27 we flew back to New Delhi, and shortly later we flew on to Rome. I looked out the window at the earth so far below and remembered the flight in so many months ago. It seemed a year. As the jet flew above Persia and Arabia, the pilot emerged from the forward compartment to speak a bit with the passengers. He announced rather proudly that we were now flying at an altitude of 23,000 feet. I couldn't resist turning to Norm and saying in a loud voice, "Hell, we *walked* higher than that."

XIV

AFTERMATH AND REFLECTIONS

It was over a year before my left arm regained its full strength. It was about six months before my weight came up to where it had been. Because I was perpetually hungry, my weight eventually went above even what it had been. I hated to think that I might have to go to Everest all over again—there should be some less expensive way of losing weight. It was about two months before I walked at a normal speed. I took small, slow, hunched-over steps like a very old man. Finally, it was only about one month before it was no longer true to say that I hated mountains. In fact I could contemplate the whole trip with pleasure.

Many have asked if I would do it again. If they mean would I do what I did even knowing what the outcome would be, the answer is, of course, yes. As a matter of fact, I would say that doing what I did and *not* knowing what the outcome would be might be more difficult. If, on the other hand, they mean, would I repeat the identical trip, I would think probably not. Once was enough.

Finally, if they mean would I try something similar again, then I would have to say yes, as far as I myself am concerned. But as far as those around me are concerned, no. My next expedition will be the very first traverse of Central Park with oxygen.

Nevertheless, I am back climbing rocks again. One can't take a breath large enough to last a lifetime; one can't eat a meal big enough so that one never needs to eat again. Similarly, I don't think any climb can make you content never to climb again. In the next chapter I will say more fully what I get out of climbing, but certainly there are such values as warm friendship tested and strengthened through shared danger, the excitement of obstacles overcome by one's own efforts, or the beauty of the high, quiet places on the world. But these values can't be stored like canned goods. They need to be experienced live—many times.

My wife and the children met me in Rome, and we had a wonderful motor trip through Italy, France, and Spain. Even before returning to the United States at the end of August, however, various transatlantic calls began to make me aware of a big squabble ahead. It all hinged on the question of publishing the facts of our trip. It was claimed that Nepal was in precarious balance between Communist and Western influences. If our trip into Tibet became known, the Communists might put pressure on Nepal to retaliate against the United States. Furthermore, the second American expedition to Everest, under Dyhrenfurth, might be harassed or even canceled out.

I certainly didn't want to jeopardize this expedition. Nor did I want to embarrass the Kingdom of Nepal. They are a wonderful friendly people who had been in every respect kind and helpful to me. Still, I couldn't quite believe that all these dire consequences would really occur. The trouble was that I had no disinterested information to guide me. After so many years of preparation, it was quite understandable that Dyhrenfurth would not want to take the slightest risk of hurting his chances by my publishing the facts. Moreover, nobody enjoys having a mountain stolen from him. The State Department, also, had everything to gain by exaggerating the dangers in order to keep me silent. On the other hand, the dangers might be very real.

A veritable campaign of letters was initiated. Pressure was put on *Life* magazine not to publish my account. Pressure was put on Tufts University to silence me. Letters were written to my family, to the State Department, even to President Kennedy. Dyhrenfurth said that as a minimum his expedition would be canceled. It was likely that Nepal would be driven into the arms of the Communists—ten years of foreign aid would go down the drain. As a maximum, our whole position in Southeast Asia might well be threatened. I wondered that I wasn't charged with responsibility for losing the space race as well. The State Department added the suggestion that I was presenting the Communists with a ready-made opportunity to accuse the United States of spying.

Personally, I felt that these countries were mature enough to distinguish between the acts of a government and the acts of a few individuals who were undoubtedly crazy anyway. It wasn't the United States Government that had invaded Tibet. Also, I rather thought that the Chinese Communists would not be terribly proud of the fact that an expedition had traveled without detection for over a month through territory they controlled. It seemed to me they would be more inclined to try to hide this fact than to publicize it by making a protest. Indeed, if they made too much of a fuss, if they accused the United States of spying, mightn't they look a little bit ridiculous? For what country publishes the exploits of its spies in a national magazine? And what is there to spy on up there? Finally, since the Chinese are not the legal government of Tibet, why should we wait fearfully for them to protest? Why not attack their right to protest in the first place?

The image of the United States abroad is of the huge, the organized, the rich, the overpowering. People would expect a United States expedition to have the last word in scientific equipment and the biggest budget in history. None of these qualities have exactly endeared us to other countries, many of whom are intimately acquainted with poverty and struggle, and the fight merely to stay alive. I think this was why our small expedition inevitably met with genuine interest, surprise, and friendly appreciation. People had an immediate sympathy for the problems of the little fellow pitted against the machine. Spontaneously, we received all kinds of help. Having experienced this firsthand, I can't help thinking that our State Department thought too defensively about this whole affair. Here was an actual example of the "pioneer" spirit, the spirit of adventure and individual initiative to which we pay such lip service. *If* any official position should have been taken, therefore, I would have thought that an effort to publicize this story rather than to hide it would have been far more appropriate. In fact, I am glad that no such official position was taken, but I am sorry for the timidity or lack of imagination that not doing so indicates. Here was one chance to say loudly, "See, the United States isn't *all* bigness and wealth." It is something we need to say.

However, for a long time I weighed the matter most carefully, undecided whether to publish or not. Finally, I was given independent information, which I considered authoritative, that the Communists would not make a fuss. I decided to go ahead. Just in case, it was agreed to postpone the publication until the forthcoming expedition was safely on its way towards Base Camp.*

Looking back on the expedition, I feel that at least

* The account was published in *Life* magazine in the March 22, 1963, edition.

some conclusions can be drawn. On the side of accomplishments, the primary one, no doubt, for any expedition is to arrive at one's objective, perform more or less as one had planned, and retire in good order without loss of life or limb. This we did. We came out under our own power and if our Base Camp had not been incredibly pulled out from under us, we would have come out in even better order than we did.

Secondly, we struck a blow for a tradition that I personally hope is not dead—the tradition of the small expedition. Our mobility and our modest expenses should encourage others who are attracted to the idea of a small expedition anyway.

Considering mobility, we demonstrated that a small group can move freely in even the highest terrain under its own power. One can have a radius of action from the original dump of supplies at Base Camp of at least 25 miles, and the freedom in time to be gone for at least thirty days before returning. Actually, we were gone forty-one days, but I think it would be better to plan for only thirty, so that there would be a margin to spare in case of bad weather or emergencies.

Most people do not realize that a small expedition can be so self-sufficient. This, I think, is because this self-sufficiency depends on new developments in lightweight food and equipment which have taken place very gradually. Even a little while ago it would not have been possible to go such a distance from Base Camp without Sherpas. Now it is. And the fact that it is, if exploited, should open up whole new areas of Himalayan exploration.

Considering cost, we demonstrated that a Himalayan expedition can be financed for less than $3,000 per man. Again, this depends on the fact that we could carry everything. We avoided the expense of equipping and paying high-altitude Sherpas. We avoided the expense of establishing and equipping many fixed camps. Finally, we avoided the expense of transporting and

212

supplying oxygen equipment. If we had gone by boat, we could have cut the cost still further. And yet our equipment was of the best. Whatever misfortunes we may have suffered, none of them can be attributed to poor equipment. After such budgets as the third of a million dollars to finance the mass migration under Dyhrenfurth, it should again be encouraging to a small group to know that a very modest outlay will still get you to any peak you set your heart on in the Himalayas. In this connection, one of our statisticians figured out the daily cost for each member of our expedition. He calculated that we did Everest on $25 a day!

We might have struck an even better blow for the small expedition if we had not had certain weaknesses. For instance, I think it was unfortunate that all four of us had not climbed together before. If we had, we would have known each other's strengths, weaknesses, habits, and quirks. Then any major incompatibility would have been found and eliminated, or else we wouldn't have been on the trip together. Surely there were enough obstacles without leaving unknowns in this area.

This is all bound up with the question of morale. The small expedition has a natural advantage in morale. One reason for this is that everyone already likes and respects each other, they have had fun climbing together, and so they have a warm sense of unity. The members of the large expedition, on the other hand, quite often have never met before. Since we, too, had not all met before, we were sacrificing one of our potential advantages.

We did possess the other natural advantages in morale. For example, in the small expedition, every man is needed and every man knows he will have the chance to go as high as his strength or his skill will allow. There is then no cause for jealousy, and this helps morale. In the large expedition, however, there is some pretty cutthroat competition and some pretty obvious politics in getting chosen as a "summit man", a member of "the first team". If a member is not chosen, there is bound to be some inner hurt and disappointment, no matter how much he smiles about it on the surface. Traditionally, he is given numerous bouquets. He is told that the team effort never could have succeeded without him or, again, that it was his sacrificial donkeying of supplies that made all the difference. But such compliments don't really make up for the fact that he was not allowed to try a climb which he wanted very much to make and which, probably, he thought he could make. Someone else, no better than himself, did get the chance.

Again, we had the morale advantage that we could be relaxed. There was no objective we had to attain. The big expedition does have to attain its objective. National prestige is involved. You are reminded that, "the eyes of the world are upon you." This can lead to unnecessary tension and friction.

Lastly, I think overall morale is affected by the function that the climbers make all the decisions. It is their show and they run things as they see fit. But in a large expedition the climbers are just one among several groups of specialists. At a given moment they are called on to do their stuff. But elsewhere the administrators and the logistics experts and the other specialists run things. I think morale is higher when you make your own decisions.

One of the weaknesses, then, of our expedition was that although we had many of the usual advantages in morale which a small expedition has, we denied ourselves the full effect of this edge. For we did not have the close unity of having climbed together as friends over a considerable period.

Another weakness we had, which is characteristic of small expeditions, was our lack of reserves. When Roger and I fell, there was no one to step into the breach. The expedition was in effect ended. I think there are various ways this deficiency might be met. One way, of course, would be simply to increase the size of the party to six or even eight members. But I rather like the mobility and independence of the four-man party. So another possibility, which might even be the best, would be to have two independent four-man parties. They could organize, travel, and finance themselves more or less separately. But they would arrange to meet at the mountain. In this manner, at the point of maximum difficulty, the strength of the party would be doubled. Then, if either party had been badly weakened, there would still be sufficient strength to mount an attack.

A third weakness, possibly, was our lack of experience and training. It is conceivable that some of our difficulties might have been avoided if we had had a little more of both. But I rather doubt it. Indeed, I regret that we had not all climbed together before, and I regret that we did not have reserves, say at least two more climbers, but I do not at all regret going to the mountain with little or no experience.

For one thing I felt we would be getting that experience on the difficult ice cliffs immediately above Base Camp. This was the ideal spot to do it, for we would be in position to retreat if anything went wrong. Then if we got up the cliffs, we would automatically be able to handle most of Everest. For the technical difficulties on Everest are relatively minor up until the last 900 feet.

For another thing I don't think technical proficiency is so very important. The good amateur, or even the poor amateur, can have just as much fun trying to climb a peak as the professional. He may have less chance of getting to the top, but why should that matter? It depends on your goal. If your goal is to put an American on the top of Everest in one particular year, then, no doubt, you should pick the most completely qualified climbers available. But my goal was not to put *an* American on the top of Everest. My goal was simply to be on the mountain myself, to feel it and touch it and rub my nose into it, and of course go as high as my luck and skill allowed. This goal was something that I could attain with a very moderate technical proficiency.

Here, quite a few of the "mountaineering fraternity" disagree violently. They argue that amateurs should not be allowed to attempt the most difficult peaks, not because they are unlikely to succeed, but because it is unsafe. Their ignorance and lack of skill will get them into trouble. Again I have to ask why this should matter. If the amateur wants to take the extra risk, why shouldn't he?

Such a question raises the whole complicated matter of safety in mountain climbing. Since it seems to concern so many people, I will close the chapter with a few reflections on the subject. Actually, I feel that overconcern with safety is a mistake in any activity. In the last chapter I will argue that it is bad in society generally. Here I will argue that it is bad in mountaineering.

On the face of it, it seems almost a contradiction for a climber to be preoccupied with safety. At least historically mountaineers have shied away from what is safe and secure. In the first place they climbed the mountains when they could have stayed safely in the valleys. Indeed, I am sure that they could have had a superb safety record if they had all stayed home in bed. Then, when most of the hardest peaks had been climbed, they began to try more and more difficult routes. The relatively easy and safe routes were ignored. In Switzerland today everything has been done, so now they are trying the hardest ways, in winter. As these, too, are mastered, they are trying the most difficult routes in midwinter, and at night! All this hardly looks like the pursuit of safety.

The truth is that part of the essence of mountain climbing is to push oneself to one's limits. Inevitably this involves risk, otherwise they would not be one's limits. This is not to say that you deliberately try something you know you can't do. But you do deliberately try something which you are not *sure* you can do. You deliberately stack the cards against yourself in one way or another. The traditional way is to try a harder-than-usual route. But it may also be done by making a climb with less than the usual amount of equipment or by trying it with less than the usual amount of experience, the way we did. These last two ways are less common, but in principle they amount to the same thing. That is, I se no logical difference between a fine expert trying an extremely difficult route and a rank amateur trying a moderately difficult one. If you don't criticize the first, why criticize the second?

One answer, often given, is that the rank amateur doesn't know what he is up against. He cannot judge accurately whether he is trying something far beyond his limits or not. The expert can. However, traditionally, this important matter of judgment has always been left up to the climbers themselves. They clear such decisions with their own family and their own conscience. Then, if they make mistakes, it is they who pay, and so it is they who ought to decide. Indeed, by what right does any man decide for another what risks he may take? If someone wants to try Everest in just a cummerbund and a pair of ear muffs, it is, after all, his life. I think it is part of the freedom for which men go to the mountains that they should decide for themselves what limits to tempt. It is, if you like, the right to be foolish, the right to make your own decisions even when they are wrong. The forces of order and reason are doing their best to wipe this right off the face of the earth. It is very precious nonetheless.

In this connection I regret an increasing trend in America towards "those who know best" making the decisions. Many of the finest peaks are in national parks and the park officials have all been alerted to prevent unqualified and ill-equipped climbers from trying an ascent. You practically have to be certified in six copies to be allowed to climb. Most of the climbing clubs have strongly backed such programs. And yet climbing clubs are the very place where you would expect to find the keenest appreciation of the importance of other values besides safety, such as the value of pushing to your own limits and the value of making your own decision as to what these limits are. I have no objection to a group of people deciding that they will climb in a particular way according to certain strict standards of safety. It may even have some value to demonstrate to the public that climbing is not necessarily as dangerous as it believes. But I think it is wrong for such groups to impose their standards on everyone else. I would like to see the peaks open to all comers. Warn them, if you like, but then let them discover their own "impossibles".

One of the stock answers that has been made against the view that each should make his own decision is the question of rescue. It is all very well, they say, to let the fools and incompetents climb all over the mountains, but then good men are going to have to go in and risk their lives to rescue them.

But this is not necessarily so. If the rules were changed to allow everyone to climb, they could also be changed to state clearly that you do so at your own risk. The Swiss did exactly this for the North Face of the Eiger. There is no reason why it could not be a general policy. Actually, someone who is willing to try something particularly difficult is usually quite willing to accept the extra risk of not being rescued. Our expedition certainly felt that way.

From another point of view most climbers, in fact, love to join a rescue effort. Far from being an unfair imposition, it is a welcome excitement. People volunteer from all over the country to help in a rescue. Why is this so?

Initially, a climber declares his independence from the standards of the public. The fact that he climbs at all proves that he does not value safety as highly as the public does. But the public retaliates subtly, sometimes by mere reiterated puzzlement, at other times by direct criticism for "irresponsibility". Eventually, many climbers seem to feel guilty that they are climbers, that they enjoy so much what "no sane man" should enjoy.

This guilt leads them to try and become respectable. They wish to prove that climbing is really very safe. They then become very disturbed every time there is national publicity about another accident. With almost self-righteous indignation they assert that those fools shouldn't have been where they were. The accident could have been predicted. They become almost frenetically concerned about the "public image" of mountain climbing. But an accident occurs. Someone is trapped high on an inaccessible ledge. A wonderful thing then happens. For the first time they are not pulled in two different directions—the desire to climb pulling them one way, and public disapproval pulling them the other. Now they can take the risks they like to take, even unreasonable risks, and yet be approved of by public opinion. Indeed, they are heroes. In a rescue, at last, they are at peace with themselves and society. No wonder they enjoy it.

I would say, then, that there will always be volunteers for most rescues. But a definite policy that none can be counted on, or expected, should be established. Then there will be no reason to ride herd on potential climbers or to try and insist that they climb according to some set standards of safety. Live and let live. Or perhaps, better, die and let die.

Personally, I can't see why the public image of the mountain climber has any importance at all. Surely no one climbs mountains to be popular. So why not let the public condemn the activity as much as it pleases? I tend to believe that lack of safety is an integral part of climbing. If one does not walk the feather edge of one's own limits, it is not worth doing. Nevertheless, I should practice the tolerance which I insist upon for myself. If others find sufficient values in climbing without any danger at all, why should they not pursue it in that manner? They should. But let them not try to impose their view, directly or indirectly, on all other climbers. Let people climb "unsafely" if they so desire.

I find a parallel here with the issue between the small and the large expedition. Just as an overconcern with safety is not to my taste, so coming to a mountain with a thousand or more people is not to my taste. But there is no reason why others who enjoy it should not climb that way. I do not criticize them. I do not thus criticize the large American expedition under Dyhrenfurth. In fact, they did a fine job. It is not something I would want to do, but it was nevertheless very well done. I would ask only an equal tolerance on the part of that expedition for their small cousin who preceded them by a year. We had different methods and ideals, but valid nonetheless.

So much for the question of safety and "proper" climbing methods. So much also for the aftermath and reflections. Of course, the aftermath is never really over. Only the other day, for example, at a friend's house, I incautiously complained about a small draft on the back of my neck. Immediately my friend replied, raising his eyebrows to their full height, "And *you* were going to climb Mt. Everest?"

XV

WHY MEN CLIMB

Why do men climb? The question is asked so often one would think the answer was one of the great mysteries of all time, on a par with the answers to such questions as "What is Beauty?" or "What is Truth?" At every one of my lectures or discussions somebody is sure to bring it up. Often they do so with an air of triumph. For, however little they may know about mountain climbing they have somehow heard that this is *the* question to stump the experts. Actually, the question is not particularly difficult. It has seemed so mainly because of confusion over what the question is really about. Because of this confusion there is an equal confusion over what makes a satisfactory answer.

But first, let's look at Mallory's famous answer. When asked once at a lecture why he climbed Everest, he replied, "Because it is there." Many people have been tremendously impressed with this answer. I think it is a tribute to their vivid imaginations. For, as it stands, it really doesn't say anything. It is too ambiguous.

Does it imply a challenge? Does it imply some kind of inevitability? Or does it simply mean that there is no reason? And what does there-ness have to do with it? Not far from my home is an impressive pile of junk which is called the town dump. It also is "there", and yet I have no desire at all to climb it. So something more than there-ness is needed as a reason for climbing.

Maybe it is the it-ness that counts. "Because *it* is there." The particular character of Everest itself is what attracts. This amounts to saying you climb it because you climb it. It is a reason, but not a very deep one.

Interpreting Mallory's answer to mean, "because it is a challenge", the question still remains: *why* is it a challenge? Why does it challenge that particular breed of men called mountaineers, whereas the vast majority couldn't care less?

My own guess would be that Mallory meant by his answer: "Please, dear questioner, ask me some other question. I am terribly tired of that one." For I am sure that all that Everest meant to him could hardly be put in a brief answer. And I suspect that setting forth all that he really felt was not something he would care to do again and again and again before a lecture audience. Wouldn't he, perhaps, be amused by the *mystique* built up around his actual reply?

For a long time I was puzzled why this question couldn't just be answered, "I climb mountains because I like to." Certainly this would be a perfectly good answer for most other activities. Why do I play tennis? I play tennis because I like to. Why do I ski or swim? Because I enjoy them. Now, why doesn't that kind of an answer satisfy anybody when it comes to mountain climbing? Why is a lecturer on mountain climbing asked again and again why he climbs, whereas a lecturer, say, on golf would almost never be asked why he played golf?

Eventually, I realized the root of the difference. The question about climbing is not a question about motivation at all. If it were, then the answer, "I climb because I like to," would be a perfectly appropriate answer. It is really a question about relative values. What the question is really asking is: "Look, this mountain climbing business is dangerous. It costs money. It is hard, exhausting work. You have to disrupt the family to do it. Now what values do you gain from climbing mountains that can possibly offset these *disvalues?*"

Put this way it is a perfectly straightforward question which is capable of a perfectly straightforward answer. It is not particularly difficult to list the values which I derive from mountain climbing which do in fact *for me* offset the disvalues—if such they be—of cost, family disruption, unnecessary risk, and so forth. I will do this in the next part of this chapter. So the question, why do I personally climb mountains, is capable of a reasonably precise answer.

If the question is generalized to "Why do *people* climb mountains?", the answer will have to be much less precise. For there is no reason to suppose that what I get out of climbing mountains is exactly the same as what another climber gets out of it. His lists of values may very well leave out a value that is on my list, and, of course, my list may leave out a value that is on his. Furthermore, the order of preference may be different. That is, my main value may only be a secondary one for him, or perhaps not even on his list at all.

I suppose one could make a combined list of all the values that anyone ever found in mountain climbing and present it as the answer to the general question of why people climb. But it would be rather bulky and not too significant. A better plan would be to try and find values that are common to everybody's, or nearly everybody's, list. This can be done and as far as I can see that is about all that can be done in answering the general question. So, after I have listed the values that I derive from climbing I will indicate the values that are most commonly acknowledged by other climbers. then, at the very end of the chapter I will give a brief justification of these values.

First on my list, but not necessarily first in importance, I would mention beauty. There are the colors: black rock and ultramarine shadows, pure white swell of snow, turquoise and amethyst crevasses, and the diamond glitter of sun on ice. In the afterglow of sunset the air itself becomes pink and gold. And there are the infinite clean shapes: wind-carved snow, fluted ice, weathered stone, and cloud-brushed sky. Most of all, there are the great mountains themselves set in their rivers of ice, changing grandeur in every light and every weather. If a person will cross the ocean just to look at the beauty of a cathedral, why would he not do as much or more to see sights such as these?

Very closely associated with the beauty of the mountains are some special emotions which the highest and wildest peaks provoke. I feel a special excitement when I look out over thousands of square miles of untouched country. I feel it again when I walk where only a handful of men have walked in the history of the world, when I explore some hidden ridge or crag, or when I make the first track across a great unbroken snow field. I feel a special happiness to be alone in the high, silent places of the world tucked close under the sky. Such things are worth a little insecurity and sacrifice.

Speaking of "aloneness" this brings up two other important values which I find in mountain climbing: solitude and companionship. Paradoxically, the mountains provide both.

The companionship provided by climbing together is almost universally valued by mountaineers. The friendships established are lasting and irreplaceable. When you have walked the feather edge of danger with someone, when you have held his life at the end of a rope in your hand, and he has later held yours, you have an almost impregnable foundation for a friendship. For the deepest friendships spring from sharing failure as well as success, danger as well as safety. There is really no substitute.

Indeed, this is one of the regrettable trends in our present civilization. Real friendship is increasingly difficult. We hurry so much, we move, we change jobs, we juggle a hundred responsibilities. How often do we see even our best friends? Once a week? Once a month? Less than that? And frequently, when we do see them, it is at a cocktail party or some occasion where the conversation remains superficial. If we hardly see them, how can we really share joy and tragedy with them? I think men are made for a deeper sort of friendship. If they miss it, they miss something very important in life. Men are made for the close warmth of a friendship tested in danger and adversity. It is not impossible without this testing, but it is much more difficult.

In most primitive societies this testing is an established custom. There is the hunting party, the war party, or games and rituals involving danger and difficulty. But in our society testing depends on individual initiative or on accident. In war, of course, men find the closeness of shared danger—the men of a gun crew or an infantry patrol, for example—but where else is the opportunity? At any rate mountain climbing is one way of providing it.

As for solitude, that, too, is a great value and is something which the mountains can provide. It is a great value because it is just as essential as companionship. A man is unhappy unless he has both. He needs to be with his fellow man, and he needs to be apart from him. If he is forced to be completely apart, that is the torture which is called "solitary confinement". If he is forced to be completely with his fellow, that also is a torture. It has no name, but it is equally harrowing. When personnel were chosen for the early Antarctic expeditions they had to be specially screened because of the psychological strain of living so closely together. Each man was forever in the public view. In their winter quarters they were packed so tightly that a man couldn't walk across the hut without another man moving out of the way. According to prisoners the absence of all privacy is a torture that has often been used by the Communists.

Once again, going to the mountains is not the only way to get this essential solitude. But our civilization is making it more and more difficult to do it any other way. As a boy I used to know frog ponds and hidden glades where no one ever came. Now they are housing developments. I used to know streams where I could fish. Now you have to wait in line just to get to the bank. The national parks are more and more committed to herd living. Even the great empty deserts are filling. Increasingly they are cut up with jeep tracks and shacks and billboards and telephone wires. The largest untouched areas left are the oceans and the poles and the highest mountains. And the demographers assure us that in less than a century it will be "Standing Room Only" even there. The human race is almost like a mold that inhabits a glass jar. The mold multiplies and grows until it so crowds the jar that it poisons itself in its own wastes. People are wonderful, but an infinite number of them are not. A man must refill the inner springs of his being in solitude and reflection. I think there is a deep inner need for this. Without this refilling life becomes increasingly hurried, it becomes increasingly insensitive.

So this is a need which the mountains can fulfill. There are many hours, especially in a small expedition, when you walk the trails completely alone. And this aloneness depends in large part on unspoilt, untouched nature. I would say that there is need for alternation here too. We need to experience nature with the friendly marks upon it of human work and struggle and hope. But also we need to see nature apart from even the smallest sign of human interference. For this the high mountains are perfect.

If it is a bit of a paradox that the mountains should provide both solitude and deep companionship, it is also a bit of a paradox that society should not provide those values. That is, in spite of all the crowded "togetherness" increasingly required of us, real companionship is nevertheless hard to find. And on the other hand, in spite of all the solitude—in the sense of loneliness—that there is in society today, nevertheless, the solitude that I have been describing is absent. It involves being alone where no voice reaches and no foot falls, where there can be and is no other sign of a human. Only then does the person turn deeply inward. Loneliness is not enough.

Thus, mountain climbing tends to furnish an antidote to much that is wrong or overemphasized in society. The pendulum has swung much too far towards "together"; mountaineering redresses the balance. Society tends to make human relationships superficial; mountaineering deepens them. Other values can be added.

For instance, our society catches us up in a great hurry and rush of activity. Mountaineering returns one to the slower natural rhythms of the rising and setting sun, the changing weather, and the simple physical needs of the day. Headlines and frenetic concern for the universe fade away.

Again, our society imposes tighter and tighter routines on us. Mountaineering relaxes them.

Finally, I will mention that society tends to submerge our self-reliance and individuality in a great mass-handling of people treated almost as statistics. Mountaineering reverses this. It forces self-reliance. For instance, we were often weeks from help of any kind. If a piece of equipment broke or an accident occurred, we had to handle it entirely from our own resources. We did, and felt a good proud feeling for having done so.

Thus, in one blow, as it were, many corrective values are achieved by climbing. Any one of them could be achieved in other ways. But it is an especially valuable activity that can achieve them all at the same time.

I will set down only three more of the values on my

227

list. First, there is the obvious value of adventure. It is exciting to discover new lands, new situations, new places. The thought of what may be just over the next ridge is intriguing. Many have been attached by adventure, and I confess a weakness for it also.

Secondly, knowledge and understanding have a value. Certainly there is increased understanding of oneself, as well as of others, for on a trip of this nature one is strapped down to the basics. One sees relationships more realistically than ever before. Also there is increased understanding of many matters traditionally discussed in the classroom: courage, friendship, death, fear, even hunger and suffering. As a teacher of philosophy I think direct acquaintance with such subjects as these is not at all out of place. I cannot be satisfied with mere book learning.

Lastly, I think that there definitely is an element of challenge in any mountaineering. One cannot help dreaming of meeting some particular problem better than anyone else has met it. Indeed, there are no more provocative words for at least some of us than the phrase "It can't be done." Immediately you think of ways that it might be done. Toni Hiebeler describes how he first was attracted to the North Face of the Eiger by having the impossibilities pointed out to him when he was still a boy. How many hours have been spent by people trying to trisect an angle with straight-edge and compass just because they were told that it was impossible?

From the point of view of society it is good for men to meet their challenges. In fact, if man ever loses his attraction for the impossible all that is generally called "progress" would cease. From the point of view of the individual it is also good to pursue those goals which have caught one's imagination. It is exciting to try the impossible; it is even more exciting to accomplish it.

These, then, are the main values that I derive from climbing. For me they overbalance the expense, the risk, and all the rest. It is not a particularly unusual list of values, but it answers the question why I climb.

The question why climbers in general climb cannot be answered so precisely. As I said earlier, one can only list the most commonly shared values. Most of these are on my list, too. Most widespread, probably, is the pleasure of meeting, and if possible overcoming, some particular challenge. Next, and almost equally widespread, is the value and depth of the friendships made while climbing. Then usually at least one of the values derived from getting away from society, which I mentioned on my list, is also included on others' lists. Also quite common is the value of beauty and adventure. Finally, there is a value which I did not include on my list. This is the sense of communion with God. Those who experience it quite often feel it to be the most important value of all. I have not included it on my list, not because I do not think it has a very great value, but simply because it is not specifically one of the reasons why I climb.

This list of the most universally acknowledged values which climbers derive from climbing is imprecise in two respects. For one thing, the reason, or reasons why any particular climber climbs may not be on the list at all. He may climb for quite unusual reasons. Secondly, the list does not give one unambiguous answer to the question why men climb. I think that if it had been realized that the question was actually a question of relative values, then no one would ever have expected that there should be a *single* answer which was valid for all climbers. An approximate list, valid for most, but not all, would have been seen as the only significant answer to the question.

Some justification of the values on this list should probably be made. This can be done in two ways. I can show that these values are more important than most people realize, or I can try to show that the usual competing values are less valuable than is generally realized. To some extent I have already done the former. I argued that solitude and deep friendship and self-reliance were, in fact, very important and were more easily available on a mountain than in ordinary "civilized" society. It remains, then, to show that some of the competing values are less valuable. I shall confine myself to the chief one. This is the tremendous value that American society places on safety and security.

I think we have made a fetish of this value. Job interviewers report that the first question that they are asked by college graduates seeking jobs is what kind of a retirement program does the company have. Consider these diverse random examples. In the name of safety the Fourth of July is now only a spectator celebration. The ban on fireworks is justified, it is claimed, if the life of one child is saved thereby. In the name of safety every holiday weekend is publicized endlessly in advance as a death dealer. The exact death toll is predicted with gruesome futility. And there is obvious disappointment if a new record, one way or the other, is not achieved. Americans insure everything. Finally, a corollary of preoccupation with safety is the prevention of death, apparently forever. We will do anything to add one minute, or one hour, or one month to the life of some poor being who can never be anything more than a vegetable. The Christian doctrine of the infinite worth of every soul is perverted to the infinite worth of mere physical existence.

But it is not mere existence that counts. As Socrates said, any man can extend his life a little longer if he is willing to do or say anything. And as he also said, it is not how long you live, but how well that is important. Mere security is a barren ideal. We need to pay attention to what is done with that security. And we also need to ask whether security itself does not have its own dangers. Is a parent really better who tries to protect his child from every conceivable danger and difficulty? I think not. Neither, then, is a society better for trying to protect every one of its members from all danger and difficulty. People grow through overcoming dangers and difficulties. They are not better off for being carefully wrapped in cotton batting. Deep within us I think we know that we need challenge and danger, and the risk and hurt that will sometimes follow. "Dangerous" sports would not be as popular as they are if this were not so.

Again, mountain climbing is not the only way of dealing with an over-organized, over-protective society. But it is one good way.

Contemplating all the values achieved by climbing mountains, I am tempted yet again to try the impossible and summarize it all in a single sentence. Men climb mountains because they are not satisfied to exist, they want to live—climbing the heights is one way.

APPENDICES

Appendix A

GLOSSARY

Mountaineering equipment

Ice axe

The most important piece of equipment for a mountaineer is the ice axe. With this he can belay, cut steps, control a glissade, maintain his balance, and perform a variety of important tasks. It has been described as a mountaineer's third leg. It is made of ash with a sharp spike at the bottom. At the top there is a flat blade in one direction and a sharp pick in the other.

Rope

The second most important piece of equipment is the rope. This allows one climber to safeguard another. It can also be used to make quick descents by rappelling.

Crampons

These are metal frames with from eight to ten metal spikes on them. They can be attached to climbing boots with straps, rather like roller skates. With crampons a man can walk up a very steep slope of hard ice without slipping.

Piton | Pitons are metal spikes which can be driven into ice or rock to help safeguard the climbers. They have an open eye at one end through which one can snap a metal link, called a carabiner. The climbing rope can be passed through this link, thus furnishing a secure point which will hold the climbers in case of a fall.

Carabiner | A metal snap-link, which can be snapped onto a piton, and through which the rope can be passed in order to protect a climber from a possible fall.

Mountaineering maneuvers

Belay | To secure another climber against a possible fall, either with one's own body, a natural projection, or an artificial projection such as a piton or ice axe. When used as a noun, it is a particular case of securing someone.

Traverse | To cross a slope horizontally or diagonally. It is sometimes used as a general term for crossing anything.

Rappel | Rappelling is essentially descending a slope or cliff by sliding down the rope. It is the most photographed of all

233

mountaineering maneuvers, because, although it is one of the safest of all procedures, it invariably looks daringly spectacular.

Glissade   When one slides down a snow slope, either sitting or standing, it is called a glissade. Technically this slide should be controlled in direction and speed usually by using the point of the ice axe. When it is not controlled, it is simply described as a fall.

Lead   When the first man on the rope advances, it is called a lead. If he should have to surmount any major difficulties, it would be called a difficult lead. Success would be a good lead.

To come off   When a man slips from an ice or a rock cliff, he is said "to come off."

To go   To say "it goes" or "I think it will go" is to assert that the route ahead looks climbable with the means at hand.

Terms referring to the terrain

Col   The low point between two high points. For instance, a ridge connecting two peaks would be called a col. Also the low point in that ridge would more correctly be called the col. This is why it is often called a pass, even if no one ever uses it as such.

Couloir   Literally, corridor. A gully in rock or snow or ice.

Pitch   A steep section of ice or rock.

Glacier   A river of ice. At these altitudes only
                     snow falls. It accumulates in the high
                     bowls or valleys (called cirques or
                     cwms). The great weight hardens these
                     tons of snow into ice which starts flow-
                     ing downward slowly toward the lower
                     elevations.

Icefall   As the ice cascades over rocky cliffs in
                     the glacier bed it makes what are
                     called icefalls. These correspond to
                     rapids or falls in a river. Only, because
                     they are frozen, they move much more
                     slowly.

Crevasse   As the rivers of ice flow downward,
                     the tremendous weight fractures the
                     ice into cracks and fissures of all sizes.
                     These are the crevasses. They are
                     especially deep and numerous in the
                     icefalls.

Moraine   The moving ice of the glacier also
                     gouges rocks from the mountainsides
                     and from its rocky bed. These rocks
                     get squeezed into long ribbons of
                     broken material which may stretch for
                     miles along the glacier. The piles of
                     rocks at the edge are called lateral
                     moraines, the ribbons in the center,
                     median moraines, and mounds at the
                     end of the glacier, terminal moraines.

Serac   Stagnant blocks of ice become fantas-
                     tically carved by sun and wind into

235

pinnacles of all sorts. These are called seracs.

Local terms

Chang   A local beer.

Rakshi   A local liquor distilled from rice—somewhat brandylike.

Sherpa   A high-altitude porter belonging to the race of mountain men who live in the environs of Mt. Everest.

Sirdar   A straw-boss or leader of porters.

Appendix B

CHRONOLOGY OF THE EXPEDITION

November 1961   First request made to Royal Nepalese Embassy in Washington, D.C., for permission to travel through Nepal to Gyachung Kang and climb on it and in adjacent areas. First requests for leave of absence from jobs for the period February 1962 through June 1962.

December 1961   Equipment lists and logistics worked into final form.

January 1962   All plans suspended until permission to climb is granted or refused by the Royal Nepalese Government.

January 17   Letter from Nepalese Embassy in Washington gives preliminary approval of our route and climbing plans.

January 24	Orders for first items of equipment sent out.
February 1962	Equipment orders completed. Packaging for overseas air shipment completed. Passports, visas, and program of immunizations completed.
February 26	Expedition leaves Boston by air for Europe.
March 1962	Purchase of additional supplies and equipment in Switzerland. Separation and packaging of all food into ration-units for convenient use on the climb.
March 20	Final permission received from Nepalese Government.
March 22	HansPeter Duttle agrees to become the fourth member of our expedition.
March 24	Expedition departs for Nepal via direct flight to New Delhi, India.
March 26	Expedition flies from New Delhi to Kathmandu, capital of Nepal (4,423 feet above sea level).
April 1962	Customs passed. Porters hired. Sherpas hired. Additional food and equipment purchased. Final packaging of ration-units completed.
April 3	Expedition leaves Kathmandu for Namche Bazar.

April 4	HansPeter Duttle arrives Kathmandu by plane. We meet and double march to join the expedition that night.
April 3–18	(16 days) Expedition moves 160 miles by foot to Namche Bazar (12,800 feet).
April 20–24	(5 days) Expedition moves about 25 miles up the Dudh Kosi River and the Ngo Jumbo Glacier to Base Camp at approximately 16,500 feet.
April 25–May 8	(14 days) Expedition moves to top of icefall (19,100 feet). Sherpas depart.
May 9–27	(19 days) Expedition moves about 25 miles over various glaciers to the foot of the North Col (about 21,300 feet).
May 29–31	(3 days) North Col climbed. Food and equipment for six days moved to its top (23,000 feet).
June 2–5	(4 days) Push to highest camp at over 24,000 feet, and climb higher to over 25,000 feet. Return to top of North Col.
June 6–17	(12 days) Expedition returns from top of North Col to Base Camp, finding it deserted.
June 18	Forced march down to first inhabited village (Nang).
June 20–21	(2 days) Expedition returns to Khum-

239

jung, immediately adjacent to Namche Bazar.

June 23–24   (2 days) Expedition flies out by helicopter to Kathmandu. HansPeter stays in Khumjung.

June 28   Expedition leaves by air for home.

Totals: Kathmandu to Kathmandu   82 days
Base Camp to Base Camp   47 days
Number of days without Sherpas
   or porters, completely self-
   sufficient   41 days
Boston to Boston (if we had
   flown directly home from
   Kathmandu)   124 days

Appendix C

EQUIPMENT USED ON THE EXPEDITION

In the lists below, all necessary equipment for our trip is set down item by item. The items have been grouped into two categories: first, what was required for the trip into Base Camp; second, what was required for the higher altitudes above Base Camp. If an item appears on both lists, it means that it was needed throughout the trip. Weights are only given for items taken to the high altitudes. This is because we carried these items ourselves and so the weights were critical. Until Base Camp it did not matter so much, because porters were always available.

I. EQUIPMENT NEEDED FOR MARCH TO BASE CAMP

    A. *Personal Equipment* (This is equipment each man would have to have.)

        1. *Clothing*
          1 pr. hiking boots (well broken-in)

1 pr. low sneakers (to rest feet from boots, especially in camp)
2 pr. medium-weight socks (nylon or nylon-wool is necessary, or else more pairs will be required, as they will wear out)
2 pr. lightweight socks (also nylon or nylon-wool)
2 pr. undershorts (cotton)
1 pr. shorts or very light cotton trousers
1 pr. wool trousers (extra heavy)
1 belt
1 light cotton or khaki shirt
1 wool shirt
1 lightweight sweater
1 heavy wool sweater
1 muffler or scarf (wool or silk)
1 poncho or loose cycling raincoat that will cover pack as well
1 wide-brimmed sunhat
1 towel

Optional
2 cotton undershirts or T-shirts
1 handkerchief (large)
1 pr. pajamas (cotton or silk)
1 toilet kit: toothbrush, toothpowder or paste, dental tape, razor and blades, shaving cream, brush, comb, nail clippers with file

2. *Gear*
1 sleeping bag
1 insulated sleeping-bag cover
1 pack: aluminum frame and waterproof nylon sack
1 wristwatch
1 pr. dark glasses (must fit over regular glasses, if any)
1 cup (pint size; soft plastic best)

1 plate (plastic or aluminum)
1 knife (Swiss army "scout" knife is good with scissors, leather punch, 2 blades, can opener, etc.)
1 spoon (large, aluminum)
2 one quart canteens
1 diary plus paper, pencil, pen, and plenty of envelopes
1 flashlight plus 4 extra batteries and 1 extra bulb

Optional

2 pr. glasses should be taken if glasses are needed
1 air mattress (A good deal can be said for saving your mattress until Base Camp and after, when it is vital. The wear and tear of the walk-in may weaken it so that it is unserviceable.)

Reading matter, as desired

3. *Drugs and medicines*
   1 cake soap
   2 packets toilet paper
   1 nose inhaler and/or 1 bottle nose drops (the nose must be kept clear at night for sleeping soundly)
   1 bottle cough syrup
   2 boxes cough drops
   1 tube Vaseline
   1 can talcum powder
   2 packets Kleenex
   1 tube of heavy protective sunburn ointment
   1 packet of large Band-Aids

B. *Community Equipment* (This is equipment of which each individual can be considered to have a quarter.)

1. *Gear*
    1 Base Camp tent with large supplementary tent-fly, poles, pegs
    2 tent-repair kits (includes extra nylon and canvas material, needles, cotton and nylon thread, twine)
    2 mattress-repair kits (includes patches and tube of adhesive)
    1 sewing kit (includes variety of needles and thread, pins and buttons of various sizes)
    1 tool kit (includes a combination tool—pliers, adjustable wrench and screwdriver, 1 mill-file with Phillips head tang, extra leather and rawhide lacing, spare parts for pack-frame, canvas, leather, a variety of metal screws)
    General cooking equipment (includes large pots, large knife, kettle, skillet, cast-iron griddle, stirring spoon, small knives, paring knife, sharpening stone, chopping board, funnels, strainer, soap, scouring pads, towels, sponge, etc.) The Sherpa cook will advise on the complete list and his preferences. Everything is locally available, but it is best to bring knives from outside. The best quality is expensive and not always available.
    1 canvas water bucket
    2 candle-lanterns with 24 extra candles
    2 flashlights and extra batteries (for kitchen use)
    1 small army-ration can opener
    1 pr. binoculars
    1 pocket compass (with mirror in lid)
    2 spring scales, capable of measuring together 88 pounds

2 rolls of strong adhesive "Scotch"-type tape (very strong)
1 Magic-Marker pen
1 ball twine
250 feet of light nylon line for porters' loads and miscellaneous use as needed.
7 canvas marine sacks for porters' loads.
18 gunny sacks and string for porters' loads
1 set of maps of Everest region and trail in from Kathmandu
2 books on Everest
1 complete set of records—payment of money to porters and Sherpas, cigarettes, advances, and incidental expenditures, receipts
1 sack of Nepalese paper money in smallest denominations for payment to Sherpas and porters and incidental purchases
1 thermometer (outdoor, pencil-type)
5 cameras and film: 1 Bolex movie camera with three lenses and 1,500 feet of Kodachrome film; 1 Contax 35mm with 2 lenses (50mm and 85mm); 1 Contessa 35mm; 45 36-exposure rolls; 1 Polaroid camera with 10 rolls, and 1 Stereo camera

2. *Drugs and medicines*
1 First-aid kit. It totaled 10 pounds and included the following items: 1 tooth extractor; 3 hemostats; 1 scissors; 1 scalpel and blades; 1 tweezers for stitching; 2 hypodermic needles; 12 disposable syringes; 130 tablets aureomycin; sufficient morphine to sedate one man for three weeks; 1 bottle paregoric (tincture of codeine)—to save weight it was strong enough so that 10 drops constituted one dose; sutures for fine and coarse wounds with needles; Leritine (for pain) 20 25mg tablets; 4 tubes of Nupercainal (medicated

petrolatum; 12 Librium tablets (tranquilizers); 25 Dexedrene (stimulants); 25 Nembutal; 25 Seconal; 2 tubes bacitracin (disinfectant); 100 sterile pads; 4 Ace bandages; 4 rolls of adhesive tape; assorted bandages (take extra for the local population); safety pins; 25 malaria pills (once a week on the walk-in); pills for amoebic dysentery (enough for each person to take a full course); wire splint; Antepar; Halazone tablets for water purification; 2,000 aspirin tablets; 400 multivitamin tablets; 1 bottle sodamint tablets; 1 tube eye ointment (for snow blindness); extra cough syrup and nose drops; 1 bottle mosquito repellent; moleskin self-adhesive for blister pads; 200 salt-tablets; glucose pills; Coramine (heart stimulant).

II. Equipment Needed For Climbing Above Base Camp

A. *Personal Equipment* (What each man carries)

1. *Clothing*

	lb.	oz.
*1 pr. Korea boots (large, rubber, vapor-barrier principle)	5	12
*2 pr. very heavy rag socks (Norwegian all wool)		10
*2 pr. light nylon undersocks		2
*1 pr. undershorts (cotton)		4
*1 pr. soft wool long underwear (or fishnet thermal)		6
1 heavy wool pants	1	8
*1 down pants	1	13
*1 down parka and hood	2	11
*1 suit of nylon windproofs (pants and parka) We had extra outside pockets sewn on these.	1	2

	lb.	oz.
†1 pr. canvas overboots, with hook-eye lacings		10
*1 pr. down-filled mittens		8
*1 pr. silk gloves		1½
*1 cotton undershirt, T-shirt, or light wool shirt		4
*1 wool shirt		10
*1 medium-heavy sweater	1	2
*1 muffler (wool or silk)		4
†1 balaclava		4
1 wide-brimmed sunhat		2

Optional
1 large handkerchief		½
(note: no toilet articles)		
Total	18	2

2. *Gear*

	lb.	oz.
*1 air mattress	1	12
*1 sleeping bag	6	2
†1 sleeping-bag insulated cover	2	4
*1 pack (frame and sack)	4	4
*1 wristwatch		1
*1 pr. extra dark glasses		2
†1 pr. dark goggles to go over dark glasses		3
*2 canteens		14
*1 diary and pencil		14
1 whistle for signaling		1
*1 pr. crampons	2	11
*1 ice axe	2	7
Total	21	11

3. *Drugs and medicines*

*1 packet toilet paper		1

† Some took this item on up the Col and some didn't. In other words, it was optional.

*1 nose inhaler	½
*2 boxes cough drops (1 box only on final assault)	1½
*1 tube Vaseline (shared tube on final assault)	2
*1 can talcum powder (shared can on final assault)	4
*1 packet Kleenex	1
*1 large tube of special protective sunburn ointment	3
Total	13

B. *Community Equipment* (Each man carries approximately a quarter of this.)

1. *Gear*

	lb.	oz.
*2 high-altitude tents with poles	23	8
*2 butane stoves	2	—
*44 butane cartridges (6 were taken on assault)	28	12
*1 flint-and-steel cigarette lighter	less than	½
*1 tool kit		9
*2 tent-repair kits (only one taken on assault)	1	—
*2 mattress-repair kits (only one taken high)		14
*1 sewing-kit		6
1 roll of repair tape		4
*2 snow shovels (only one taken on assault)	3	8
4 ski poles	4	12
25 willow wands (for marking trail and caches)	4	—
*1 army-ration can opener (for opening sardine cans)	(negligible)	
*300 meters of 4mm nylon cord	7	11
300 meters of 5mm nylon cord	12	—

		lbs	oz
2	climbing ropes (9mm, 132 feet). These ropes were used in the icefall but were not taken beyond because of their weight; therefore the weight is not calculated in this table.		
2	emergency down suits (down parka and pants convertible into sleeping bags if caught out)	10	–
*2	piton hammers (only one taken high)	1	4
*12	carabiners (aluminum) (only 4 taken high)	1	4
*10	rock pitons of various types (4 taken high)	2	2
10	ice pitons (only 4 taken in assault)	6	6
4	prussik slings		14
1	pr. binoculars	2	10
1	pocket compass		5
1	thermometer		1
1	flashlight and extra batteries	1	4
1	map of Everest region		1
3	cameras: *1 Bolex with lenses	7	–
	*9 reels of Kodachrome (only 3 were taken high)	2	4
	*1 Contax with lenses and case	3	8
	*6 rolls of Kodachrome film (only 3 taken high)		14
	1 Stereo camera and film lens brush, filters, protective case, chamois cloth	3	–
			5
*4	pint-cups (metal best, doesn't crack)	1	4
*2	spoons (aluminum; 2 men share a spoon)		1

      *2 aluminum cook-kits; each kit has
          2 nesting pots, a holder, a cover
          which is also a frying pan, and a
          leather strap to bind it together in
          a single unit   10
       2 candles   1
      *2 plastic funnels   ½
      *2 knives, Swiss army or scout-type   7
      *Polyethylene bags in which each item
          of food was wrapped (This dimin-
          ished as food was consumed and
          the bags were discarded.) Original
          weight: 5   –
                                          _____
                                   Total 139   13½

2. *Drugs and medicines*
      *1 First-aid kit: Many items were cut down or
          discarded, for example, malaria pills, dysen-
          tery pills and salt tablets were omitted. Far
          fewer vitamin pills were required and only
          measured quantities of many items such as
          bandages. Thus the total weight was reduced
          to approximately 8 pounds.

          On the final assault up the North Col and
          above, the total weight was cut to only 2½
          pounds.

GRAND TOTALS:
     —The grand total of all com-
       munity equipment taken
       from Base Camp to the foot
       of the North Col was   147 lb., 13½ oz.
     —One person's share of this
       community equipment (one
       quarter) which each man
       had to carry was   37 lb.,(approx.)

_____
*This item in part or in whole was taken, not only to the foot of the North
Col but also on up it and during the final push toward the summit.

—In addition each person carried his own personal equipment which amounted to a total of   40 lb., 10 oz.

—The total, therefore, that each person carried on his person, exclusive of food, comes to   77 lb., 10 oz.

—It is to be noted that while more than 77½ pounds were carried on the person, much less than that was actually carried on the back. This is because there are many items which are worn, or carried in the hand. The total back-load we had to carry averaged   54 lb.

(This is only an average figure because, for instance, on a hot day we would stuff more items in the pack, whereas on a cold day we would be wearing them. It is well to realize in one's calculations that a climber in cold weather is likely to carrying some 23 pounds on his person or in his hands. And this weight goes with him everywhere. Thus, when we were making three relays down the West Rongbuk, we were carrying our back-loads only once, but 23 pounds we were wearing we were carrying back and forth *six* times. All this should be calculated as part of the total effort required.)

—The grand total of all community equipment taken on up the North Col and beyond amounts to   63 lb., 2 oz.

—Each person's share of this comes to   15¾ lb.,(approx.)

—In addition each person's personal equipment was (including optionals)   38 lb., 10¾ oz.

—The total that each person carried, exclusive of food, then was   5¾ lb.,(approx.)

—But 19 pounds, 12 ounces of this was worn or carried in the hand, so the backload only came to   34¾ lb.

—At the top of the icefall we started out for Everest with 63 pounds of food apiece (roughly 2 pounds per man per day). Added to the 54½ pounds of equipment carried by each man, this meant that each man had to transport 117½ pounds on his back. It was done in three loads of about 40 pounds apiece. By the foot of the North Col we had eaten and cached enough food so that we only carried up 17 pounds of food apiece. Added to the total equipment load of 34½ pounds, this meant that each man moved 51¾ pounds up to the North Col. It was done in two trips. The totals moved are accurate. But the division of the totals for each climber are somewhat theoretical. For one climber on any given day often carried considerably more than another.

Appendix D

FOOD USED ON THE EXPEDITION

The food we took is divided into three categories: food for the approach march from Kathmandu to Base Camp, food for the high-altitude march from Base Camp to the foot of the North Col, and food for the highest altitude on the assault itself. This is done mainly because what you eat and how much you eat varies at different altitudes, so the requirements must be calculated separately.

A. *Food for Approach March:*

Here the total figures will be given of the food that we actually brought with us, as well as the food which we purchased locally. However these figures are not too significant, and so may be taken only as a rough guide. This is so for a variety of reasons:

For *one* thing, we brought with us food for only three. HansPeter was to bring about 40 pounds of additional food with him as his share. When he did not do this, it meant that our totals had to be stretched among four people, instead of the three we had planned.

Second, the food we brought had to be further stretched because KC insisted on eating exactly what we did and he had a huge appetite. The Sherpas also partook of some items in a rather haphazard manner.

Finally, these totals of food were indeed sufficient to get us to Base Camp, but they would have been insufficient to get us back to Kathmandu. If we had not come back by helicopter, we would have had to live off the country, which can be done well enough with a small expedition, but which is probably not what one would have planned.

I think the best way to go about planning the food requirements for the approach march to Base Camp is to make a basic list of the Western foods that each climber will require each day on the walk-in over and above the foods that can be secured locally. This list will certainly include: the meat for supper; nuts, raisins, chocolate, and jams for lunch; eggs, milk, cereals, and perhaps bacon for breakfast, and ingredients for the various beverages, such as cocoa, lemonade, orangeade, bouillon, and soups. Multiply this list by the number of climbers and by the number of days you expect the walk to Base Camp to take. Make fairly generous estimates to provide for delays and contingencies. Then add extra for your liaison officer, sirdar, and cook(s). It will always be somewhat variable how much you should add. But all of them will probably consume full rations of the protein foods. Perhaps half-rations of the others will be sufficient. Note that porters, as distinct from the Sherpa cooks and sirdars, provide all their own food (at their own expense). Finally, add sufficient amounts to bring you back from Base Camp. You may let the return trip take care of itself, if you prefer, and live on foods obtainable locally. After the climb, this choice is a matter of preference. But on the way in, a healthy balanced diet is essential, so supplementary Western foods must be taken.

Item	Amount of Western food (food one can not count on obtaining locally) needed by each man for each day, calculated in ounces: Amounts were exaggerated somewhat to cover expected use by cook or liaison officer.	Total amounts of Western food taken: The amount is calculated on the basis of 3 men, traveling for 52 days—21 days to Base Camp, 21 days back, plus 10 days living at Base Camp while climbing the icefalls. For convenience, we calculated the totals for 160 man-days of rations.
1. Meat bar	5.25 oz.	52½ lb.
2. Steaks and chops (freeze - dried in cans) for special occasions.		2 lb. (10 cans)
3. Bacon (smoked)	4.0 oz.	40 lb.
4. Powdered milk	2.7 oz.	27 lb.
5. Guigoz (sweetened powdered milk)	(Items 4 and 5 are here calculated as a combined weight.)	
6. Lemonade powder	.95 oz.	9½ lb.
7. Orangeade powder	(Items 6 and 7 are here combined.)	
8. Tea	We took 2 tea bags per person per day for a total of 320 bags. In addition we carried about 5 pounds of bulk tea for the Sherpas and whoever might drop in on the trail.	
9. Maggi (bouillon cubes)	We took 200 cubes in all.	
10. Assorted soup cubes	1.0 oz.	10 lb.
11. Ovomaltine	.6 oz.	6 lb.

12. Eggs (powdered)	.7	oz.	7	lb.
13. Hard candy	.5	oz.	5	lb.
14. Chocolate	.4	oz.	34	lb.
15. Nuts	1.0	oz.	10	lb.
16. Dried apples, dried peaches, dried pears, and raisins	1.2	oz.	12	lb.
17. Jams	2.0	oz.	20	lb.
18. Butter	2.0	oz.	20	lb.
19. Cheese	.25	oz.	2½	lb.
20. Cereals (dehydrated)	3.0	oz.	30	lb.

21. Anchovy paste in tubes, tomato sauce in tubes, and soybean sauce

> *Totals:*   28½ ounces approx. or
> 1¾ pounds per person
> *Bulk Total:*   290 lb. (approx.)

To these Western foods were added locally purchased foods:

22. Sugar: about 100 pounds was bought at Kathmandu and more later in Namche Bazar. These were the only places where it could be counted on.

23. Rice: about 60 pounds was bought in Kathmandu. Other towns are likely not to have it.

24. Flour: about 100 pounds was bought at Kathmandu and more later in Namche Bazar for the trip to Base Camp. The best quality exists only in Kathmandu, although a nice, rough dark flour, which we preferred, was available at Namche Bazar.

25. Potatoes: From Those on, potatoes were available at every village.

26. Salt: We brought about 5 pounds of salt from Kathmandu.

27. Condiments: In Kathmandu we purchased various condiments to give variety to the evening meal. These included: pepper (red), mustard, curry, chutney, pepper (black), and a few spices.

28. Tea: As stated above, we bought our bulk tea in Kathmandu. The tea bags were brought with us from Switzerland.

Bulk Total of Local Food as We Left Kathmandu: 270 lb. (approx.)

Grand Total On Leaving Kathmandu: 560 lb. (approx.)

B. *Food for High-Altitude March:*

Item	Daily amount per man	Total (for 4 men for 20 days, or 80 man-days)	Calories contained in each 1-day ration for 1 man
1. Meat bar	3.0 oz.	15.0 lb.	500
2. Steaks and chops	1.5 oz.	7.5 lb.	250
3. Bacon	3.0 oz.	15.0 lb.	600
4. Guigoz	1.75 oz.	8.75 lb.	135
5. Lemonade powder or orangeade powder	.5 oz.	2.5 lb.	50
6. Tea bags	3 bags apiece	240 bags	—
7. Maggi (bouillon cubes)	1 cube	80 cubes	—
8. Ovomaltine	.75 oz.	3.75 lb.	123
9. Biscuit (sweet)	1.0 oz.	5.0 lb.	50
10. Logan bread (a hard molasses and egg bread)	2.0 oz.	10.0 lb.	100
11. Eggs (powdered)	1.0 oz.	5.0 lb.	160
12. Hard candy	.5 oz.	2.5 lb.	50
13. Chocolate	3.0 oz.	15.0 lb.	435

	Daily amount per man	Total (for 4 men for 20 days, or 80 man-days)	Calories contained in each 1-day ration for 1 man
14. Nuts	.5 oz.	2.5 lb.	70
15. Raisins	.1 oz.	.5 lb.	5
16. Jam	2.0 oz.	10.0 lb.	72
17. Dried apples, pears, or peaches	.4 oz.	2.0 lb.	—
18. Butter	1.5 oz.	7.5 lb.	274
19. Cereals (dehydrated)	3.0 oz.	15.0 lb.	300
20. Sugar	10.0 oz.	50.0 lb.	1,000
Totals:	35.5 oz.	177.5 lb.	4,174

21. Condiments   1 small sack each of salt, black pepper, and curry were taken. Daily weight was negligible; they furnish no calories.

C. *Food for Assault:*

Item	Daily amount per man		Total for 4 men for 10 days, or 40 man-days	
1. Meat bar	3.0	oz.	7.5	lb.
2. Sardines (in cans)	1.2	oz.	4.0	lb. (10 cans)
3. Condensed milk (in tubes)	3.0	oz.	7.5	lb.
4. Lemonade powder	1.0	oz.	2.5	lb.
5. Tea	3	bags	120	bags
6. Sweet biscuit	1.0	oz.	2.5	lb.
7. Logan bread	2.0	oz.	5.0	lb.
8. Candy (hard)	.5	oz.	1.25	lb.
9. Chocolate (semisweet)	2.5	oz.	6.25	lb.
10. Nuts	.5	oz.	1.25	lb.
11. Raisins	.25	oz.	.625	lb.

Item	Daily amount per man		Total for 4 men for 10 days, or 40 man-days	
12. Dried pears	.25	oz.	.625	lb.
13. Jam	2.0	oz.	5.0	lb.
14. Butter	.5	oz.	1.25	lb.
15. Cheese	.5	oz.	1.25	lb.
16. Cereal (dehydrated)	3.0	oz.	7.5	lb.
17. Sugar	9.0	oz.	22.5	lb.
Total:	30.2	oz.	76.5	lb.*

Total weight of all food at departure from Kathmandu:
    Bulk total of food for approach march   560.0 lb.
    Total of food for high-altitude march   177.5 lb.
    Total of food for assault   76.5 lb.
                              Grand Total: 814.0 lb.

This total of food constitutes almost exactly half of the total weight which we carried out from Kathmandu, since we had around 1,600 pounds in all. Twenty-two porters carried 60- to 66-pound loads. The remainder was carried by the four of us, the Sherpas, and the Liaison Officer in packs that averaged a half-load.

* The extra pound comes from the weight of the sardine cans.

Appendix E

FINANCES OF THE EXPEDITION

I. Actual Expenses:

A. *Travel and Freight:*

1. Three round-trip tickets, Boston-Kathmandu (economy fares) $3,685.05
2. Air-freight on 200 pounds food and equipment shipped to Geneva, Switzerland, in three cartons   115.00
3. Travel in Geneva on expedition business via trolley car and taxi   15.00
4. Hotels for 3-week stay in Switzerland   315.00
5. Air-freight Geneva to Kathmandu on 840 pounds of food and equipment (7 marine sacks, 3 cartons)   760.40
6. Freight-handling in transfer of luggage between airports at New Delhi, India   9.80
7. Hotel in New Delhi (plane schedules necessitate at least a one-night stopover)   15.66

8. Excess baggage New Delhi to Kathmandu   10.25

9. Travel in Kathmandu on expedition business via bicycle and taxi   33.15

10. Hotel Snow View, 8-day stay   102.80

11. Travel, Kathmandu to Banepa (once by truck with expedition gear, once by jeep April 4)   30.00

12. Himalaya Society fee for hiring porters   6.50

13. Pay for 22 porters from Kathmandu to Namche Bazar (full pay for the 16 days' going, plus half-pay for the 16 days of their return)   397.30

14. Pay for 22 porters, Namche Bazar to Base Camp. Wages were paid for 5 days of travel plus half-wages for the 5 days of return   99.60

15. Lodging for 2 Sherpas in Kathmandu   7.26

16. Wages to Sherpas for acting as *sirdar* and cook, manning Base Camp, and carrying gear back to Kathmandu   135.00

17. Equipping Sherpas with equipment they were lacking (as required by Himalayan Society): air mattress, $9.21; boots, $11.00; sleeping bag and jacket, $32.89; miscellaneous, $5.00   58.10

18. Lodging, Nang   6.50

19. Lodging in various monastery courtyards, with charge for firewood included   7.93

20. Lodging in Khumjung   4.40

21. Porters to recover cache at Base Camp   4.73

22.	Porters to carry, Nang to Khumjung	10.40
23.	Porters to carry, Khumjung to Kathmandu	31.20
24.	Helicopter, Khumjung to Kathmandu	1,316.25
25.	Hospital, Kathmandu, observation and testing	206.70
26.	Hotel, New Delhi	31.50
	Total:	$7,415.48

B. *Fees and Duties:*

27.	Passports (3 at $10 apiece) visas and passport photographs	$ 52.00
28.	Duty on items taken into Switzerland	2.38
29.	Duty on items taken into Nepal	425.44
30.	Climbing fee to Nepal for expedition	412.00
31.	Liaison Officer's salary for 3 months	110.44
32.	Equipping Liaison Officer as required with such items as boots, socks, underwear, heavy and light pants and trousers, gloves, sweaters, warm jacket, air mattress and sleeping bag, walking stick, wristwatch, sunhat, warm hat, towels, and so forth	101.00
33.	Lodging for Liaison Officer	16.25
34.	Airport taxes	14.50
	Total:	$1,134.01

C. *Food* (for details of type and quantity, see Appendix D)

Purchased in the United States:

35.	Meat bars	$ 368.07
36.	Cans of freeze-dry steaks and pork chops	86.77

Purchased in Switzerland:

37.	Bacon, jam, chocolate, and all other special or dehydrated foods not obtainable later	370.05
38.	Vitamin tablets	34.21
39.	Glucose tablets	1.86

Purchased in Nepal:

40.	Supplies in Kathmandu	91.83
41.	Rice in Those	1.97
42.	Potatoes on trail	1.18
43.	Eggs on trail	1.96
44.	Namche Bazar, flour, rice, potatoes	31.58
45.	Nang, 1 sheep and potatoes	11.80
46.	Khumjung, food supplies	4.17
47.	Chang for porters and ourselves at various times	2.60
	Total:	$1,008.05

D. *Equipment* (for details of type, quantity and weights, see charts in Appendix C)

Purchased in the United States:

48.	High-altitude tents (2)	$ 350.00
49.	Down suits (4), includes hood, parka, pants	372.20
50.	Wind-suits (4), parka and pants	151.60
51.	Sleeping bags with insulated covers (4)	332.80
52.	Air mattresses (3)	34.05
53.	Down-filled mittens (3 pairs)	45.75

263

54. Packs, frame and nylon sacks (3)   141.00
55. Emergency suits (2)   263.10
56. Polyethylene bags (1,300) assorted sizes   12.65
57. First-aid kit components   87.49
58. Film for cameras; 15 rolls of Kodachrome 16mm movie film, 97.95; Polaroid Land (secondhand) Camera, 27.00; 10 rolls of Polaroid film, 12.60; 45 36-exposure Kodachrome 35mm rolls of film, 95.85   233.40

Purchased in Switzerland:

59. Climbing rope (9mm, 120 meters)   29.29
60. Nylon cord (4mm, 300 meters)   41.86
61. Nylon cord (5mm, 300 meters)   48.88
62. Ice pitons (20)   32.78
63. Rock pitons (30)   9.41
64. Pockets on parka installed (2 on each)   6.91
65. Sunburn cream (8 tubes)   7.75
66. Adhesive tape (3 rolls)   1.87
67. Magic-marker pen   1.69
68. Whistles (4)   1.61
69. Metal marking tags (20)   1.16
70. Piton hammer   6.92
71. Carabiners   18.34
72. Woolen mittens (4 pairs) canvas outers with leather palms (later given to Sherpas and Liaison Officer)   49.36
73. Canvas water bucket (1)   2.46
74. Silk gloves (4 pr.)   6.63
75. Balaclava wool head coverings (4)   13.92
76. Sunglasses (5 pair)   16.60
77. Poncho rain coverings (4)   7.94
78. Crampons (5 pair)   68.90

79.	Sponge	.61
80.	Specially made canvas marine sacks (7)	52.80
81.	Specially made canvas overboots (4-pr.)	31.62
82.	Collapsible candle-lanterns (2)	4.09
83.	Butane stoves, 1 large, 2 small	30.00
84.	Butane cartridges for stove (at high altitudes one cartridge lasts two men for over two days)	22.67
85.	Butane, large canisters (good for 40 hours of cooking; these were used at Base Camp only)	13.30
86.	Chamois cloth for camera lenses	1.32
87.	Lens brush	.56
88.	Flashlights (4)	1.51
89.	Toilet paper	4.09
90.	Flashlight bulbs (4)	.34
91.	Flashlight batteries	1.36
92.	Candles (24)	.81
93.	String in ball	.81
94.	Large goggles (4)	10.60
95.	Plastic funnels (2)	.23
96.	Towels (3)	4.02
97.	Malaria pills	1.00
98.	Polyethylene bags (100 large size)	13.99
99.	Canteens (7)	11.44
100.	Ice axes (4)	46.80
101.	Refinishing ice axes and adding straps	7.26
102.	Ski poles (4 pr.)	20.25
103.	Snow shovels (1)	4.80
104.	Prussik slings (4)	20.25
105.	Plastic pint-cups (3)	4.10
106.	Aluminum cooking pots	9.30
107.	Plates, aluminum (4)	2.70
108.	Light cord	.60
109.	Tent-repair kits (2)	2.30

110.	Mattress-repair kits (2)	1.60
111.	Balances, spring (2)	1.40

Purchased in Nepal:

112.	Crampon straps and buckles made	3.10
113.	Shorts, light shirts	3.51
114.	Heavy wool pants	7.49
115.	Miscellaneous drugs (cough syrup and nose drops)	.93
116.	Willow-wands (actually purchased on trail)	.79
117.	Kitchen equipment, pots, soap, etc.	19.50
118.	Burlap bags for porters' loads and string	2.00
	Total:	$ 2,726.97

E. *Miscellaneous*

119.	Postage stamps	$ 9.00
120.	Phone, local and overseas calls	42.00
121.	Deduction by banks for changing money	20.00
122.	Cables, to Boston and Kathmandu	17.35
123.	Miscellaneous supplies	12.38
124.	Immunization shots	11.00
125.	Photostating Nepalese custom lists	15.35
	Total:	$ 127.08

TOTALS:—*Grand Total of all Actual Expenditures:* $12,411.59

Note: To this total one could add personal expenses which averaged $65.00 per week for two of us while in Europe, somewhat less for the third. Also one could add in some purchases such as cameras and watches which we bought in Switzerland. These, however, were not strictly necessary. Also they could have been minimized if we had sold the cameras when we returned to the United States. We preferred to keep them. Thus the figure above is the most accurate figure that can be given for the actual *expedition* expenses.

Total Cost for Each Individual: $3,102.90

II: Expenses One Could Reasonably Expect:

It seems worthwhile to modify the total of actual expenditures by adding those items which we did not spend, but which normally would be spent, and by subtracting those items which we did spend, but which normally would not. In this section in summary this new total is calculated:

In item *1* another $1,228.35 should be added. HansPeter Duttle paid his own transportation from Switzerland out of personal funds, but normally round-trip transportation all the way from America would be required—at least for an American expedition.

I think it would be more efficient to skip the four-week stay in Europe. Chocolate, jam, and butane stoves could be picked up in a single day's stopover. This would add to the air-freight cost from America, but it would save on the costs of the long stay in Switzerland. Moreover, all items are actually in stock in the United States, whereas often long delays are required in Europe in order to make the item specially. If the stay in Europe were eliminated then: items *3* and *4* would be eliminated for a savings of $330.00.

Normally Base Camp would not be abandoned and the members of the expedition would not be tempted so strongly to fly out. The debilitation of the last days of starvation made this temptation overwhelming. Normally, then, items *21*, *24*, and *25* could be omitted, for a saving of $1,527.68.

Also, item *33* would be deleted, if the Liaison Officer had remained in camp, a saving of $16.25.

Some items we felt were actually unnecessary. Specifically we could have done without items *55, 68, 69, 72,* and in item *102* two pairs of poles would have been ample. If these items were eliminated there would be a saving of $325.35.

The net saving of all these adjustments
would be: $ 970.93
Expedition costs would then *total:* $11,440.66
    Total Cost for Each Individual: $ 2,860.17

Appendix F

GENERAL COMMENTS ON FOOD, EQUIPMENT, AND FINANCES

In this section I propose to suggest some of the things that we might have done differently, as well as some of the things that worked out particularly well. In fact it is a catch-all section for bits and pieces of knowledge which we gleaned from experience. It is presented here simply for whatever help it may give others in similar circumstances.

FOOD:

1. In general, a simple repetitive diet simplifies packaging and planning. It is quite acceptable if one makes up one's mind to it.

2. Beyond Base Camp everything should be packed into polyethylene bags containing complete rations for one day. If the expedition travels in teams of two, as we did, then the bag should contain all that these two men

will require for a single 24-hour period. The bag is opened for supper, used again for breakfast, and the remaining lunches are put in one's pocket to be eaten later on the trail. This procedure helps avoid the erratic overuse and underuse of individual items, it facilitates packing and repacking, and it keeps all supplies safely packaged until the actual moment of use. Only such items as salt and condiments should be packaged in amounts greater than the quantity needed for a single day.

3. The polyetheylene bags should be inspected in advance for holes. Some manufacturers are careless about this. Once on the trail, there are no replacements.

4. Wire twist closures are efficient for sealing and unsealing these bags easily, especially those, like salt, which require opening and closing dozens of times.

5. Chocolate should be of the semisweet black type. Because it melts at a higher temperature than other chocolates, it will survive the tropical temperatures which are inevitably encountered at one point or another on the way to Base Camp.

6. Hard candy is good, not only for its quick energy on the trail, but also for keeping the mouth wet at high altitudes. One must breathe through the mouth and this dries it out and irritates the mucous membranes. The hard candy counteracts this.

7. Some reward items are invaluable. They depend somewhat on taste, but we were most pleased with the freeze-dry steaks and chops at the lower altitudes and the sardines at the higher altitudes. The sardines were the only item we did not repack into lightweight containers. We didn't dare take the chance of the new container breaking and spreading the oil over everything.

8. Besides the variety of our "reward" items, we got considerable variety from the use of various condiments. They can make an otherwise bland diet seem quiet exciting. It is to be noted that these condiments are more and more diluted as you leave civilization behind. It is best to take full-strength supplies with you from the first.

9. We did not bring enough soup-cubes and bouillon cubes with us. The variety of flavors was delightful. Two cubes per man per day for the whole trip would not be excessive.

10. Polyethylene tubes with no sharp corners are vital for packaging jam and condensed milk. We did not do this and many of the tubes broke and their sharp corners tore the polyethylene bags. We should have transferred the contents into these polyethylene tubes.

11. The condensed milk in tubes is ideal for a sore throat at the high altitudes. It is cool and fresh and soothing.

12. The dried fruits are a matter of taste. Only half the group could tolerate them. Even the ravens rejected them. Less of these items should therefore probably be taken.

13. Our bread, Logan bread, was an Alaskan innovation. It is a heavy, nourishing bread that becomes hard —and so does not crumble—and yet remains fresh and edible under almost all climatic conditions.

14. In general all foods must be packaged and chosen with an eye to the fact that they will have to withstand both tropical and arctic conditions.

15. We had trouble getting canned bacon, powdered eggs, unsweetened powdered milk, and unsweetened plain lemon and orange powder in Switzerland. It is probably simplest and most efficient, therefore, to take all such special foods with you. They are easily obtainable in the United States. However, the Swiss chocolate and the Swiss jams are unbeatable. Also I developed a passion for the sweetened milk powder (Guigoz), so that I would now recommend taking it.

16. One should not depend on finding Western food supplies beyond Europe. We did buy canned butter in New Delhi, and saw it, as well as condensed milk and powdered milk, on the shelves of some of the stores in Kathmandu. But it would be risky to count on these.

17. In Kathmandu we bought our salt. They sold us rock salt at first. This would be completely unsatisfactory. Insist on ground salt.

18. Three native foods turned out to be palatable additions to our diet on the walk-in to Base Camp. For breakfast there were *chapatis* made from the flour. These looked and tasted pretty much like Mexican tortillas. We spread jam and butter on these for lunch also. For supper *tsampa* was good. It is a native "iron ration" made by kneading water and flour and grain together into a ball about the size of a baseball. Finally there is *dahl* which tastes like a peasoup and is delicious.

19. Meat can be bought on the trail in the form of eggs, chickens, or even a sheep.

20. The meat bars we took are about a pound of pork and beef dehydrated and compressed into 3-ounce bars. Then they are sealed and wrapped in aluminum foil so that they do not spoil even under extreme heat and over long periods.

21. We purchased these meat bars—as well as the steaks and chops from Wilson Bros., Chicago, Illinois. Our other groceries we secured in Switzerland chiefly through the kindness of P. Matthey in Geneva who was recommended to us by the Lamberts. Then, later, what we bought in Kathmandu was purchased for us through the kindness of Mrs. Mendes of the Snow View Hotel.

EQUIPMENT

22. In general, it is easier to get all equipment in the United States. All necessary articles are stocked and the weight and design are always of the best. We found that even European-made items, such as ice axes, were just as cheap in the United States. In Europe, pitons, cara-biners, ice axes and many other items were not available in sufficient numbers because it was not the "climbing season." We had to resort to handmade, specially ordered items which took time and were not always the best and lightest design.

23. One notable exception was the butane stove and disposable refills of gas. At present this is obtainable only in Europe. They are immensely superior to anything else. When they are compared with the old British stoves used on the early expeditions, one feels that this item alone might have meant success. The old stoves took hours to heat very little with solid fuel alcohol as its burning base. The butane stove gives instant heat to the degree required with complete reliability. Moreover its disposable fuel containers and lightweight construction are exactly what is needed at high altitudes.

24. Our boots were the U.S.-surplus Korea boots, sometimes called thermal boots. For our route these were ideal. An expedition planning to do delicate rock-

work would no doubt want something less heavy and cumbersome. The boots designed for the climb of the North Face of the Eiger in winter might be just the thing. Still these would probably wear out if there is a long approach march over moraines and other obstacles. Consideration should be given to having two sets of boots: one general utility boot, and one extra-light boot for the assault itself.

25. We found the whistles we brought for signaling were not powerful enough to break through the background noises of the glaciers and weather. We had to rely on our own voices.

26. We found that our metal marker tags for the porters' loads were unnecessary. Paint or a Magic-Marker pen is better for easy identification.

27. The need for a special sun cream that does not become transparent as it dissolves into the skin is fundamental. We neglected to provide ourselves with this extreme protective ointment before we left. Then we could not find any in Europe. We made do with adhesive tape and gauze protective masks, but a good, white, permanent ointment would have been better. The reflected sun is brutal on the snow and glaciers.

28. Pockets should be sewn on the outside windproofs. They have innumerable uses.

29. About ten feet of light nylon cord is needed for each porter to tie on his load.

30. Cigarettes and matches constitute part of the unofficial pay of the porters and Sherpas. We gave each porter five cigarettes a day and a half package of matches. We gave the Sherpas and Liaison Officer twice that.

31. We were not allowed to keep the matches we brought with us. They were confiscated in customs. But the native matches were only 50-percent reliable. Thus our flint-and-steel cigarette lighter was one of the most necessary items of equipment we had. No expedition should rely solely on matches.

32. Ski poles are favored by some for stability in walking on the loose rock and ice at lower altitudes. Half the party used them, half didn't. They were useful also as status symbols for the *sirdar* and Liaison Officer. Each of them carried one. Probably one pair of poles for each two climbers would be ample. They are not strictly necessary at all.

33. We found aluminum canteens superior to thermos bottles. The bottles often break and are heavy. The canteens can be prevented from freezing by putting them under your legs at night and by carrying them on your person during the day.

34. The silk gloves are helpful for doing jobs that require finger manipulation in the coldest weather—but they tended to wear out.

35. Our Swiss sunglasses, "Suval" type, were excellent for normal use. But in the severest weather goggles are preferable.

36. In the tool kit we would add a zipper tool for repairing zippers. Zippers are efficient but some of them invariably break.

37. One funnel per tent is very useful for filling the canteens from the general pot.

38. The wide-brimmed sunhat is indispensable. Even up to the North Col we found it useful in protecting against the glare.

39. We took two tent-repair kits and two mattress-repair kits since each tent should have one of these at all times.

40. In the first-aid kit we should have had flea powder. Also we neglected to include any laxatives although they were not in fact required.

41. It is characteristic of climbing at high altitudes that everyone is afflicted with a perpetual cough. This is why the first-aid kit should go heavy on cough syrups and lubricants for the throat.

42. In general the first-aid kit is going to have unpredictable demands on it if all the local population is treated on the approach march. Since we had no doctor we had fewer demands on our supplies than we would have had if we were competent to treat every illness which appeared.

43. We used two scales for measuring porters' loads, since we had no scale strong enough to measure up to 66 pounds. A single 75 pound scale would have been preferable.

44. Good stout envelopes are practically nonobtainable. Take plenty from home.

45. The insulated mattress cover should be considered optional.

46. Materials for night illumination can be saved by planning to go to bed and rise with the sun.

47. The base-tent slept four to five. It provided an invaluable general meeting place and lounging area. The large fly was sufficient to cover all our supplies in case of rain during the march in. At Base Camp the tent provided sleeping quarters for the Sherpas and Liaison Officer. It should be considered an essential piece of equipment.

48. Our canvas marine sacks were useful in transporting our gear all the way from Europe to Base Camp. They are a most adaptable item. The Sherpas even used them as extra ground-covering beneath their sleeping bags at Base Camp.

49. Having spent nights in the open without any emergency suits, these items are really not necessary. One's ordinary down clothing is sufficient.

50. Our tents worked very well. It would, nevertheless, be worth considering the reputedly more rugged type of tent which has the poles on the outside.

51. At all times someone from the expedition should have the gear under personal custody. This is true throughout the trip. The only exception is where the goods are responsibly signed for by a transporting agency.

52. Our main sources of supply for equipment were: (in the United States) Gerry of Boulder, Colorado; Eddie Bauer of Seattle, Washington, and Ski Hut of Berkeley, California; (in Switzerland) Hofstetter Sports, Geneva; Au Grand Passage, for general items in Geneva; Zurcher Sports Goods, for conscientiously produced handmade items, also in Geneva.

FINANCES

53. Extra money, beyond what is budgeted should always be taken. Off the beaten track, personal checks cannot be cashed and, of course, the United States embassies are not going to help you out on financial matters.

54. There will be unbudgetable expenses, such as duties and personal expenditures and emergencies of all kinds. The customs charges keep changing, so that they cannot be predicted exactly. Also it is hard to predict what expenditures will be required to equip the Sherpas and Liaison Officer for travel to Base Camp. In general a 20-percent cushion is advisable. The extra money can always be brought back if you should happen not to use it.

55. Traveler's checks and other types of "safe" methods of carrying funds always involve service charges. On a large amount of money this can mount up. We found that cash (fifty- or hundred-dollar bills) was really the most convenient of all. They are honored everywhere.

56. Don't forget to allow extra money for the gifts you are sure to want to bring back. (You are actually saving money by spending it! —they say.)

Appendix G

NOTES ON PHOTOGRAPHY

1. The bulk of the photographs in this volume were taken by Norman C. Hansen on a 35mm Contax, model IIIA, with two lenses: 50mm and 85mm. The remainder were taken by the other members of the expedition and by bystanders on our Polaroid camera, the 35mm Contessa, or the Stereo camera belonging to Roger Hart.

2. We did not find it necessary to winterize any of the cameras. The daytime temperatures were usually above 10°F so that no undue slowing of the shutter speed and other mechanisms occurred. If we had arrived earlier in the season, it might have been necessary to do this. If the camera is to be winterized, especially in the case of the Bolex, it involves sending the whole camera back to the factory. At least a month should be allowed for this.

3. It is important to keep the camera and film at the same temperatures otherwise static electricity can ruin

the film. This means that neither the film nor the camera should be carried inside one's clothing. Fogging from moisture is another danger if cameras are not kept at all times in the free air, unprotected by the climber's clothing.

4. Ideally, a tripod should be taken for the movie camera. Some steadying device is especially necessary when using the telephoto lens. A single leg support is helpful. Weight being so critical for us, we got by with using an ice axe for support, or a rock, or a snow or ice pinnacle. This works satisfactorily, although it is not the best.

5. We found the Land camera was a happy item for morale. It was the first exposure our porters and Sherpas had had with instant development. They were quite thrilled with the whole procedure and begged for pictures which they would proudly show to all their relatives and friends. We could have used many more rolls of film than we brought with good effect. Incidentally, our own families were pleased to have some immediate pictures of our progress toward Base Camp.

6. For all amateur photographers, the advice cannot be too often repeated. Take people, people, and more people. However intrinsically exciting the shot may be, it will be improved by including a person in it doing something characteristic. The exceptions to this are very rare. When taking people, it should be added, take a good half of the photographs from other than the usual "middle" distance. Show people as dots on a great snowfield. Show people in complete close-ups—trying to undo a frozen strap with their teeth, for instance. Deliberately imagine shots you have never seen, and then take them.

Appendix H

HISTORICAL SUMMARY
OF NORTH FACE EXPEDITIONS

1921   *Nationality:* British.
      Leadership: Lt. Col. C. K. Howard-Bury.
      Results: The first detailed reconnaissance of Mt. Everest. The North Face route was chosen as the most promising. The first obstacle on this route, the 23,000-foot North Col was climbed for the first time by Captain Wheeler, G. H. Bullock, George Leigh-Mallory, and three Sherpas.

1922   *Nationality:* British.
      Leadership: Brig. Gen. Charles G. Bruce.
      Results: Lt. Col. E. F. Norton, T. Howard Somervell, and Leigh-Mallory without oxygen equipment pushed to 26,986 feet. A second team, with oxygen equipment, consisting of Geoffrey Bruce and George Finch, reached 27,300 feet.

1924   *Nationality:* British.
       Leadership: Charles G. Bruce. When he became
                    ill, E. F. Norton took over.
       Results: Climbing without oxygen, Somervell
                  and Norton reached 28,000 feet. Nor-
                  ton went the farthest, reaching 28,126
                  feet. A second team, A. C. Irvine and
                  Leigh-Mallory, climbed with oxygen.
                  They may have gone higher—possibly
                  even to the top—but they never re-
                  turned. N. E. Odell climbed without
                  oxygen to at least 27,000 feet looking
                  for them.

1933   *Nationality:* British.
       Leadership: Hugh Ruttledge.
       Results: Wyn Harris and L. R. Wager climbed
                  without oxygen to over 28,000 feet, the
                  same spot as Norton in 1924. Eric
                  Shipton and Frank S. Smythe, also
                  without oxygen, practically repeated
                  the struggle of Somervell and Norton.
                  In this case it was Smythe who went
                  the extra hundred feet or so alone.

1934   *Maurice Wilson,* a Britisher, got to the base of
       the North Col at around 21,300. He refused to
       return with his Sherpas and died there in his
       tent.

1935   *Nationality:* British.
       Leadership: Eric Shipton.
       Results: Everest was tried for the first time by
                  a small party during the monsoon. The
                  North Col was climbed, but nothing
                  much more could be done because of
                  snow conditions.

1936   *Nationality:* British.
       Leadership: Hugh Ruttledge.

Results: The North Col was again climbed, but the early monsoon prevented anything further.

1938 *Nationality:* British.
Leadership: H. W. Tilman.
Results: Again a small party tried Everest, but was blocked by heavy snows. Two groups of two climbers reached somewhat over 27,000 feet. Shipton, Smythe, and Tilman did it without oxygen. The fourth climber, Peter Lloyd climbed with oxygen.

1947 *A Canadian-born climber, Earl Denman,* tried Everest with two Sherpas. One of them was Tenzing who later made the first successful ascent of Everest with Edmund Hillary in 1953. It is apparent from Denman's book that they climbed part way up the North Col. Denman probably operated on the lowest budget in Everest history.

1951 *R. B. Larsen, a Danish mountaineer,* and some Sherpas reached the foot of the North Col. Since his equipment was inadequate, the Sherpas refused to go on, and he was forced to return. He was the first to visit both the Nepalese and the Tibetan side of Everest in the same climbing season.

1958? *The Chinese Communists* sent in one large expedition of which we personally saw traces. They claimed to the Swiss to have reached the top. However their pictures were shown not to have been taken from the top. Thereupon they claimed to have reached the top after dark.

Unfortunately, no complete record of expeditions made on the North Face by the non-Western world is available. There is only hearsay and speculation. There are rumors of tremendous disasters springing from orders to get to the top or don't bother to return. Whether these are true or not, nobody seems to know.

The most persistent rumors seem to be that there were two expeditions. Neither of them was successful. There was loss of life. And the last one was in 1958.

THE TOWER NATURAL HERITAGE SERIES

TOWER DO-IT-YOURSELF BOOKS
SAVE YOU MONEY

T-095-27   **FIX IT YOURSELF! HOME REPAIRS**   95¢
MADE FAST AND EASY
A Tower original by Bruce Cassiday, home
repairs editor of Argosy magazine. Here is
an economy-oriented guide to home repairs
that will start putting money back in your
wallet. From the basement to the peak of
the roof, you can learn to handle crisis
repairs, plumbing, painting, and insulation.
Hundreds of tested tips. Must reading for
every inflation-strapped home owner.

T-095-20   **175 MONEY SAVING TIPS FOR EVERY**   95¢
CAR OWNER
A Tower original by Carl Sifakis that can
save every car owner $300 to $900 a year.
Included in this must-reading guide are
tips on buying new and used cars; how
to spot gas station, tow truck and dealer
frauds; what accessories to avoid. A complete guide to buying, maintaining and
selling your car—and saving money in the
process.

T-095-46   **INDOOR GARDENS**   95¢
Ware Budlong's bestseller is a collection of
original ideas on how to create indoor gardens that will add freshness and beauty to
your home, office or classroom. Fully illustrated with hundreds of ideas for everyone
with a green thumb and thin wallet.

TOWER NON-FICTION TELLS THE STORY
OF THE REAL WEST

T-125-7   COMPACT HISTORY OF THE
INDIAN WARS by John Tebbel $1.25
Fascinating account of the Indian Wars that raged
in America for 300 years. Fast-paced, readable narra-
tive of uprising and revolt by an acknowledged
American expert.

T-095-13   THE GHOST DANCE MESSIAH
by Paul Bailey   95¢
A Tower original. The story of Wovoka, a Paiute
Indian who became the Messiah of the Indian na-
tions and founded a mystic religion based on the
Ghost Dance.

T-075-17   THE SNAKE DANCE OF THE HOPI
INDIANS by Earle R. Forrest   75¢
An exciting, colorful account of the dance still danced
by the Hopi Indians. Holding deadly rattlesnakes in
their arms and mouths, the Hopis petition the gods
for life-giving rain.

T-095-40   LOS HERMANOS PENITENTES
by Lorayne Horka-Follick   95¢
The story of the secret brotherhood self-exiled in
New Mexico since the 16th century. They practice
flagellation to atone for their sins and crucifixion to
celebrate Christ's death.

T-125-16   BOOK OF INDIAN LIFE CRAFTS
by Oscar E. Norbeck $1.25
Complete handbook of North American Indian crafts,
designs, customs and life styles. 300 unique civiliza-
tions each with its own language and customs. Fully
illustrated.

T-095-59   INDIAN SLAVE TRADE IN THE
SOUTHWEST by L. R. Bailey   95¢
A little-known horror of American history. A barbaric
slave trade in Indians went on until 1935 in the
Southwest United States. Thousands of Indians were
forced to work in mines.

T-095-71   VAST DOMAIN OF BLOOD
by Don Schellie   95¢
Exciting, violent saga of the Camp Grant Massacre
in Arizona. One of the bloodiest incidents in the
history of the American Indian when an Apache
camp was massacred and the whites responsible were
brought to trial.

T-095-66   ON THE BLOODY TRAIL OF
GERONIMO by Lt. John Bigelow, Jr.   95¢
An exciting, first-hand account of the famed Negro
Tenth Cavalry and their relentless pursuit of Geroni-
mo, the most feared Indian in the Southwest.

T-095-76   WHO KILLED CUSTER? by Jack Parks   95¢
Tower Original. More than a historical account of
Custer and his defeat, this is an exciting account of
the parallel lives of Custer and White Bull, the Sioux
who claimed to have killed Custer at the Little Big-
horn.

Please allow 3 weeks for filling orders.